Education and Social Theory

Series Editor: Stephen J. Ball, *Institute of Education, University College London, UK*

Social theory can help us to make sense of many aspects of contemporary education by providing analytic concepts and insights. Social theories are tools of analysis and interpretation for educational researchers that enable us to make sense of the processes, effects, and outcomes of educational experiences and institutions.

Drawing together selections from the best work previously published in Taylor and Francis journals to create powerful and effective collections, this series highlights and explores the social theories critical to educational writers, researchers and scholars. Each book focuses a different key writer or field of theory, with the overarching aim of providing an overview of the social theories important to education research, but also of showing how these theories can be applied in a practical manner in the current education landscape.

Books in the Series:

Feminist Posthumanisms, New Materialisms and Education
Edited by Jessica Ringrose, Katie Warfield and Shiva Zarabadi

Freud, Lacan, Zizek and Education
Edited by Claudia Lapping

The Education Assemblage
Edited by Greg Thompson

Bourdieu and Education
Edited by Diane Reay

Judith Butler and Education
Edited by Judith Butler

Nancy Fraser, Social Justice and Education
Edited by Carol Vincent

Basil Bernstein, Code Theory, and Education
Women's Contributions
Edited by Parlo Singh

Basil Bernstein, Code Theory, and Education

Women's Contributions

Edited by
Parlo Singh

Routledge
Taylor & Francis Group
LONDON AND NEW YORK

First published 2020
by Routledge
2 Park Square, Milton Park, Abingdon, Oxon, OX14 4RN

and by Routledge
52 Vanderbilt Avenue, New York, NY 10017

Routledge is an imprint of the Taylor & Francis Group, an informa business

British Library Cataloguing in Publication Data
A catalogue record for this book is available from the British Library

ISBN13: 978-1-138-49125-0

Typeset in Baskerville
by Newgen Publishing UK

Publisher's Note
The publisher accepts responsibility for any inconsistencies that may have arisen during the conversion of this book from journal articles to book chapters, namely the inclusion of journal terminology.

Disclaimer
Every effort has been made to contact copyright holders for their permission to reprint material in this book. The publishers would be grateful to hear from any copyright holder who is not here acknowledged and will undertake to rectify any errors or omissions in future editions of this book.

Contents

Citation Information

The following chapters were originally published in Taylor and Francis journals and books. When citing this material, please use the original page numbering for each article/chapter, as follows:

Chapter 1

Ways of Meaning, Ways of Learning: code as an explanatory concept
Ruqaiya Hasan
British Journal of Sociology of Education, volume 23, issue 4 (2002) pp. 537–548

Chapter 2

Pedagogic practices in the family socializing context and children's school achievement
Isabel P. Neves and Ana M. Morais
British Journal of Sociology of Education, volume 26, issue 1 (February 2005) pp. 121–137

Chapter 3

Literacy and Pedagogy in Flux: constructing the object of study from a Bernsteinian perspective
Gemma Moss
British Journal of Sociology of Education, volume 23, issue 4 (2002) pp. 549–558

Chapter 4

Explorations in policy enactment: feminist thought experiments with Basil Bernstein's code theory
Parlo Singh, Barbara Pini and Kathryn Glasswell
Gender and Education, volume 30, issue 4 (May 2018) pp. 417–434

Chapter 5

Britton and Bernstein on Vygotsky: divergent views on mind and language in the pedagogic context
Moira Inghilleri
Pedagogy, Culture & Society, volume 10, issue 3 (2002) pp. 467–482

Chapter 6

Pedagogic discourse and sex education: myths, science and subversion
Gabrielle Ivinson
Sex Education, volume 7, issue 2 (May 2007) pp. 201–216

Chapter 7

From psychic defences to social defences. Recontextualizing strategies and Klein's theory of ego development
Claudia Lapping
Lapping, C. (2011). *Psychoanalysis in Social Research. Shifting Theories and Reframing Concepts.* Chapter 5, pages 140–172. London, New York: Routledge.

Notes on Contributors

Kathryn Glasswell was an Associate Professor in the Department of Literacy and Reading in the College of Education at California State University, Fullerton, USA. She is now based in the School of Education, RMIT University, Melbourne, Australia.

Ruqaiya Hasan who passed away in 2015, was an Emeritus Professor of Linguistics at Macquarie University, Australia. She was based in the School of Education, RMIT University, Melbourne, Australia.

Moira Inghilleri is a Professor, Director of Comparative Literature, and Director of Translation and Interpreting Studies in the College of Humanities and Fine Arts at the University of Massachusetts Amherst, USA.

Gabrielle Ivinson is a Professor of Education and Community in the Faculty of Education at Manchester Metropolitan University, UK.

Claudia Lapping is a Reader in Psychosocial Studies and Education at the UCL Institute of Education, UK.

Ana M. Morais is a Professor Emeritus of Didactics of Mathematics at the University of Lisbon, Portugal.

Gemma Moss is a Professor of Literacy and Director of the International Literacy Centre at the UCL Institute of Education, UK.

Isabel P. Neves is an Emeritus Associate Professor of the Institute of Education at the University of Lisbon, Portugal.

Barbara Pini is a Professor in the School of Humanities, Languages and Social Science at Griffith University, Australia.

Parlo Singh is a Professor in the field of Sociology of Education, based in the Institute for Educational Research at Griffith University, Brisbane, Australia.

Introduction

Parlo Singh

Sara Delamont (2014: 470) suggests there are two main ways to engage with the work of a great thinker, either through their publications or through those who engaged with their work. In this book, I indulge in the latter, by turning to women's encounters with, and innovations of, the theoretical and methodological sociological oeuvre developed by Basil Bernstein. My aim is not to silence the voices of women by claiming their allegiance and contribution to the works of a great thinker.[1] Rather, my aim is to highlight the intellectual projects of women colleagues as generative engagements with what remains one of the most important sociological theories of education.

Bernstein's sociological corpus has already received extensive attention in the research field (Atkinson, Davies & Delamont, 1995; Moore, 2013; Sadovnik, 1995). This edited collection contributes to this research field by focusing on the significant methodological and theoretical innovations of women scholars with a long association with Bernstein's code theory work. It adds to the scholarship of Madeline Arnot (2001: 70) who has previously written about the ways in which the 'active' and 'powerful' intellectual encounters of women scholars with Basil Bernstein's theory of pedagogy have contributed to the development of gender theories in the sociology of education.

In what follows, I outline my own engagement with Bernstein's code theory and the reasons that I continue to use this work in my most recent scholarship. In the second section, I provide an account of Bernstein as a conceptualiser and the sets of concepts developed in his sociological theory. In the third section, I introduce the papers in this collection under three separate sections: (i) studies in family pedagogic codes and orientations to meaning; (ii) studies in languages of description: theory–method nexus; and (iii) studies in recontextualising.

Personal engagement with Bernstein's sociological corpus

I first came across Bernstein's work in the early 1980s when I was studying part-time for a Bachelor of Education Studies degree in Brisbane, Australia, having completed a Diploma of Teaching (Primary) prior to entering the teaching profession. While studying and attending classes in the evening, I worked full-time as a primary school teacher. Bernstein's (1975) papers titled 'On the Classification and Framing of Educational Knowledge'[2] and 'Visible and Invisible Pedagogies' reprinted in *Class, Codes and Control Volume 3* were listed as essential readings in the university sociology of education course. The final assessment piece required an empirical analysis of schooling, drawing on concepts introduced in the course.

There was something in Bernstein's writing, particularly his metaphor of symbolic boundaries, and social interaction or communication within and across boundaries, which resonated with my own experience, offering an 'unarticulated familiarity' (Grimshaw, 1976: 557). I felt I came to understand schooling differently through these concepts. Bernstein did not offer tips for teaching, but a conceptual language for thinking differently about schooling. His papers helped me to articulate my own 'sensed knowledge' (Grimshaw, 1976: 557) about the boundaries between school and local knowledge; the organisation of classroom space and time; the structuring of curriculum (daily, weekly, monthly, yearly); the strength of the insulation boundaries between curriculum subjects; and safe and risky school knowledge. They also helped me to think about the difference between progressive (invisible) and conservative/traditional (visible) pedagogies, and the underpinning theories of the teacher, teaching and learning implicit in such pedagogic designs.[3] Most importantly, the papers allowed me to think about schooling outside the confines of my classroom. I could think not only about the gendered division of labour of the teaching workforce within my school, but also across different types of schools situated within different socio-economic areas (Arnot, 1995, 2001). In Bernstein's (1975, 2000) terms, classification refers to the strength of the insulation boundaries (permeable or non-permeable) demarcating categories of knowledge, spaces, people and artefacts, within and between schools. By contrast, framing refers to 'the specific pedagogical relationship of teacher and taught… to the strength of the boundary of what may be transmitted and what not… in that relationship and… to the degree of control teacher and pupil possess over the selection, organization, and pacing of knowledge transmitted and received' (Bernstein, 1975: 88–89).[4] As Daniels (1993: 59–60) states:

> Bernstein's work on the school shows his continuous engagement with the interrelations between changes in organizational form, changes in modes of control and changes in principles of communication. Essentially… the analysis in the early papers focuses upon two levels: a structural level and an interactional level. The structural level is analysed in terms of the social division of labour it creates and the interactional level with the form of social relation it creates. The social division of labour is analysed in terms of strength of the boundary of its divisions, that is, with respect to the degree of specialisation… The interactional level… comes to refer to the pedagogic context and the social relations of the classroom or its equivalent… The solution to linking the structural and interactional levels in such a way that these levels *up to a point* are in relation of free variation, was to distinguish in the school three message systems: curriculum, pedagogy (practice) and evaluation.

My first encounter with Bernstein's concepts, nearly four decades ago, led me down a research path in the sociology of education. His sociological ideas continue to be a source of inspiration not only for me, but also for many of my doctoral students. Women now constitute the majority of the workforce in teacher education and teaching in Australia, and the majority of my research students are women. Many of these research students read Bernstein's sociological work in conjunction with, or through other work such as: postcolonial scholarship (Dooley, 2001; Hu & Singh, 2018); Indigenous research (Whatman, 2004; Whatman & Singh, 2015); sociology of the professions (Exley, 2005); sociologies of mobilities, cultural globalisation (Doherty, 2006); ethnomethodologies (Nicolson Setz, 2007); refugee education (Standage, 2015); and Goffman's frame analysis (Thompson, 2016). Many of these former research students, all women, now hold senior positions in universities across the globe. Collectively, this group of women have mobilised social media sites to build on and take Bernstein's sociological ideas in different disciplinary directions: Facebook: www.facebook.com/PCPRgroup/; EDJEE videos: https://vimeo.com/edjee.

There are many reasons why I continue to find inspiration in Bernstein's writings. **Firstly,** Bernstein's concepts help me to think about the global education reform movement (GERM), and the ways in which international policies are recontextualised and enacted in national and local contexts (Singh, 2015, 2017, 2018). **Secondly,** Bernstein's models of pedagogy help me to think about the contestations and struggles over different pedagogic codes (i.e. radical, critical, visible, progressive), as well as the ways in which pedagogy is increasingly being framed within standardised, online templates and algorithms of learning (Ivinson & Singh, 2018). **Thirdly,** I find Bernstein's work on the sociology of pedagogy and his prediction of the emergence of a totally pedagogised society useful in thinking about the evolution of education systems and the accelerated pace of edu-business, edu-scapes and edu-worlds (Singh, 2015, 2017, 2018). **Fourthly,** I find Bernstein's work on knowledge codes and knowledge structures useful for thinking about what constitutes powerful knowledge, for whom, when and where (Ivinson & Singh, 2018). **Fifthly,** the sociology of education is currently caught up in struggles over truth, expertise and forms of realism (social, critical, agential, speculative).[5] On the one hand, what constitutes valid educational research is being narrowly defined by government and private funding agencies in the logic of randomised, control trials and learning analytics. A commonsense, putative, naive realism dominates these versions of research. On the other hand, some scholars (Ivinson & Singh, 2018), whose work is re-presented in this volume, are reading Bernstein's sociology diffractively and working in the spaces of agential and speculative realism.

This edited collection positions itself within struggles over pedagogy, curriculum and evaluation codes; theory–method contestations; and the purposes of schooling and educational research.

Bernstein as conceptualiser and Bernsteinian concepts

Bernstein's work on the set of ideas and concepts[6] that constitute the theoretical corpus of *Class, Codes and Control* persisted over a career spanning four decades. Bernstein's interest in reworking the same set of ideas and concepts, and attempting to link micro to macro processes, sets his work apart in the sociology of education. However, his re-working of concepts also built theoretical complications, so that his writing became convoluted and hard to follow at times.[7] Bernstein remained focused on the problematic of schooling inequality and its relation to social-class structures for his entire career. As Sadovnik (2001: 612) argues, all of Bernstein's scholarship was related to one overall project: 'to develop a systematic theory that provides an analytic description of the way in which the education system is related to the social division of labour'[8] (see also Sadovnik, 1991a, 1991b). He engaged in this project by attempting to explain how socialisation into macro power and class relations happens through the micro processes of schooling (selection and organisation of curriculum, pedagogic practices, evaluation methods). In explaining the processes by which he developed concepts and built theory, Bernstein states:

> I wanted to set the analysis of the school against a broader canvas of changes in **forms of social control**... I am sensitive to inter-actions and once these are part of **my experience**, I can begin to **intuit** what I take to be structural principles which they embody. But it takes a long time, at least for me, to condense **experience** into a concept, and even longer to extract from the concept what one has not in the first place directly experienced... When a set of concepts do not work, it is as if one's own sense of the social is obscured. When they do, then one's **own biography** is continuous with the formulation. Concepts, I believe, for some, look outwards and inwards. Their generality finds its springs in the **analysis of inner space**. The relationships between concepts and the conceptualizer are not only the product of the intellectual market place, nor a *simple* reflection of the ideological ambience although clearly neither of these two forces can *ever* be discounted.
>
> (Bernstein, 1975: 2–3, emphasis added)[9]

Bernstein (1975) argued that the concept of symbolic boundaries or membranes drove a lot of his thinking. He wrote about the insulation strength or permeability of boundaries, drawing on his own experience of growing up poor in East London in a Jewish community, and his engagement with schooling, as both student and teacher (see Atkinson, 1985; Halliday, 1995; Moore, 2013; Sadovnik, 2001). As a sociologist of education, Bernstein (2000) wrote about making explicit the criteria for theory generation, development and growth. His model of scientific research remains firmly within the logic of social realism where the theory comes first, then the research problem, data collection/production, and finally the testing and refinement of the theory (Bernstein, 2000; Moore, 2013). His pre-occupation with the theory remained at a very abstract level. His engagement with the empirical was often through the deep investments he made in the work of graduate students.

Bernstein developed his code theory[10] across five volumes. The first four volumes were titled *Class, Codes and Control* (CCC) and respectively sub-titled: Volume 1 – *Theoretical Studies Towards a Sociology of Language*; Volume 2 – *Applied Studies Towards a Sociology of Language*; Volume 3 – *Towards a Theory of Educational Transmissions* and Volume 4 – *The Structuring of Pedagogic Discourse*. The final book produced by Bernstein (1996), subsequently revised and published in 2000, is the only volume not to have the title CCC. I understand that he did try to publish a fifth volume with *Class, Codes and Control* in the title which included chapters of empirical work testing out his theoretical ideas but could not find a British publisher interested in this work in the 1990s (see Delamont, 2014). The last volume titled *Pedagogy, Symbolic Control and Identity: Theory, Research, Critique*, originally titled *A Sociology for Pedagogy*, was published by Taylor and Francis (1996) and a revised version of this book was published by Rowan & Littlefield (2000). In this volume, three chapters make explict reference to code theory in their title: Chapter 1 – *Pedagogic codes and their modalities of practice*; Chapter 6 – *Codes and research*; and Chapter 10 – *Codes and their positioning: A case study of misrecognition*. In addition, the back of the original and revised version states: 'This book, the fifth in the series developing Bernstein's code theory, presents the most recent developments of this theory and, importantly, shows the close relationship between this development and the empirical research to which the theory has given rise'. Dickinson and Erben (1995: 260–261, emphasis added) provide a particularly rich explication of the concept of code:

> How a person sees the world, interprets the world, and brings that world back inside them is done in terms of some sort of coding. Bernstein employs the term code, which he has used from his earliest to his most recent works, to mean the acts (normally hidden) that valorize regulation; acts which he has analyzed to reveal the regulatory processes themselves. Codes are then the acts of cultural transmission by which society is sustained... Codes, whether linguistic, whether regulating the performance of social roles or regulating conduct, or whether mediating learning, are culturally accepted frameworks of meaning that govern the responses of individuals in the gamut of social situations in daily life... Codes for Bernstein will axiomatically become complicit in whichever **forms of narrative** are associated with power.

In other words, narratives are culturally transmitted through pedagogic interactions (home, school), and become the coding devices by which children interpret, make sense and meaning, and narrate their own lives. Not all narratives are equally valued, nor do all narratives produce the same life possibilities or pathways for children. The differential distribution of narratives and coding orientations through schooling thus became a focal concern for Bernstein and other scholars following in this tradition.

Code theory : Generative diverse trajectories of research

The complex thinking undertaken by Bernstein in the sociology of education provides a generative reservoir of ideas and concepts that have inspired different trajectories of scholarship. Some of the papers in this collection are by scholars supervised by Basil Bernstein in their doctoral studies or research projects, others by those who worked in a research relationship as colleagues, and still others by scholars who had only a distant connection with Bernstein himself. Many of the contributors to this volume maintained a long working relationship with Basil Bernstein spanning several decades. Ana Morais (2001: 3), whose own doctoral studies were supervised by Bernstein, argues that the 'way Bernstein has developed his theory can be seen as having features of the way theories in experimental sciences have developed'. In the experimental sciences, the first task is to construct a model, and then a methodological approach is designed to test the model; engagement, modification and elaboration of the model follow. Yet for many women scholars this 'scientific' model of research seems too linear, rational and logical, and driven from top-down changes in modes of social control or regulation. As Claudia Lapping (2008, 2011a, 2011b; 2017) and Gabrielle Ivinson (2011, 2014a, 2018) argue, Bernstein also writes in ways that are not formulaic and not structuralist.

Ruqaiya Hasan's (1999, 2001a, 2001b, 2002a, 2002b, 2004, 2006) linguistic research corpus sits alongside the Bernstein scholarship, and there remained a productive dialogue between the two scholars throughout their lives. Hasan's linguistic studies were informed by the sociological theories developed by Bernstein, and Bernstein's work on interactional and speech codes drew on the linguistic scholarship of both Hasan (1999, 2004, 2006) and Halliday (1973; 1975; 1995).

The scholarship of Isabel Neves and Ana Morais might be said to provide one of the most sustained and practical applications of Bernstein's theoretical ideas to the field of teacher education, and specifically science teacher education (see: Morais, 2001; Morais & Neves, 2001, 2004, 2018; Neves & Morais, 2001, 2005). Based in Portugal, Ana Morais and Isabel Neves not only used Bernstein's models to describe the curriculum, pedagogy and assessment practices of science educators through the use of coding theory, but also worked with these same teachers to help re-code (re-classify and re-frame), that is, re-model and re-design, schooling practices to improve student learning outcomes.

The theory–method nexus is also central to the scholarship of Gemma Moss, Gabrielle Ivinson, Claudia Lapping, Moira Inghilleri and Parlo Singh. Lapping and Singh explore the ethics of interpretation, while Inghilleri explores the ethics of translation. Moss and Ivinson explore the space or gap between what Bernstein described as the language of the theory and the language of the empirical world.

In what follows, I briefly introduce the papers in this collection and position these papers within the wider corpus of scholarship of each scholar. I have categorised the scholarship into three groups: (i) studies in family pedagogic codes and orientations to meaning; (ii) studies in languages of description: theory–method nexus; and (iii) studies in recontextualising.

Studies in family pedagogic codes and orientations to meaning

Mothers, young children and orientations to meaning

Hasan (this collection) suggests that what children learn and internalise is constrained by social location. In other words, families are positioned in the social division of labour, and in turn, this positioning constitutes social relations (interactional orders) which are internalised as communication codes and culturally transmitted to children via local (home, community) and official pedagogies (schools). Differential positioning within the hierarchically ordered division of labour for the production of material and symbolic resources generates different interactional practices and so different coding orientations. Bernstein (1971: 144) expresses it this way: '... every time the child speaks or listens, the social structure is reinforced in him and his social identity shaped. The social structure becomes the child's psychological reality through the shapings of his speech acts'. Hasan (1999: 19) argues that in Bernstein's work, 'society and the individual are brought in a dialectical relation through the workings of semiotic exchanges which are themselves sensitive to and which sensitize the interactants to the social foundations of their own social positioning'.

Hasan's (2001a, 2001b, 2002a) linguistic empirical research engages in a meta-dialogue with Bernstein's sociological hypotheses drawing on data generated from two groups of mothers, workers in higher and lower autonomy professions, as indicated by the degree of control in the workplace environment. The 24 mothers were asked to audio-record naturally occurring talk with their children (age 3.5 to 6 years) at home in Sydney, Australia. Hasan differentiates between the two categories of mothers in terms of two modes of meaning habitually displayed to children, and contributing to the children's ways of making sense of their social world. Moreover, Hasan distinguishes between two modes of meaning: informative (elaborated code) and formative (restrictive code), explaining these as follows: 'the informative mode is an explicit mode of attempting to inculcate some concept, irrespective of the domain within which the concept is located' (this collection). The formative mode is not so much about concept development, but about setting up interpersonal relations between the dyads. There is a connection between location in the social structure, higher and lower autonomy professions, and speech code – ways of orientating to meaning and conveying meaning in interactions. Hasan suggests that the mother–child pedagogic relationship with its question–answer routines is founded on assumptions made by the mother about the child, about knowledge of the child's mental maps, about similarities and differences of the child's mental map to that of the mother, and the need or otherwise of bridging differences in mental mapping through discursive explication. She argues that the communicative talk of the LAP (Lower Autonomy Profession) mothers 'signifies that the mothers view the child as an extension of themselves, similar to them in essential ways, so that there exists an *interpersonal trust* between them' (this collection). By contrast, the HAP (Higher Autonomy Profession) mothers' communication with their children placed emphasis on 'individuation, on precision, and explicitly conveyed information' (this collection). So for example, HAP mothers tended to weaken the framing of communication (what was allowed to be brought into the parent–child conversation by the child) and engage for longer periods of time in explaining concepts when pressed by 'why' questions from the child. This is not to suggest that both groups of mothers spoke exclusively in one mode of communication, formative or informative. Rather, it suggests that one group, positioned in the dominating occupational positions (HAP), spent more time engaging in the informative. The informative mode of communication provides information in an explicit manner on specific topics that have not been actually experienced (sensorial/bodily) by the child. Rather, the topics deal with virtual, abstract or imagined realities and deploy disembedded or decontextualised language that is essential for the development of abstract thought. Hasan (2001a: 53–54) suggests that:

> ...a discourse is decontextualized/disembedded not because what it refers to is not present to the senses here and now, but because it refers to something that is by its very nature incapable of being present in any spatial-temporal location whatever. It is simply not sens-ible. The virtual context of a situation is an entirely text-based reality, brought into existence by constitutive verbal action... Virtual contexts are non-material and removed from situational realities, they simply cannot be directly and physically experienced: they are intellig-ible,

> not sens-ible. They reside only in a conceptual universe, and consist simply of the said and the imagined.

Hasan develops complex arguments about socialisation; home and school pedagogies; social positioning, class structures and interactional orders. She writes about the ways in which children learn to make and convey meanings; and the importance of dis/embedded or abstract meaning-making systems for the development of higher-order thinking. As a linguist, Hasan (1999) draws on Bernstein's sociological ideas to go beyond deficit and difference theories in attempting to explain how schools persistently fail children from disadvantaged communities (see also Halliday, 1978, 1995).

> The goal of schooling is the search for new meanings, and an understanding of how prior meanings need to be re-thought in light of new evidence and understanding. The school need not and should not ignore past experiences and pretend that the child comes to school without a past or past experiences **(the deficit view)**. Nor is it enough simply to note differences in assumptions, values and performance criteria **(the differences position)**. Educators must recognize the power of language to shape how the world is viewed and understood. Code theory provides a way to recognize some of these shaping factors and move beyond them.
>
> (Danzig, 1995: 166, emphasis added)

Significantly, Hasan (1999, 2001a, 2001b, 2002a, 2002b, 2004, 2006) does not simply apply, extend or adapt the theoretical and methodological resources of code theory. Rather, Hasan (1999: 11) suggests that she was fascinated by a general problem based on her early work in the 1960s in the Sociolinguistic Research Unit, Institute of Education, University of London.

> A general problem fascinated me as I witnessed the meta-dialogue between the disciplines of sociology and linguistics: What does it take for theories to engage in dialogue? Could any linguistic theory dialogue with Bernstein's sociology? Could any sociology dialogue with Halliday's linguistics? If not, how do we explain this selectivity?

Hasan (1999: 12) suggests that meta-dialogue pre-supposes reciprocity of a positive kind, not only around a problem of concern, but also around how an 'object of study' is conceptualised. The meta-dialogue between Bernstein's sociology and Hasan's linguistics was possible, Hasan (1999) argues, because both conceptualised the 'objects of study' as components of open, dynamic systems, changing and being changed through engagement with other components of the open system. Within both theoretical orientations (Bernstein's sociology, Halliday and Hasan's linguistics), classified as exotropic rather than endotropic theories,

> ...the genesis, fertilization and change in the object of study are accounted for to a large extent by reference to its relation with the different components of the dynamic open system. As a consequence of this constant exchange, the object of study... appears to be always on the move, presenting a different facet with every change in the observer's vantage point.... the gaze of the... theory is relational: its problematic is at the centre of different kinds of processes.
>
> (Hasan, 1999: 13)

Bernstein's enduring 'object of study' or 'central problematic' focused on class relations and processes of cultural re/production, centring specifically on the role of schooling (curriculum, pedagogy and evaluation codes). He paid particular attention to power and control struggles between factions of the middle class over the three message systems of schooling (what is taught, how it is taught and how it is evaluated). This object of study – class relations, cultural re/production, schooling/education – is not fixed and static but dynamic, fluid and constantly changing and morphing. Consequently, the theoretical framework had to be flexible enough to account for, describe and make meaning of these changes, as well as openly engage in dialogue with other theories such as linguistics (Halliday, 1973/2003, 1978, 1995; Hasan, 1999), social psychology (Daniels, 1993, 2011a, 2011b, 2012) and anthropology (Douglas, 1996). Although Bernstein described himself as a sociologist, his work could 'never easily be placed within the fashionable intellectual categorizations of sociology or sociology of education' (Arnot, 2001: 71).

Parents, family codes and orientation to school science

Isabel Neves and Ana Morais (this collection) also explore socialisation practices in the home and the constitution of family pedagogic codes. They consider the coding orientation, 'that is, the meanings that are present in the family's discourses and practices' (this collection). Data for their study were collected by informal interviews with the parents (mothers and fathers) of children. The families are described in terms of their positioning within the occupational division of labour. At the same time, however, Neves and Morais are specifically interested in the relation between family pedagogic codes and children's learning achievement in science. Specifically, they want to explore the complexity of the pedagogic codes generated in families by interviewing both parents, and try to work out why some children from families positioned in lower occupations may achieve high science learning outcomes. Consequently, they differentiate between the pedagogic codes constituted by mothers and fathers in their interactions with children, exploring both the instructional (what is taught) and regulative (how it is taught) aspects of these codes. Moreover, they explore how different interactional networks inhabited by mothers and fathers through work practices, as well as through hobbies and other interests, might generate different pedagogic code modalities. The authors stress the importance of designing school pedagogies that connect with the complexity of experiences of working-class children, including the complexity of interactional modes inhabited by families. Such pedagogic connections are the first step in introducing children to the discourses of school science, and suggest a weakening of the framing between school and local knowledge to allow for the 'exchange of ideas and experiences between children from different cultural universes and opens up interaction relations teacher–child and child–child' (this collection). This position is close to that advocated by other scholars reporting on studies of educational disadvantage (see Barrett, 2017; Semel, 1995; Singh, 2001).

Morais (2001, 2002) and Morais and Neves (2001, 2004, 2018) have undertaken significant empirical work in science education classrooms in Portugal, drawing on and extending Bernstein's work. In so doing, they continue to contribute to methodological designs aimed at describing pedagogic practices, and also redesigning such practices to improve scientific learning outcomes for disadvantaged groups of students. Morais (2001: 3) argues:

> [t]he way Bernstein has developed his theory can be seen as having features of the way theories in experimental sciences have developed. It is extremely interesting to think of it as within a rationalist view, where a model is firstly constructed and a methodological approach is defined to open the way for the work of researchers, to its testing, modification and enlargement.

Studies in languages of description : Theory–method nexus

Languages of description : Dialogues across theory and empirical worlds

In her paper presented in this volume, Gemma Moss draws on Bernstein's analytic concepts, particularly around visible and invisible pedagogies and competence and performance pedagogies, to describe the ways a new literacy curriculum settlement has unfolded over time in England. As Moss argues, Bernstein does not align with or favour one pedagogic code. Rather, he is interested in the different middle-class factions promoting different pedagogic codes, and the 'respective costs and social investments of running' respective pedagogies.

Moss is particularly interested in 'how Bernstein's theoretical language can be used to bring different elements of the empirical data on literacy into an analytic relationship; and how juxtaposing different elements in the data can react back on Bernstein's theoretical formulation' (this collection). Specifically, she is interested in tensions that surround the adoption of particular pedagogic approaches in the home and school, because as she argues, 'the tensions are there, not so much because visible pedagogies are inherently weakly defined, but because the invisible pedagogies in a literacy arena are always to some extent stalked by their shadow other, visible pedagogies' (this collection). The boundary line between different pedagogies becomes a contested resource.

Moss proposes that Bernstein's elastic and flexible ways of delinating dichotomies (e.g. visible and invisible pedagogies, competence and performance pedagogies) makes his theory particularly useful for mapping out changing boundary relations in a given field, in her case literacy discourses and practice. Such an analysis shows Bernstein's categories in a dynamic relationship to each other and to the data. The data are not consumed by the theory. On the one hand, Bernstein's models conceptually structure the field by bringing different elements into association with each other, establishing what goes together and what stays apart. On the other hand, Bernstein's models make the opposition between visible and invisible pedagogies clear and throw into relief the ability of these two categories to interact, as they attempt to rewrite each other.

In several papers, Moss (2002, 2013, 2014, 2015, 2018) reads or interprets Bernstein's models as dynamic rather than static entities, energising his concepts of 'relations within' and 'relations to' categories. Moss argues that if the relationship between categories is accepted as dynamic then it is possible to look for changes in the realisation of symbolic boundaries over time. In addition, a dynamic reading of Bernstein's models allows for the possibility of exploring the fluctuating boundary relationships between home and school literacy practices, as well as the dominance of different models of literacy (critical, progressive, traditional) in the curriculum, and the target groups for literacy interventions (girls, boys, socio-economically disadvantaged students). 'Such an element of flux becomes amenable to study once the categories are interpreted as operating, not as hermetically sealed entities, but as always in active dialogue with each other. That dialogue changes over time' (this collection).

Parlo Singh, Barbara Pini and Kath Glasswell also work through the meaning of Bernstein's languages of description, and specifically the relation between theory and empirical data. The authors produce three accounts of analysing and writing up data. This exercise is not about exploring different perspectives on a singular reality. Such an exercise would enact the fable of the elephant and the blind men, with the argument that each blind man can only 'see' from a particular perspective, but is blinded from 'seeing' the whole picture. It is only when the different perspectives or ways of seeing are joined together that it is possible to put together the puzzle of the big picture singular reality. By contrast, the position taken by Singh et al. (this collection) is that the three different research accounts perform multiple realities, through the acts of theory engagement, data collection, analysis and reportage (see also, Singh, Heimans, & Glasswell,

2014; Singh & Glasswell, 2016). So, the first reality produced is about a continuum of school leadership discourses ranging from welfarism to new managerialism. The second reality is about the gendered division of the labour of policy enactment in primary school education generally, and primary schools servicing high-poverty communities specifically. The implication is that processes of policy interpretation and translation may produce gendered enactment codes. Consequently, high-stakes education policies on national curriculum, pedagogic frameworks and assessment may be recontextualised within welfarist discourses by women school leaders. Such recontextualisation processes may manage to contain some of the fear and anxiety generated by such high-stakes policies. The third reality is about 'care' and how care can be analysed, represented and performed in research practices. The research interview is not something happening at a distance, from a god-like position, generating data about the 'Other'. Rather, the research interview is 'potentially a space for participants' to think together about schooling work. The interview thus performs 'relational realities, not only through the relationships between researchers and researched, but also through the various instruments and artefacts introduced into the school through the research partnership project' (this collection). In other words, code theory is not neutral, but attunes researchers and the researched to pay attention to particular practices, and in so doing produces realities. Any tool 'co-producers the thinker' (Stengers, 2005: 191). The authors argue that 'theoretical sensitivity treats research objects, including interview data, as recalcitrant with the capacity to push back and contribute to collaborative thinking, rather than as passive objects moulded to fit generalizable theoretical frameworks'.

Studies in recontextualising

Recontextualising : Zones of proximal development as social contexts of learning development

Moira Inghilleri, a sociolinguist, was inspired by Basil Bernstein's scholarship to complete her doctoral studies at the Institute of Education, University of London (Inghilleri, 1996; 2002). Her research topics ranged from an analysis of the 'intellectual field of English education' (this collection), to an analysis of interpreter training and practices, specifically relating to political asylum interviews and adjudication (Inghilleri, 2003, 2005). Inghilleri (this collection) draws on Bernstein's concepts of pedagogic discourse and recontextualisation to show the ideological work undertaken to politically neutralise a concept such as 'zones of proximal development' (ZPD) so that communication is devoid of its social, cultural and historical context. This work is particularly important given the ways in which the ZPD concept has been appropriated and recontextualised within the global education reform movement to justify a narrow view of quality teaching and learning attainment. Inghilleri argues that 'consciousness' is 'sociologically and culturally patterned' and this in turn suggests that within the ZPD, 'conflict and/or strategic negotiation over meaning would naturally occur' (this collection).

> Furthermore, for Bernstein, **the zone** would be the cognitive representation of a social world, and hence the meanings as well as the 'tools' that were employed or made available within it – the social context of learning – would be subject to the uneven social regulation and distribution of the content and framing of the knowledge to be acquired and/or transmitted.
>
> (This collection, emphasis added)

In a number of papers, Inghilleri (2005: 4) takes up and synthesises Bernstein's concept of pedagogic discourse with postcolonial concepts of contact zones and transculturation (see also Singh

& Doherty, 2004), to elaborate on the concept of zone of proximal development. This re-working of a key concept deployed within the educational research field, through engagement with Bernstein's theoretical ideas, makes Inghilleri's work particularly interesting. In addition, Inghilleri takes Bernstein's concept of pedagogic discourse out of the schooling context to explore zones of uncertainty in interpreter agency and activity during political asylum adjudication cases. Zones of uncertainty are defined as 'contradictory and potentially liberatory spaces within a social structure in which contradictions emerge from a convergence of conflicting world views' (Inghilleri, 2005: 4). This position directly contests dominant/official discourses which position interpreters as occupying a 'neutral space *between* different cultural and linguistic practices', "ideological voids" rather than contact zones of uncertainty of 'potentially conflicting or competing ideologies' (Inghilleri, 2005: 9). By viewing interpreting activity 'as a *pedagogic discourse*' Inghilleri (2005) pays attention to processes of recontextualisation, that is, the principles of selecting, ordering and focusing texts to make cases for political asylum. She argues that '[t]he conceptualization of interpreting activity as a pedagogic discourse clarifies the means by which zones of uncertainty, although they represent relatively weak social positions, are nevertheless endowed with the potential to create new forms of legitimate social practice (Inghilleri, 2005: 4–5).

Recontextualising : Scientific and common-sense knowledges in school curriculum and pedagogic codes

Gabrielle Ivinson (this collection) takes up, elaborates and experiments with Bernstein's (1999) concepts of vertical and horizontal discourses, and vertical and horizontal knowledge structures with weak and strong grammars, in a study of sex education enactment in junior secondary school curriculum subjects in England. She proposes that while the term 'sex' signifies an 'almost limitless' array of symbolic potential, when it is framed within a discourse, its meaning potential is limited and bounded. Ivinson then contrasts the ways in which the term 'sex' might be framed within 'a collection of scientific or specialist discourses' and 'common-sense discourses' within schools. The scientific schooling discourses framing the meaning of 'sex' include the curriculum subjects of English, Art, and Physical Education. The common-sense discourses include Personal, Social and Health Education. Ivinson argues that it is possible to analyse the meaning potential of 'sex' within these schooling curriculum discourses by analysing the structuring rules of the respective discourse. Following Bernstein (2000), Ivinson distinguishes between the structuring of knowledge within scientific, pedagogic and common-sense discourses, as well the fluid, shifting relation between these discourses. So the scientific realm 'provides a reservoir of terms, vocabularly and resources that people appropriate when they need to make sense of unfamiliar situations in everyday life' (this collection). The rules for inventing and re-inventing ideas in this realm are made explicit and coded in institutional rituals, routines, procedures and processes, broadly known as the 'scientific method'. The patterning, association and alignment of ideas within this realm are made explicit. Consequently, the ways in which the meaning of the term 'sex' evolves over time in scientific discourses can be traced through archaeological and genealogical research (Foucault, 1972, 1988, 1989). By contrast, 'the norms, beliefs and myths that make up common sense are not shaped by the relatively visible structures of institutions' (this collection). Ideas travel across the realms of scientific and common-sense discourses, and what constitutes common-sense and scientific shifts over time, as both realms recontextualise ideas from the other. In schooling institutions, pedagogic recontextualising rules, rituals and processes convert common-sense and scientific discourses into curriculum discourses. Ivinson (this collection) argues that skilful teachers can recontextualise scientific and common-sense discourses to construct a school curriculum that is meaningful and engaging for students. Teachers can usefully deploy scientific discourses to challenge negative and debilitating common-sense myths about sex and sexually transmitted diseases. However, the problem is that the vertical discourses of scientific knowledge 'suppress embodied knowledge, evacuate subjectivity and deny emotions' (this collection). Consequently, teachers need to make use of the 'tipping points' in classroom interactions when students introduce 'unruly topics such as body and sex into classroom discourse' (this collection). Students' subversion of the pedagogic discourses of schooling can be successfully re-deployed by teachers for their pedagogic potential. Ivinson (this collection) also explores the ways in which common-sense discourses about sex are recontextualised in schools. Such pedagogic recontextualising practices firstly deny students access to scientific discourses and secondly denigrate the common-sense knowledge of young people. Ivinson makes clear that schools need to develop internal school cultures that 'privilege instructional discourse over regulative discourse' and ensure that there is a 'shared understanding that the *raison d'etre* for regulative rituals and discourses is the pursuit of knowledge' (this collection).

Gabrielle Ivinson has written extensively on school curriculum and pedagogic codes and children's representations of these codes, drawing on Bernstein's sociological corpus (see Ivinson, 2011, 2012a, 2007, 2014a, 2018; Ivinson & Duveen, 2006). The significance of Ivinson's work is her re-interpreting, re-translating and re-working of Bernstein's concepts through new philosophies of science and new material feminisms. As Morais (2001) argues, Bernstein based his scientific approach on the dominant models of science of the time. The beauty of Ivinson's work is that she speculates on how Bernstein's concepts and methods might be read diffractively with the work of new material feminisms (see Ivinson, 2018; Ivinson & Renold; 2013, 2018). In addition, Ivinson (2011) examines the limitations of Bernstein's code theory. The theory, she suggests, draws attention to the different forms of meaning-making of children from different social classes. However, the rapid movement of ideas, information, people and money across national boundaries has meant that social-class divisions and differences are not easy to categorise, nor are they homogenous. Furthermore, new forms of social groupings have emerged, including generations of people who are under-employed or unemployed, as well as state-less people, refugees and others on the move.

While Bernstein used code theory as an attempt to predict how different social groups might engage in schooling codes, there has been less work on how children read classroom codes (see Daniels, 2012). Moreover, Bernstein's code theory focused on orientations to meaning, and in so doing, perpetuates a split between the body and mind, consciousness (rational thought) and emotions. Scholars working in the fields of health, sports and physical education have extended Bernstein's work to examine the ways dominant cultural codes around health and well-being produce affects and are internalised in the body (see Evans & Rich, 2011; Evans, Davies, Rich, & DePian, 2012; Evans, Rich, Allwood, & Davies, 2008; Evans, Rich, Davies, & Allwood, 2005; Whatman & Singh, 2015).

Sociological code theory still has much to offer scholars working in the field of education studies. But inspiration for how to use the resources of code theory/methods needs to come not only from Bernstein's corpus, but those scholars (post-Bernstein) who have appropriated, adapted, modified and extended this work in innovative and interesting ways.

Recontextualising : Psychic to social defence mechanisms in disciplinary knowledge codes

Claudia Lapping also draws on Bernstein's (1999) latter work on vertical and horizontal discourses and knowledge structures to explore disciplinary knowledge codes in higher education institutions. Lapping recalls reading Bernstein's (1996) work during her doctoral studies and 'getting to the conceptions on the thinkable' and unthinkable, and 'the suppression of contradictions and dilemmas, and about psychic defenses' feeling that this was exactly what she had been looking for in terms of her research problematic (email communication, 31/08/2018). After completing her doctoral studies, Lapping (2008, 2011a, 2011b, 2017) retained a lingering interest in the relation between Bernstein and psychoanalysis, especially the work of Melanie Klein and Jacques Lacan (email communication, 31/08/2018). This interest in the relation between two very different theories/methodologies operates at a number of levels. Lapping distinguishes between two aspects of theory, firstly the speculative inferential narrative, and secondly the sets of concepts that define possible relations between components of the narrative. So for example, Bernstein develops a speculative inferential narrative around the struggles of middle-class factions to exercise power and control over the production, distribution and evaluation of educational codes, and thus maintain their position within social-class hierarchies. Concepts such as classification and framing, knowledge, curriculum, pedagogy and evaluation codes are formulated to empirically test out the speculative narrative. Appropriation and recontextualisation of theories can then take place at the speculative, narrative level and/or at the level of specific concepts.

In addition, Lapping (this collection) unpacks different forms of recontextualisation by exploring how 'free floating signifiers in the symbolic order are articulated and ordered within discourse', and can be rearticulated and reordered, but also 'excluded through psychical mechanisms of substitution, such as disavowal'. This is a new way of thinking about recontextualisation, a concept formulated by Bernstein in relation to the appropriation and embedding of instructional discourses in regulative discourses. Based on this hypothesis of recontextualisation, Lapping makes some interesting analytic moves in her paper in this edited collection. Firstly, she explicates the psychoanalytic theories of Melanie Klein and then demonstrates how scholars have appropriated and recontextualised this work. Specifically, she explores the ways in which Kleinian concepts are appropriated, disembedded from the speculative narrative of individual ego development and psychic processes and recontextualised to study the social workings of groups in factories and nurses' practices in health institutions. Then, in a further analytic move, Lapping proposes that Bernstein appropriates and makes use of Kleinian concepts to develop his theoretical work on knowledge codes: singular, regional and generic. However, unlike scholars working within the psychoanalytic tradition, Bernstein and his contemporary, Bourdieu, do not acknowledge or reference Klein or other psychoanalysts as they develop their sociological narratives. Firstly, Lapping exposes this silence in the work of prominent sociologists of education, including Bernstein. Secondly, she identifies where Bernstein has appropriated Kleinian conceptual vocabulary, but not clearly defined these concepts, nor unpacked the implications of these concepts for thinking about educational knowledge codes and institutional identities. Thirdly, Lapping articulates theoretical work around the 'psychic structuring of fields of knowledge'. And finally, Lapping suggests that while the Kleinian concepts in conjunction with the Bernsteinian go some way in theorising the formation of fields of knowledge, perhaps the work of Lacan is more closely aligned to the Bernsteinian project (see also Clarke, 2019; Davis, 2005; Moore & Clarke, 2016).

Discussion

This book takes papers produced in different times/spaces by women scholars engaging with Bernstein's theoretical corpus and puts them in one collection as a 'thought experiment'. The experiment is not intended to produce a coherent, grand narrative about the Bernsteinian project or Bernstein's legacies, or to make claims about the universalistic appeal and applicability of Bernstein's ideas. The scholars in this collection have all engaged in reading Bernstein with/

against a wide variety of theoretical and methodological orientations. Such readings have produced powerful, original knowledge contributions to the sociology of education. As Karen Barad (2007: 91, emphasis added) argues:

> [M]aking knowledge is not simply about making facts but about *making worlds*, or rather, it is about *making specific worldly configurations* – not in the sense of making them up ex nihilo, or out of language, beliefs, or ideas, but in the sense of *materially engaging as part of the world in giving it a specific material form.*

My own recent engagements with Bernsteinian concepts have taken me in two different directions. Firstly, I have been interested in the ways in which Asian scholars who have studied in Western universities have appropriated, recontextualised and made use of Bernstein's work in 'Asia' (see Hu & Singh, 2018). Secondly, I am interested in thinking through the possibilities of reading Bernstein alongside the work of feminist philosophers (Barad, 2007) and object-relations psychoanalytic theories (Bion, 1988; Britzman, 2017; Bollas, 2007; Taubman, 2012, 2017; Winnicott, 1963/2018).

For me, doing research is not simply a matter of designing theories and instruments to collect data and report on an external 'putative', 'common-sense reality'[11] (Law, 2009). From an ethico-onto-epistemological position, the researcher, research concepts/theories and research instruments are entangled in and with the empirical world. As Barad (2012: 207) argues:

> [d]oing theory requires being open to the world's aliveness, allowing oneself to be lured by curiosity, surprise, and wonder. Theories are not mere metaphysical pronouncements on the world from some presumed position of exteriority. Theories are living and breathing reconfigurings of the world. The world theorizes as well as experiments with itself.
>
> Thus, theory and theorising are embodied 'thought experiments' (Barad, 2012: 208). Theory is produced through 'the touch of entangled beings (be)coming together-apart… The idea is to do collaborative research, to be in touch, in ways that enable response-ability'.
>
> (Barad, 2012: 208)

In this introductory chapter, I have taken responsibility for re-presenting the work of women colleagues, and in so doing I have performed another reality – the material configuration of this edited book. I hope I have done justice to their creative work, which I think, has made significant original contributions to the sociology of education.

Notes

1 The position I have taken in this paper is very different from that assumed by Dowling (1999) and Power (2010). Paul Dowling (1999: 1) suggests that, 'in some respects, we are all Bernsteinians now', and then goes on to group education scholars into four categories: disciple, vulgariser, heretic, and exploiter. Sally Power (2010) asks about the relationship between Bernsteinian concepts and empirical research, and groups research studies published in the *British Journal of Sociology of Education* into two categories: Bernstein-independent and Bernstein-dependent. The first group undertake empirical research and make passing reference to Bernstein's work; the second group are dependent on Bernstein's concepts for the empirical research and test out and develop his ideas. This second group, Power (2010) suggests, have to be socialised 'within the Bernsteinian theoretical frame' in order to do empirical research. Researching 'within the frame' is only possible through extensive research association and induction by Bernstein himself, or by those who were supervised by Bernstein.

2 The opening sentence in Bernstein's *Classification and Framing* paper written four decades ago still is pertinent in terms of thinking about struggles over international, national, state and school-based curriculum reforms: 'How a society selects, classifies, distributes, transmits and evalutes the educational knowledge it considers to be public, reflects both the distribution of power and the principles of social control' (Bernstein, 1977: 85).

3 In the early 1980s, the architectural design of new classrooms in Queensland, Australia encouraged open spaces to support progressive pedagogies. My initial teacher education emphasised the importance of progressive pedagogies with school curriculum organised around topical themes of interest to children. Thematic organisation of the curriculum meant that boundaries around disciplinary areas such as subject English, Mathematics, Science, Geography, History, Music, Art were weakened. The knowledge incorporated in these disciplines was to be taught in an integrated fashion centred around the thematic topic of interest to the class of students (see Whitty, Rowe (Ivinson), & Aggleton, 1994). However, when I entered the practical world of primary school teaching, I found that temporary barriers closed off the open classroom spaces, and student desks arranged in a traditional format, mitigated against the enactment of progressive education policies. Moreover, students were grouped into age-based classes and were expected to progress through the curriculum at the same pace. The school day was rigidly organised with mathematics taught in the morning, followed by subject English in the middle session, and then social studies, science and music/art, and physical education relegated to the afternoon session. This classification of the curriculum, as well as time and space, belied an implicit disciplinary hierarchy.

4 I distinguish between three concepts: *frame*, *framing* and *classification*. Goffman (1974) distinguishes between frames and framing, but doesn't apply these concepts to schools or education settings. Drawing on Goffman (1974) and Bernstein (2000) I use the concept of *frame* as a metaphor illustrated by the frame around a painting or picture. *Frame* refers to the symbolic boundaries demarcating what is in and outside of the metaphorical picture, and *framing* refers to what is happening in the picture, roles taken up by people, routines and rituals adopted, modes of interaction, tools and artefacts of teaching – curriculum documents, worksheets, assessment rubrics, observation schedules, smart boards, and so forth. Frames are the symbolic categories that help people (teachers) to store, manage and make sense of information. So frame as articulated by Goffman is similar to Bernstein's concept of classification, because for Bernstein the tacit metaphor for classification is '"boundary" (inside/outside, intimacy/distance,here/there, near/far, us/them)' (Bernstein, 2000: xiii). Crucially, however, Bernstein focused on the strength of the boundary – varying degrees of weakness and strength within and between categories. Thus, classification is used to think about 'the means by which power relations are transformed into specialized discourses' (Bernstein, 1996: 3) and thus the strength of the insulation boundaries, or permeability of frames. So while I can use the concepts of frames and framing to think about forms of social control and social change, classification enables me to think about power structures/relations constituting boundaries, and what these boundaries come to signify.

5 Some scholars working within the Bernstein tradition have positioned themselves as either critical or social realists and argued against the relativism of post-structural theorizing (see Moore, 2009). By contrast, a number of the women contributing to this volume (Singh, Ivinson) take an alternative position on realism, and argue for a performative, agential and speculative realism. From this perspective, reality is not external to the researcher, viewed from a god's-eye position. The approach here acknowledges 'the 'ongoing-ness' of reality, so that realities are not secure until they are practised (see Barad, 2007); they are indeterminate. This places 'us' in the thick of the 'ontological action' and brings to the fore the responsibility that goes with being 'involved' in what comes to matter' (Heimans & Singh, 2018: 188).

6 Following Patton (2007) who cites the philosopher John Rawls, I distinguish here between ideas, concepts and conceptions. '*Ideas* are relatively indeterminate and often fundamental objects of belief and value' (Patton, 2007: 7). For example, Bernstein (2000: 17) proposes a set of ideas as assumptions 'about the necessary and effective conditions for democracy', and then derives from these assumptions 'a set of pedagogic rights for evaluating democracy in education which will provide principles for examining schools'. In contrast to ideas, '*concepts* specify the meaning of the general terms employed in elaborating such ideas in particular contexts' (Patton, 2007: 8). So Bernstein's concepts specify the meaning of the general terms of democracy and pedagogic rights in the workings of schooling institutions. Conceptions add further specificity to the meaning of ideas. So in addition to concepts, conceptions provide particular

principles and criteria for deciding 'which distinctions are arbitrary and when a balance between competing claims is proper' (Rawls cited in Patton, 2007: 8). So for example, Bernstein (2000) develops principles of power (classification) and control (framing), as well as criteria for pedagogic practice and research that might disrupt educational inequalities for students in poverty (see Singh, 2001).

7 I owe this insight to Gabrielle Ivinson.

8 Bernstein (1996: 2) argues that his theory 'attempts to integrate macro to micro levels of analysis, that is, interactional levels, institutional levels and macro-institutional levels', explaining that [e]ducation is central to the knowledge base of society, groups and individuals [and is] 'central to the production and reproduction of distributive injustices' (Bernstein, 1996: 5). He goes on to state: 'social class is a major regulator of the distribution of students to privileging discourses and institutions… we have to consider the constraints and grip of class-regulated realities. Further we have to consider their interactions with underlying structural pressures arising out of the changing complexity of the division of labour' (Bernstein, 1996: 11). Davies (2000) states: 'His intention has always been to "fit it all together", to produce work on pedagogic practice that spanned social institutions that, necessarily, involved the deepest questions of the relationships between knowledge and power, identity and communication, consciousness and change' (see also Davies, 1994, 2011: 486).

9 Grimshaw (1976: 569) suggests that Bernstein is being 'richly thoughtful' and 'naively defensive' in articulating this position. However, it seems to me that Bernstein includes these very personal discussions in all his books and is being explicit about his intellectual journey. For example, in his writing about changes in forms of social control over the last 500 years, and new modes of social control which may emerge, Bernstein (1996: 82) talks about 'intuitions, rather than worked-out positions', an 'embryonic outline, rather, than a completed painting ready to be signed and framed' (Bernstein, 2000: 65).

10 At the time that Bernstein was formulating a theory of educational codes, research in the natural sciences was beginning to formulate a theory of the structuring of DNA and hence gene codes. It seems that Bernstein appropriated and applied the term 'code' to the structuring of experience through the coding of curriculum, pedagogy and evaluation in education systems. Bernstein's full list of publications around code theory are provided in the reference list (see: Bernstein, 1958, 1959, 1960, 1961,, 1964,, 1971/2003, 1973/2003/2005, 1975/1977, 1977, 1985, 1987, 1988a, 1988b,, 1990/2003, 1994, 1995a, 1995b, 1996, 1999, 2000, 2001a, 2001b, 2001c; Bernstein & Diaz, 1984; Bernstein & Solomon, 1999).

11 Law (2009: 1) provides a sketch of 'common-sense realism' as follows: 'First it tells us – it assumes – that there is a reality out there. Second it tells us that whatever is out there is largely independent of our actions. (A qualification: it is obvious that our actions sometimes influence reality). Third, it tells us that whatever is out there substantially precedes our actions or attempts to know it. Fourth, it assumes that whatever is out there is definite in form. Fifth, it takes it for granted that there is a single reality, that it is singular. And sixth, probably (perhaps less certainly) it assumes this reality to be coherent.'

References

Arnot, M. (1995). Bernstein's theory of educational codes and feminist theories of education: A personal view. In A. Sadnovik (Ed.), *Knowledge and Pedagogy* (pp. 297–322). Norwood, NJ: Ablex Publishing Corporation.

Arnot, M. (2001). Bernstein's sociology of pedagogy: Female dialogues and feminist elaborations. In K. Weiler (Ed.), *Feminist Engagements: Reading, Resisting, and Revisioning Male Theorists in Education and Cultural Studies* (pp. 109–139).. New York: Routledge.

Atkinson, P. (1985). *Language, Structure and Reproduction: An Introduction to the Sociology of Basil Bernstein.* London: Methuen.

Atkinson, P., Davies, B., & Delamont, S. (Eds.), (1995). *Discourse and Reproduction. Essays in Honor of Basil Bernstein.* Cresskill, NJ: Hampton Press,Inc.

Barad, K. (2007). *Meeting the Universe Halfway. Quantum Physics and the Entanglement of Matter and Meaning.* Durham, NC: Duke University Press.

Barad, K. (2012). On touching—The inhuman that therefore I am. *differences*, *23*(3), 206–223. doi:10.1215/10407391-1892943

Barrett, B. D. (2017). Bernstein in the urban classroom: A case study. *British Journal of Sociology of Education*, *38*(8), 1258–1272. doi:10.1080/01425692.2016.1269632

Bernstein, B. (1958). Some sociological determinants of perception. *British Journal of Sociology*, *10*, 159–174.

Bernstein, B. (1959). A public language: Some sociological implications of a linguistic form. *British Journal of Sociology*, *10*, 53–69.

Bernstein, B. (1960). Language and social class. *British Journal of Sociology*, *11*, 271–276.

Bernstein, B. (1961). Social structure, language and meaning. *Educational Research*, *3*(3), 163–176. doi:10.1080/0013188610030301

Bernstein, B. (1964). Social class, speech systems and psycho-therapy. *The British Journal of Sociology*, *15*(1), 54–64.

Bernstein, B. (1971/2003). *Class, Codes and Control: Volume 1. Theoretical Studies Towards a Sociology of Language.* London; New York: Routledge, Taylor and Francis Group.

Bernstein, B. (1973/2003/2005). *Class, Codes and Control: Volume 2. Applied Studies towards a Sociology of Language.* London; New York: Routledge, Taylor and Francis Group.

Bernstein, B. (1975/1977). *Class, Codes and Control: Volume 3. Towards a Theory of Educational Transmissions.* London: Routledge & Kegan Paul.

Bernstein, B. (1977). Sources of consensus and disaffection in education. In B. Bernstein (Ed.), *Class, Codes and Control Volume 3. Towards a Theory of Educational Transmissions* (2nd ed.) (pp. 37–53).. London: Routledge.

Bernstein, B. (1985). On pedagogic discourse. In J. Richardson (Ed.), *Handbook of Theory and Research in the Sociology of Education* (pp. 205–240). New York: Greenwood Press.

Bernstein, B. (1988a). *An Essay in Education, Symbolic Control and Social Practices.* Paper presented at the CIDE, Poder, Educacion y Conciencia Sociologia de la Transmission Cultural, Santiago, Chile.

Bernstein, B. (1988b). On pedagogic discourse (revised). *Collected Original Resources in Education (C.O.R.E)*, *12*(1), 1–86.

Bernstein, B. (1990/2003). *Class, Codes and Control: Volume 4. The Structuring of Pedagogic Discourse.* London; New York: Routledge, Taylor and Francis Group.

Bernstein, B. (1994). Edwards and his language codes: Response to A. D. Edwards, Language codes and classroom practice. *Oxford Review of Education*, *20*(2), 173–182. doi:10.1080/0305498940200202

Bernstein, B. (1995a). A response. In A. Sadovnik (Ed.), *Knowledge and Pedagogy: The Sociology of Basil Bernstein* (pp. 385–424). Norwood, NJ: Ablex Publishing Corporation.

Bernstein, B. (1995b). Code theory and its positioning: A case study in misrecognition. *British Journal of Sociology of Education*, *16*(1), 3–19. doi:10.1080/0142569950160101

Bernstein, B. (1996). *Pedagogy, Symbolic Control and Identity: Theory, Research, Critique.* London; New York: Taylor and Francis.

Bernstein, B. (1999). Vertical and horizontal discourses: An essay. *British Journal of Sociology of Education*, *20*(2), 157–173.

Bernstein, B. (2000). *Pedagogy, Symbolic Control and Identity: Theory, Research, Critique. Revised Edition* (2nd ed.). Lanham, BO; New York; Oxford: Rowan & Littlefield Publishers, Inc.

Bernstein, B. (2001a). From pedagogies to knowledges. In A. Morais, I. Neves, B. Davies, & H. Daniels (Eds.), *Towards a Sociology of Pedagogy: The Contribution of Basil Bernstein to Research* (pp. 363–368). New York: Peter Lang.

Bernstein, B. (2001b). Symbolic control: Issues of empirical description of agencies and agents. *International Journal of Social Research Methodology*, *4*(1), 21–33. http://dx.doi.org/10.1080/13645570118017

Bernstein, B. (2001c). Transcript: Video conference with Basil Bernstein. In A. Morais, I. Neves, B. Davies, & H. Daniels (Eds.), *Towards a Sociology of Pedagogy: The Contribution of Basil Bernstein to Research* (pp. 369–384). New York: Peter Lang.

Bernstein, B., & Diaz, M. V. (1984). Towards a theory of pedagogic discourse. *Collected Original Resources in Education (C.O.R.E)*, *8*(3), 1–84).

Bernstein, B., & Solomon, J. (1999). 'Pedagogy, identity and the construction of a theory of symbolic control': Basil Bernstein questioned by Joseph Solomon. *British Journal of Sociology of Education, 20*(2), 265–279. http://dx.doi.org/10.1080/01425699995443

Bion, W. (1988). A theory of thinking. In E. B. Spillius (Ed.), *Melanie Klein Today: Developments in Theory and Practice Volume 1: Mainly Theory* (pp. 174–182). Hove; New York: Brunner-Routledge.

Bollas, C. (2007). *The Freudian Moment.* London: Karnac Books Ltd.

Britzman, D. P. (2017). Mrs Klein and Paulo Freire: Coda for the pain of symbolization in the lifeworld of the mind. *Educational Theory, 67*(1), 83–95.

Clarke, M. (2019). *Lacan and Education Policy: The Other Side of Education.* London: Bloomsbury.

Daniels, H. (1993). The individual and the organization. In H. Daniels (Ed.), *Charting the Agenda: Educational Activity after Vygotsky* (pp. 46–68). London; New York: Routledge.

Daniels, H. (2011a). Analysing trajectories of professional learning in changing workplaces. *Culture Psychology, 17*(3), 359–377.

Daniels, H. (2011b). The shaping of communication across boundaries. *International Journal of Educational Research, 50*, 40–47.

Daniels, H. (2012). Institutional culture, social interaction and learning. *Learning, Culture and Social Interaction, 1*, 2–11.

Danzig, A. (1995). Applications and distortations of Basil Bernstein's code theory. In A. Sadnovik (Ed.), *Knowledge and Pedagogy: The Sociology of Basil Bernstein* (pp. 145–170). Norwood, NJ: Ablex Publishing Corporation.

Davies, B. (1994). Durkheim and the sociology of education in Britain. *British Journal of Sociology of Education, 15*(1), 3–25. http://dx.doi.org/10.1080/0142569940150101

Davies, B. (2000). Basil Bernstein: An obituary. *British Journal of Sociology of Education, 21*(4), 485–486.

Davies, B. (2011). Why Bernstein? In D. Frandji & P. Vitale (Eds.), *Knowledge, Pedagogy and Society. International Perspectives on Basil Bernstein's Sociology of Education* (pp. 34–46). Abingdon, Oxon; New York: Routledge.

Davis, Z. (2005). *Pleasure and Pedagogic Discourse in School Mathematics: A Case Study of a Problem-Centred Pedagogic Modality* (Doctoral dissertation). University of Cape Town, Cape Town, South Africa.

Delamont, S. (2014). The heavy shadow? Bernstein and his legacy. *British Journal of Sociology of Education, 35*(3), 469–474. doi:10.1080/01425692.2014.893073

Dickinson, H., & Erben, M. (1995). Bernstein and Ricoeur: Contours for the social understanding of narrative selves. In P. Atkinson, B. Davies, & S. Delamont (Eds.), *Discourse and Reproduction: Essays in Honor of Basil Bernstein* (pp. 253–268). Cresskill, NJ: Hampton Press Inc.

Doherty, C. (2006). *The Production of Cultural Difference and Cultural Sameness in Online International Education.* (Doctoral dissertation), Queensland University of Technology, Brisbane, Australia.

Dooley, K. (2001). *Adapting to Diversity. Pedagogy for Taiwanese students in mainstream Australian secondary school classes* (Doctoral dissertation). Griffith University, Brisbane, Australia.

Douglas, M. (1996). *Natural Symbols: Explorations in Cosmology with a New Introduction* (2nd ed.). London; New York: Routledge.

Dowling, P. (1999). Basil Bernstein in frame: 'Oh dear, is this a structuralist analysis?'. Retrieved from www.pauldowling.me/publications.html

Evans, J., Davies, B., Rich, E., & DePian, L. (2012). Understanding policy: Why health education policy is important and why it does not appear to work. *British Educational Research Journal.* http://dx.doi.org/10.1080/01411926.2011.647679

Evans, J., & Rich, E. (2011). Body policies and body pedagogies: Every child matters in totally pedagogised schools? *Journal of Education Policy, 26*(3), 361–379. http://dx.doi.org/10.1080/02680939.2010.500399

Evans, J., Rich, E., Allwood, R., & Davies, B. (2008). Body pedagogies, P/policy, health and gender. *British Educational Research Journal, 34*(3), 387–402. http://dx.doi.org/10.1080/01411920802042812

Evans, J., Rich, E., Davies, B., & Allwood, R. (2005). The embodiment of learning: What the sociology of education doesn't say about 'risk' in going to school. *International Studies in Sociology of Education, 15*(2), 129–148.

Exley, B. (2005). *Teachers' Professional Knowledge Bases for Offshore Education: Two Case Studies of Western Teachers Working in Indonesia.* (Doctoral dissertation). Queensland University of Technology, Brisbane, Australia.

Foucault, M. (1972). *The Archaeology of Knowledge* (S. Smith, Trans.). London: Routledge.

Foucault, M. (1988). *The Care of the Self: The History of Sexuality. Volume 3.* New York: Vintage Books.

Foucault, M. (1989). *The Order of Things: An Archaeology of the Human Sciences.* London: Routledge.

Goffman, E. (1974). *Frame Analysis: An Essay on the Organisation of Experience*. Harmondsworth, Middlesex: Penguin Books Ltd.

Grimshaw, A. D. (1976). Polity, class, school, and talk: The sociology of Basil Bernstein. *Theory and Society*, *3*(4), 553–572.

Halliday, M. A. K. (1973/2003). Foreword. In B. Bernstein (Ed.), *Class, Codes and Control: Volume II. Applied Studies towards a Sociology of Language* (Digital ed.). London: Routledge. (Reprinted from: 1973).

Halliday, M. A. K. (1995). Language and the theory of codes. In A. Sadovnik (Ed.), *Knowledge and Pedagogy: The Sociology of Basil Bernstein* (pp. 127–144). Norwood, NJ: Ablex Publishing Corporation.

Halliday, M. A. K. (1978). *Language as a Social Semiotic*. London: Edward Arnold.

Hasan, R. (1999). Society, language and the mind: The meta-dialogism of Basil Bernstein's theory. In F. Christie (Ed.), *Pedagogy and the Shaping of Consciousness: Linguistic and Social Processes* (pp. 10–30). London; New York: Continuum.

Hasan, R. (2001a). The ontogenesis of decontextualised language: Some achievements of classification and framing. In A. M. Morais, I. Neves, B. Davies, & H. Daniels (Eds.), *Towards a Sociology of Pedagogy: The Contribution of Basil Bernstein to Research* (pp. 47–79). New York: Peter Lang.

Hasan, R. (2001b). Understanding talk: Directions from Bernstein's sociology. *International Journal of Social Research Methodology*, *4*(1), 5–9. doi:10.1080/13645570010028549

Hasan, R. (2002a). Semiotic mediation and mental development in pluralistic societies: Some implications for tomorrow's schooling. In G. Wells & G. Claxton (Eds.), *Learning for Life in the 21st Century: Sociocultural Perspectives on the Future of Education* (pp. 112–126). Oxford: Blackwell Publishers.

Hasan, R. (2002b). Ways of meaning, ways of learning: Code as an explanatory concept. *British Journal of Sociology of Education*, *23*(4), 537–548. doi:10.1080/0142569022000038396

Hasan, R. (2004). The concept of semiotic mediation: Perspectives from Bernstein's sociology. In J. Muller, B. Davies, & A. M. Morais (Eds.), *Reading Bernstein, Researching Bernstein* (pp. 30–43). London: Taylor and Francis, RoutledgeFalmer.

Hasan, R. (2006). Literacy, pedagogy and social change: Directions from Bernstein's sociology. In R. Moore, M. Arnot, J. Beck, & H. Daniels (Eds.), *Knowledge, Power and Educational Reform. Applying the Sociology of Basil Bernstein* (pp. 211–225). London; New York: Routledge.

Heimans, S., & Singh, P. (2018). Putting the steam back into critique? 'Gathering' for critical–dissensual collaborations in education policy research. *Policy Futures in Education*, *16*(2), 185–201. doi:10.1177/1478210317736209

Hu, Y., & Singh, P. (2018). Western fragments, Asia as method: New modes of policy scholarship. *Discourse: Studies in the Cultural Politics of Education*, *39*(4), 664–671. doi:10.1080/01596306.2017.1362749

Inghilleri, M. (1996). *Language, Culture and the Quest for Commensurability* (Doctoral dissertation). Univesity of London, London, England, United Kingdom.

Inghilleri, M. (2002). Britton and Bernstein on Vygotsky: Divergent views on mind and language in the pedagogic context. *Pedagogy, Culture & Society*, *10*(3), 467–482. doi:10.1080/14681360200200154

Inghilleri, M. (2003). Habitus, field and discourse. *Target*, *15*(2), 243–268.

Inghilleri, M. (2005). Mediating zones of uncertainty. Interpreter agency, the interpreting habitus and political asylum adjudication. *The Translator*, *11*(1), 1–17.

Ivinson, G. (2011). Bernstein: Codes and social class. In R. Wodak, B. Johnstone, & P. Kerswill (Eds.), *The SAGE Handbook of Sociolinguistics* (pp. 40–56). London: Sage.

Ivinson, G. (2012a). The body and pedagogy: Beyond absent, moving bodies in pedagogic practice. *British Journal of Sociology of Education*, *33*(4), 489–506. doi:10.1080/01425692.2012.662822

Ivinson, G. (2012b). Boys, skills and class: Educational failure or community survival? Insights from Vygotsky and Bernstein. In H. Daniels (Ed.), *Vygotsky and Sociology* (pp. 156–174). London; New York: Routledge.

Ivinson, G. (2014a). *Pedagogy of Improvised Choreography and Dance: Restricted Codes Revisited – Developing Pedagogies for the Corporeal Device*. Paper presented at the 8th International Basil Bernstein Symposium 2014, Nanzan University, Nagoya Campus, Nagoya, Japan.

Ivinson, G. M. (2014b). Skills in motion: Boys' trail motorbiking activities as transitions into working-class masculinity in a post-industrial locale. *Sport, Education and Society*, *19*(5), 605–620. doi:10.1080/13573322.2012.692669

Ivinson, G. (2018). Re-imagining Bernstein's restricted codes. *European Educational Research Journal*, *17*(4), 539–554. doi:10.1177/1474904117745274

Ivinson, G., & Duveen, G. (2006). Children's recontextualisations of pedagogy. In R. Moore, M. Arnot, J. Beck, & H. Daniels (Eds.), *Knowledge, Power and Educational Reform* (pp. 112–125). London: Routledge.

Ivinson, G., & Renold, E. (2013). Valleys' girls: Re-theorising bodies and agency in a semi-rural post-industrial locale. *Gender and Education, 25*(6), 704–721. doi:10.1080/09540253.2013.827372

Ivinson, G., & Renold, E. (2018). Writing as bodywork: Poverty, literacy and unspoken pain in ex-mining south Wales valley communities. In S. Gannon, R. Hattam, & W. Sawyer (Eds.), *Resisting Educational Inequality: Reframing Policy and Practice in Schools Serving Vulnerable Communities* (pp. 277–293). London; New York: Routledge, Taylor and Francis Group.

Ivinson, G., & Singh, P. (2018). Special issue on 'International policies – local affects: Regenerating the sociology of Basil Bernstein'. *European Educational Research Journal, 17*(4), 461–469. doi:10.1177/1474904118784126

Lapping, C. (2008). The ethics of interpretation: The signifying chain from field to analysis. *Discourse: Studies in the Cultural Politics of Education, 29*(1), 69–83. doi:10.1080/01596300701801351

Lapping, C. (2011a). 'Psychic defences' and institutionalised formations of knowledge. In G. Ivinson, B. Davies, & J. Fitz (Eds.), *Knowledge and Identity: Concepts and Applications in Bernstein's Sociology* (pp. 143–156). Abingdon, Oxon: Routledge.

Lapping, C. (2011b). *Psychoanalysis in Social Research: Shifting Theories and Reframing Concepts.* London; New York: Routledge.

Lapping, C. (2017). The explosion of real time and the structural conditions of temporality in a society of control: Durations and urgencies of academic research. *Discourse: Studies in the Cultural Politics of Education, 38*(6), 906–922.

Law, J. (2009). *Collateral Realities*, 29 December 2009 version. Retrieved from www.heterogeneities.net/publications/Law2009CollateralRealities.pdf

Moore, R. (2009). *Towards the Sociology of Truth.* London: Continuum International Publishing.

Moore, R. (2013). *Basil Bernstein: The Thinker and the Field.* Abingdon, Oxon; New York: Routledge.

Moore, A., & Clarke, M. (2016). 'Cruel optimism': Teacher attachment to professionalism in an era of performativity. *Journal of Education Policy, 31*(5), 666–677. doi:10.1080/02680939.2016.1160293

Morais, A. M. (2001). Crossing boundaries between disciplines: A perspective on Basil Bernstein's legacy. In S. Power (Ed.), *A Tribute to Basil Bernstein – 1924–2000* (p. 4). London: Institute of Education, University of London. Retrieved from http://ioewebserver.ioe.ac.uk/ioe/index.html.

Morais, A. M. (2002). Basil Bernstein at the micro level of the classroom. *British Journal of Sociology of Education, 23*(4), 559–569. doi:10.1080/0142569022000038413

Morais, A. M., & Neves, I. P. (2001). Pedagogic social contexts: Studies for a sociology of learning. In A. Morais, I. Neves, B. Davies, & H. Daniels (Eds.), *Towards a Sociology of Pedagogy: The Contribution of Basil Bernstein to Research* (pp. 185–212). New York: Peter Lang.

Morais, A. M., & Neves, I. P. (2004). Teachers as creators of social contexts for scientific learning: New approaches for teacher education. In R. Moore, M. Arnot, J. Beck, & H. Daniels (Eds.), *Knowledge, Power and Educational Reform: Applying the Sociology of Basil Bernstein* (pp. 146–182). London: Routledge.

Morais, A. M., & Neves, I. P. (2018). The quest for high-level knowledge in schools: Revisiting the concepts of classification and framing. *British Journal of Sociology of Education, 39*(3), 261–282. doi:10.1080/01425692.2017.1335590

Moss, G. (2002). Literacy and pedagogy in flux: Constructing the object of study from a Bernsteinian perspective. *British Journal of Sociology of Education, 23*(4), 549–558. doi:10.1080/0142569022000038404

Moss, G. (2013). Research, policy and knowledge flows in education: What counts in knowledge mobilisation? *Contemporary Social Science, 8*(3), 237–248. doi:10.1080/21582041.2013.767466

Moss, G. (2014). Putting literacy attainment data in context: Examining the past in search of the present. *Comparative Education, 50*(3), 357–373. doi:10.1080/03050068.2014.921369

Moss, G. (2015). *Bernstein and His Legacy: Looking Forward, Looking Back.* Seminar presentation. Institute of Education, University of London.

Moss, G. (2018). Reframing the discourse: Ethnography, Bernstein and the distribution of reading attainment by gender. *European Educational Research Journal, 17*(4), 528–538. doi:10.1177/1474904117740112

Neves, I. P., & Morais, A. M. (2001). Texts and contexts in educational systems: Studies of recontextualising spaces. In A. Morais, I. Neves, B. Davies, & H. Daniels (Eds.), *Towards a Sociology of Pedagogy: The Contribution of Basil Bernstein to Research* (pp. 223–250). New York: Peter Lang.

Neves, I. P., & Morais, A. M. (2005). Pedagogic practices in the family socializing context and children's school achievement. *British Journal of Sociology of Education*, *26*(1), 121–137. doi:10.1080/0142569042000292752

Nicolson Setz, H. A. (2007). *Producing Literacy Practices that Count for Subject English* (Doctoral dissertation). Queensland University of Technology, Brisbane, Australia.

Patton, P. (2007). Deleuze and Derrida on the concept and future of democracy. *Distinktion: Journal of Social Theory*, *8*(2), 7–23. doi:10.1080/1600910X.2007.9672944

Power, S. (2010). Bernstein and empirical research. In P. Singh, A. Sadnovik, & S. Semel (Eds.), *Toolkits, Translation Devices and Conceptual Accounts: Essays on Basil Bernstein's Sociology of Knowledge* (pp. 239–248). New York: Peter Lang.

Sadovnik, A. R. (1991a). Basil Bernstein's theory of pedagogic practice: A structuralist approach. *Sociology of Education*, *64*, 48–63.

Sadovnik, A. R. (1991b). Connecting the macro and micro. Reviewed work(s): The Structuring of Pedagogic Discourse: Vol. 4: Class, Codes and Control by Basil Bernstein. *Contemporary Sociology*, *20*(3), 471–474.

Sadovnik, A. (1995). Basil Bernstein's theory of pedagogic practice: A structuralist approach. In A. Sadovnik (Ed.), *Knowledge and Pedagogy: The Sociology of Basil Bernstein* (pp. 3–38). Norwood, NJ: Ablex Publishing Corporation.

Sadovnik, A. R. (2001). Profiles of famous educators: Basil Bernstein 1924–2000. *PROSPECTS. Quarterly Review of Comparative Education*, *XXXI*(4), 607–620.

Semel, S. (1995). Basil Bernstein's theory of pedagogic practice and the history of American progressive education: Three case studies. In A. Sadovnik (Ed.), *Knowledge and Pedagogy: The Sociology of Basil Bernstein* (pp. 337–358). Norwood, NJ: Ablex Publishing Corporation.

Singh, P. (2001). Pedagogic discourses and student resistance in Australian secondary schools. In A. Morais, I. Neves, B. Davies, & H. Daniels (Eds.), *Towards a Sociology of Pedagogy: The Contribution of Basil Bernstein to Research* (pp. 251–276). New York: Peter Lang.

Singh, P. (2015). Performativity and pedagogising knowledge: Globalising educational policy formation, dissemination and enactment. *Journal of Education Policy*, *30*(3), 363–384. doi:10.1080/02680939.2014.961968

Singh, P. (2017). Pedagogic governance: Theorising with/after Bernstein. *British Journal of Sociology of Education*, *38*(2), 144–163. doi:10.1080/01425692.2015.1081052

Singh, P. (2018). Performativity, affectivity and pedagogic identities. *European Educational Research Journal*, *17*(4), 489–506. doi:10.1177/1474904117726181

Singh, P., & Doherty, C. (2004). Global cultural flows and pedagogic dilemmas: Teaching in the global university 'contact zone'. *TESOL Quarterly*, *38*(1), 9–42.

Singh, P., & Glasswell, K. (2016). Differences that come to matter: Leading struggles against educational inequality. In G. Johnson & N. Dempster (Eds.), *Leadership in Diverse Learning Contexts* (pp. 255–275). Dordrecht, The Netherlands: Springer.

Singh, P., Heimans, S., & Glasswell, K. (2014). Policy enactment, context and performativity: Ontological politics and researching Australian National Partnership policies. *Journal of Education Policy*, *29*(6), 826–844. doi:10.1080/02680939.2014.891763

Singh, P., Pini, B., & Glasswell, K. (2018). Explorations in policy enactment: Feminist thought experiments with Basil Bernstein's code theory. *Gender and Education*, *30*(4), 417–434. doi:10.1080/09540253.2016.1216523

Standage, S. (2015). *Changing Stories, Developing Identities, Transforming Education. A Narrative Thematic Study of Cultural Identity in Refugee Inclusive Classrooms* (Doctoral dissertation). Griffith University, Brisbane, Queensland, Australia.

Stengers, I. (2005). Introductory notes on an ecology of practices. *Cultural Studies Review*, *11*(1), 183–196.

Taubman, P. (2017). Death by numbers: A response to Backer, Sarigianides, and Stillwaggon. *Educational Theory*, *67*(1), 97–106.

Taubman, P. M. (2012). *Disavowed Knowledge: Psychoanalysis, Education and Teaching*. New York: Routledge.

Thompson, R. (2016). *Teen Girls' Online Participation: An Australian Study* (Doctoral dissertation). Griffith University, Gold Coast, Australia.

Tyler, W. (1999). Pedagogic identities and educational reform in the 1990s: The cultural dynamics of national curricula. In F. Christie (Ed.), *Pedagogy and the Shaping of Consciousness* (pp. 262–289). London: Continnum.

Whatman, S. L. (2004). *'Wis Wei Youpla Health'? A Case Study of the Nature and Extent of Community Participation in Health-Education Decision Making for Torres Strait Islander Girls at Bluewater High* (Doctoral dissertation). Queensland University of Technology, Brisbane, Australia.

Whatman, S. L., & Singh, P. (2015). Constructing health and physical education curriculum for indigenous girls in a remote Australian community. *Physical Education and Sport Pedagogy*, *20*(2), 215–230. doi:10.1080/17408989.2013.868874

Whitty, G., Rowe (Ivinson), G., & Aggleton, P. (1994). Discourse in cross-curricular contexts: Limits to empowerment. *International Journal of Sociology of Education*, *4*(1), 25–42.

Winnicott, D. (1963/2018). Fear of breakdown. In G. Kohon (Ed.), *British Psychoanalysis: New Perspectives in the Independent Tradition*. London: Routledge.

1 Ways of Meaning, Ways of Learning

Code as an explanatory concept

Ruqaiya Hasan

ABSTRACT *The aim of this paper is to offer further empirical evidence in support of Bernstein's concept of code from the social semiotic perspective of systemic functional linguistics. When the concept of code was first introduced in the 1960s, it was severely criticised by many famous socio-linguists. It will be argued that these socio-linguists failed to understand the significance of language as a meaning potential, and so they also failed to appreciate the inherent relation between meaning and mental development (Halliday, 1975; Vygotsky, 1978). The concept of code is important in any viable theory of mental development which does not hide behind a mythical homogeneity. Human beings develop different forms of consciousness, and code theory offers a detailed and coherent account of both the social origin and the nature of this variation. In fact, the panoramic scope of Bernstein's sociological theory clarifies the relations of social positioning, coding orientation, communication, and consciousness to learning in official pedagogic sites.*

In presenting some of the results of my investigation in variant forms of communication between mothers and their young children, I will show that: (a) the variation is systematic, (b) the nature of the variation needs Bernstein's code theory for its interpretation, and (c) the fact of variation can only be accounted for by its relation to social positioning.

> ... codes transform distributions of power and principles of control into pedagogic communication. Codes attempt to suppress contradictions, cleavages and dilemmas in the external order (classification) and set up psychic defences for intra-individual order through the insulation (boundaries) they produce. *But code acquisition necessarily entails both the acquisition of order and the potential of its disturbance.* (Bernstein, 2000, p. 203; original emphasis)

As members of the human species we possess an almost unlimited potential for learning: in this sense, the world is truly our oyster. However, what we actually learn in our lifetime is typically constrained by our social location, a problem that demands explanation: why and how does social location intervene in constraining what is learnt by whom? This question formed an important part of the research agenda in Basil Bernstein's working life (Bernstein, 1971, 1975, 1990, 2000). Of course, one's social location is not inalterable, as Bernstein took great pains to point out, but the conditions for such changes are fairly stringent, which may or may not be met. These conditions have little to do with our supposedly 'innate' mental capacities: in fact, recent research in the development of human brain reveals that at birth we have yet to acquire a 'mind' (Deacon, 1997; Greenfield, 2000; Boncinelli, 2001): our most precious biological assets—the plasticity of our brain and its potential for forming billions of connections—make us uniquely dependent on the social for turning that powerful brain into a usable mind. It thus transpires that the two basic supports of our existence, the biological and the social, are linked by a co-genetic logic, and what forges this link between the two is our capacity for semiosis—for making meanings by the use of shared symbolic systems. Through centuries of evolutionary trial and error, the human brain is predisposed to make sense of symbols and, among the various symbolic systems, language, due to some of its defining characteristics (Deacon, 1997) proves crucial in the enterprise of linking the biological and the social: to gain consciousness, to become a usable mind, the human brain needs experience, and language acts as a uniquely effective, immensely supple means of construing experience by acts of meaning (Halliday & Matthiessen, 1999). So, if we wish to answer our question—why and how does social location intervene in constraining what is learnt by whom?—we will need a theory that is sensitive to the complex interactions of language, culture and consciousness, for although learning is achieved by individual minds, the minds themselves are fashioned socially by means of semiotic mediation, which means largely through discursive interaction.

From this perspective, Bernstein's code theory is exceptional. For a serious socio-linguist, it is perhaps the only sociological theory that takes the power of language seriously enough to give it a definite place in his theory; and this theory has been deeply concerned with the relations of culture, communication and consciousness (see, especially, Bernstein, 1971, 1982, 1990, 2000). It thus represents a powerful resource for examining the complex interplay of the factors active in the formation of consciousness and the unequal distribution of knowledge. Developed and refined over decades, it describes on the one hand the dialectic of semiosis and consciousness, and on the other it traces the relevant macro and micro social phenomena, identifying the attributes of the social system that enable social processes. The present paper is not intended as a potted history of the development of Bernstein's code theory, as excellent and authentic accounts of this can be found in Bernstein (1990, 1996, 2000), which present particularly lucid accounts of how social class, social practice and forms of human consciousness are socio-logically related. My aim in this paper is to show the power of the concept of code in explaining systematic variation in the meanings people habitually mean, an enquiry that was inspired by Bernstein's writings on the relations of coding orientation to knowledge distribution in modern societies (Bernstein, 1971, 1975).

I am aware of the various pejorative readings of the code theory, but again this is not the appropriate place to deconstruct them: to my mind, these (mis-)readings told us more about the standards of academic (il-)literacy than they did about the nature of the code theory. For, indeed, the potential of the theory was quite obvious from its early stages (Bernstein, 1965; Halliday, 1973a; Hasan, 1973). Certainly there were problems with the data—the data used in the Sociological Research Unit research was collected via questionnaires and interviews (for some details, see Bernstein (1973)), and so it did not represent naturally occurring language in the contexts of everyday life. The second major point of code criticism was that the linguistic evidence was not valid. Again it is true that much of the lexical and syntactic evidence that was cited (see Bernstein, 1971, 1973, 1975) could not be easily interpreted as decisive instantiation of code varieties. But a thoughtful reading would have conceded that the problem lay largely with the linguistic models, none of which offered any viable resources for the analysis of meaning in discourse, and Bernstein's code theory is above all concerned with orientation to meaning and with the internalisation of orders of relevance (Bernstein, 1990). If one wished to cite evidence for how coding orientation may activate social subjects' selection and organisation of meaning, subjects' judgements of what is or is not legitimate social practice, then clearly counting morphemes and words defined by their grammatical status was not going to be much help. What was needed was the ability to relate grammar and semantics in a non-*ad hoc*, systematic manner; linguists needed to offer Bernstein a theory of grammar as a resource for meaning. As systemic functional linguistics has shown, it is the nexus of grammar with meaning, as manifested in discourse in social life, that is crucial to the formation of consciousness, and the latter is an essential element both in the reproduction of society and of social change. Meaning is thus critical to the very concept of Bernstein's code theory. But systemic functional linguists as yet had no coherent theory of semantics, while formal semantics was largely unusable in the analysis of discourse.

To me this situation presented a dual challenge: a challenge to produce a linguistic tool capable of such an analysis of discourse in social life, and a challenge to mount an investigation that would examine whether and to what extent the linguistic form of social interaction was instrumental in the formation of consciousness. In the rest of the paper, I want to present briefly an account of this research. My research project should not be seen as one that explores all the complex relations outlined by Bernstein in the explication of his code theory (Bernstein, 1971, 1982, 1987): this would be a daunting task for any single research effort (see Hasan (1999) as a linguist's account of the full architecture of Bernstein's theory). As a linguist, my interest and my training prepared me to explore that element of the code theory that is concerned particularly with the relation between forms of linguistic communication and forms of consciousness. Accordingly, the major questions that the first phase of my research asked were:

- Q1. Do mothers from different social groups/classes systematically vary in the meanings they habitually mean in talking to their three and a half-year-old children?
- Q2. If the answer to Q1 is 'yes', then: (a) does the experience of participation in different semantic varieties manifest itself in children's own ways of meaning; if so how; and (b) how can these patterns of variation be explained? What is/are the activating factor(s)?

By interrogating the results of the analysis of my data from these points of view, I hoped to be able to show whether variation in forms of communication is particularly responsive to social positioning (Bernstein, 1990), and by comparing the maternal sayings with those of the children, hoped to find some indication whether the active experience of fashions of speaking has any bearing on forms of consciousness. If there is a significant correlation between the semantic styles of the mothers and the children, this could be taken as a confirmation of Bernstein's claims about codes, communication and consciousness (Bernstein, 1971, 1990, 1996).

Beginning in the mid-1980s, with Carmel Cloran's able assistance, I directed such a research project over a period of some 6 years, entitled 'The Role of Everyday Talk between Mothers and Children in Establishing Ways of Learning' (for details, see Hasan, 1989, 1992; Hasan & Cloran, 1990). As for the tool for analysis, the main inspiration came from the systemic functional model, with its emphasis on meaning and its system-oriented description. Although Bernstein had been working as early as the 1960s with the network representation of behavioural choices in specific contexts such as that of control (Bernstein & Cook-Gumperz, 1973), my own inspiration came from the seminal work of Halliday (1973b) and Turner (1973). The former, in particular, showed how the selection and organisation of meaning can be systematically related to lexico-grammatical resources. It thus served as the starting point for devising a semantic system network, which represents, up to a certain degree of detail, the meaning potential and the grammatical resources for its realisation, available to speakers of English in the environment of everyday discourse. Bernstein's (1971) early work in the area of socialisation and code varieties suggested that the principles governing systematic variation in the distribution of knowledge had to be inculcated at the early stages of life, where identities are formed, desires acquire legitimacy, and orders of relevance become established. Accordingly, the children selected to participate in my research were quite young (3 years 6 months–4 years old; mean age, 3 years 8 months). The theory stipulated further that underlying the systematic variation in learning are relations of power and control in society: as Bernstein put it:

> 'Class relations' ... refer to inequalities in the distribution of power, and in the principles of control between social groups, which are realised in the creation, distribution, reproduction, and legitimation of physical and symbolic values, that have their source in the social division of labour. (1990, p. 1)

Keeping this in mind, the 24 mothers participating in the research were selected from families that were evenly divided between dominating and dominated social groups. The specific parameter taken as the indicator of domination was the degree of control on the workplace environment: the greater the possibility for making policy changes, and for passing on executive decisions to others as instruments for carrying them out, the more dominating the professional location. The dominating professions were referred to as Higher Autonomy Professions (HAP) and the dominated ones as Lower Autonomy Professions (LAP). To ensure the naturalness of the data, the mothers were requested to do the recording themselves. No contextual restrictions were placed; mothers were free to record at any time that suited them so long as they varied the time of recording and so long as they did the recording while carrying out their ordinary day-to-day household jobs. Some 100 hours of naturally occurring conversation was collected. When this data was examined from the point of view of what was going on at the time of these talks, three material situational settings were found to be in common to all mothers: (a) giving care to the subject child (such as bathing, providing food, putting the child to bed), (b) engaging in some cooperative activity with the child (such as tidying up a room, reading a book or playing a game together), or (c) carrying out some household jobs (such as cooking, cleaning, washing up) while the child simply hung about. Since the analysis was to be made in terms of a large number of semantic variables, say around 50, a representative sample was constructed taking just over 55 minutes per dyad divided as equally as possible across the three material situational settings described earlier. This sample consisted of just over 20,000 messages, each of which was analysed using the categories of the semantic network.

Rather than undertake here a step by step discussion of how the semantic analysis was carried out (for this, see Hasan 1989, 1992), I want to present a brief semantic profile of my data, whereby I hope to show specifically what kind of information is distributed how and where during the mother–child interactions. I will initially identify two modes of meaning habitually displayed by the mothers: both are active in enabling the children to internalise experience and to make sense of their social world, but in different ways.

I will refer to the two modes as (i) *informative mode* and (ii) *formative mode.* Neither of these corresponds exactly to any category suggested by Bernstein but the conceptualisation of both resonates with his views, as my comments during the discussion of these two modes will show. Indeed, Bernstein's insights and predictions regarding code-governed selection and organisation of meaning are strongly supported by my research. Let me begin then with some actual extracts from the data [1].

Extract 1

Mother: (1) ... you were certainly very brave
Cameron: (2) (? I wasn't) very brave
Mother: (3) yeah you were brave (4) you mightn't think you were brave (5) but I think you were
Cameron: (6) what for?
Mother: (7) because you acted in a very brave way
Cameron: (8) **no
Mother: (9) **you hurt yourself (10) and you cried (11) and that's good to cry (12) when you hurt yourself (13) but you only cried for a little while (14) and then you climbed back on your bike
Cameron: (15) **and didn't—
Mother: (16) **and when you were a little boy (17) you know what you would have done?
Cameron: (18) what?
Mother: (19) you would have run back to mummy (20) crying really loudly (21) shouting (22) and you didn't do that (23) you acted like a big boy
Cameron: (24) yes
Mother: (25) you got hurt (26) so you cried (27) because you were hurt
Cameron: (28) yeah
Mother: (29) and then after a little while you stopped crying
Cameron: (30) yes
Mother: (31) that's what big boys do
Mother: (32) yeah

Extract 2

Mother: (1) ... when you plant seeds from mandarins or oranges (2) sometimes you get very strange fruit (3) or sometimes you don't get much fruit at all (4) so you have to plant a tree that's been grafted—that's been stuck on (5) they're special trees that they make (6) by sticking one tree to another tree
Stephen: (7) how do they stick it?
Mother: (8) well, I think they cut it in a special way (9) they cut them in a special way (10) and they put them together (11) and then they bind stuff around the outside (12) to hold them together (13) till they grow together ... (14) they eventually grow together the same way as when ... (15) if you cut yourself (16) the skin grows back together again, doesn't it? (17) the two pieces of skin grow together again (18) well the tree—the two bits of the tree grow back too

Extract 3

Mother: (1) do you love daddy?

Julian: (2) mm
Mother: (3) do you love Rosemary?
Julian: (4) no
Mother: (5) why don't you love Rosemary? (JULIAN LAUGHS) (6) why don't you love Rosemary? (JULIAN CONTINUES TO LAUGH) (7) you're a [? ratbag] (MOTHER REALISES JULIAN WAS TEASING)
Julian: (8) I do
Mother: (9) (?)
Julian: (10) who else do you want me to love?
Mother: (11) you can love whoever you want to
Julian: (12) can I love Peter? ... (13) can I?
Mother: (14) no (15) I think that's more like friendship
Julian: (16) pardon
Mother: (17) thought you'd say that (18) it's like friendship, isn't it? ... (19) you're friends with Peter, aren't you?
Julian: (20) yep ... (21) mum!
Mother: (21) yes
Julian: (22) when I get as old as you (23) and (? Maree likes me) (24) could we marry each other?
Mother: (25) no (26) because Maree is your cousin
Julian: (27) oh
Mother: (28) cause cousins aren't allowed to marry
Julian: (29) why?
Mother: (30) cause the law says they're not
Julian: (31) who's that?
Mother: (32) the law?
Julian: (33) yeah
Mother: (34) the policeman ...

First, the informative mode, as is illustrated by Extract 1. What the mother is doing here is informing the child about certain concepts, which happen to be descriptive and evaluative. She is telling Cameron what it means to be described as 'a big boy', or as 'brave'. *The informative mode is an explicit mode of attempting to inculcate some concept, irrespective of the domain within which the concept is located.* This mode fits into Bernstein's category of *elaborated code*, especially if the explicit–implicit axis of differentiation is taken as crucial (Bernstein, 1971). In Extract 1, Cameron's mother explicitly identifies the child's behaviours to which the terms refer; the concepts she tells Cameron about pertain to the communal domain of life. In Extract 2, the same mode is used, but here Stephen's mother explains the concept of 'grafting' as used in the specialist field of horticulture, a domain regarding which the child has no practical experience. She recontextualises the information, so that it becomes immediately accessible to Stephen: 'if you cut yourself, the skin grows back together again, doesn't it? the two pieces of skin grow together again, well the tree—the two bits of the tree grow back too'. In both extracts the discourse is about something, be it part of specialist knowledge or an everyday concept such as acting like a big boy. The informative mode as used by mothers in conversation with their children can also be seen as resonating with Bernstein's concept of *local pedagogy* (Bernstein, 1990), which may be interpreted for our purposes as the transmission of knowledge within the contexts of everyday life (but see later comment). One respect in which Extract 2 differs from Extract 1 is that the information transmission in Extract 2 can hardly be distinguished from the instructional component of official pedagogic discourse for young children. Two issues are particularly relevant to the informative mode: what is the framing like, and how extensive is the pedagogic segment? In my research, the dominating group shows weaker framing and a greater readiness to continue with the informative mode (Cloran, 1999; Hasan, 2000, 2001). This finding is entirely in keeping with Bernstein's predictions (1975, 1990, 1996): weaker framing characterises dominating code modalities [2].

The mode I have called the formative mode is formative in the sense that, rather than instilling particular pieces of information, *it functions as a way of setting up interpersonal relations between the discursive dyads.* The two modes are not mutually exclusive: it is not that one mode characterises one group of speakers, and the other, another group; in fact, the two modes can occur within the same discourse. Extract 3 illustrates the complexity of the simultaneous play of these two modes. Ignoring for the moment the Rosemary episode, turn to messages (12)–(34). Here, the mother is providing information on three issues: (a) whether Julian can love a male friend, (b) whether he can marry his cousin Maree, and (c) who in the community represents legal authority. I am not concerned here with evaluating the items of knowledge that the mother provides: from some points of view, each is 'defective'. Some of us certainly believe that love is not restricted to members of the opposite sex, marrying a cousin is not illegal, and the police do not make the law, although they do have the reputation for maintaining it. The correctness or otherwise of information is an issue that is not relevant to my discussion here; nor does it matter that the three segments are less extensively developed than those in Extracts 1 and 2, although this is a significant parameter of variation between social groups (see Cloran, 1999). For a discursive mode to be informative, the information does not have to be extensively developed or to be factually correct, whatever the standards of correctness applied. That Julian's mother is explicitly telling him about the legal boundaries between love, friendship and marriage is all that matters for taking it as a case of the informative mode, and from this point of view, messages (12)–(34) of Extract 3 are like Extracts 1 and 2: they all provide information in an explicit manner on specific topics.

To see the working of the formative mode, take the earlier part of Extract 3, especially the mother's repeated question 'why don't you love Rosemary?' (messages (5) and (6)). Here the mother is not giving information, but seeking it. Of particular interest is the form for seeking information: the question is framed in the negative. In my semantic network, negation in certain question types (yes/no or why/how questions) realises an important choice, referred to as *assumptive*. A question with this feature does not simply seek information; it implies that the information sought is already known to the enquirer and that its nature is pre-determined. So whenever an assumptive question is asked, there is an explicitly worded meaning; namely, this or that information is needed, as for example: 'I am seeking an explanation for the fact that you don't love Rosemary'; but there is also an *implicational meaning*, which is not worded, but simply implied. In our example, the mother's question implies: 'I believe you *should* love Rosemary'. One might think the distinction between explicitly worded and implied meaning is too subtle to make any practical difference, especially to very young children, but note Julian's uptake on this assumptive question: he asks his mother 'who else do you want me to love?' (message (10)). This shows that, at some three and a half years old, he had already got the covert message. The asking of an assumptive question implies that the enquirer presumes to know what the addressee's mental map is or should be like. The personal distance between them is greatly reduced: the mother is here behaving on the assumption that she and the child share the same experiences, expectations and mental maps.

The semantic feature *assumptive* is not the only feature construed by implicational wording. Here is another example, again involving questions. Compare two questions: (i) 'are they leaving?' and (ii) 'did you know they are leaving?'. The first question seeks information about some state of affairs in the external world of our experience, and the second seeks information about the addressee's mental state: did the addressee know something or not. In the semantic network, this attribute of questions is referred to as *prefaced*: a preface such as 'did you know?', 'do you remember?', 'did you see?', 'would you like?' implies that the enquirer does not presume to know what the addressee knows, remembers, sees or likes; the addressee's mental map is an unknown territory. The mother who asks 'did you know they are leaving?' is not assuming a similarity of knowledge, feeling and expectations: it is as if there exists a personal distance between the two, which means that reliance must be placed on discourse as a means of bridging the distance. It is perhaps obvious from this account that the two semantic features of questions—*assumptive* and *prefaced*—are mutually incompatible so far as an individual's orientation to meanings is concerned: speakers who *habitually* use one feature are not likely to use the other. The features point to different expectations about one's relations to the other. In terms of the early code theory (Bernstein, 1971), these two features are indicative of two distinct codes: the theory would predict that the feature *prefaced*, which implies a greater sense of individuation, would be an element of the elaborated code; while the feature *assumptive*, which implies a greater sense of reflexivity between speaker and addressee, would be that of the restricted code.

Linguists have recognised the tendency of certain specific words to occur with certain other specific words: in fact, Firth's well-known concept of *collocation* (Firth, 1957) is built on this tendency. I suggest that there is such prehension also between specific features at the semantic level. So the semantic feature *prefaced* tends to co-occur with the features *related* and/or *elaborated*. These features refer to aspects of information management. Specifically, the feature 'related' is realised by the linking of messages, so that details about the sequencing of the states of affairs become available, as in 'you hurt yourself and you cried and that's good to cry' (Extract 1, messages (9)–(11)). The feature elaborated is realised by messages that modify and/or develop the information concerning the state of affairs, as in 'when you were a little boy you know what you would have done? you would have run back to mummy, crying really loudly, shouting and you didn't do that, you acted like a big boy' (Extract 1, messages (16)–(23)). This 'clustering' of the semantic features *prefaced*, *related* and *elaborated* makes sense: if the personal distance between the speaker and the addressee has to be bridged discursively, then the terms in that discourse need to be carefully displayed, and information has to be detailed. Now, the semantic features *related* and *elaborated* are realised grammatically as 'modification' and 'subordination', which means these patterns would be expected to occur more often. When in the 1960s Bernstein suggested that these features were relevant to the linguistic differentiation of code varieties, his claim was dismissed (Labov, 1969). With hindsight, it is obvious that Bernstein was right; my research shows that, given their meaning, certain categories of modification and subordination are relevant to code varieties. But there is more to the clusters.

In the environment of questions and answers, two additional semantic features co-occur. The addressee's message following a question is expected to be a *response*, which acknowledges that a question is on the floor; and responses are expected to be *adequate*, so they will address the query point of the question. However, if two persons keep talking, this does not necessarily entail that questions are being responded to or that, if they are, they address the question's query point. The significance of these semantic features is obvious from the following examples.

Extract 4

Mother: (1) oh hurry up ... (2) quick ... (3) sit down ... (4) you're gonna have your hair washed now ... (5) look—

Karen: (6) what? (7) what mummy? ... (8) what?

Mother: (9) nothing

Karen: (10) why did you say 'look'?

Mother: (11) alright lay down (12) and I'll wash your hair.

Here Karen repeats her question three times (messages (6)–(8)) before a response comes in message (9), and that response is not *adequate*: note, the child is not satisfied, as message (10) shows. And although, following upon message (10), the mother does produce a message, it bears no relevance to the question and so it cannot seen as a *response*. Here is another example:

Extract 5

Pete: (1) can I play with (?)?

Mother: (2) no

Pete: (3) oh why not?

Mother: (4) no

Pete: (5) oh (PETE CRIES)

Here the mother's first response is *adequate* although it is *minimal*, without any further elaboration. Contrast this with Julian's mother (Extract 1, messages (25) and (26)), who immediately elaborates on her minimal response: 'no because Maree is your cousin'. We have thus identified two clusters of semantic features, as presented in Table I.

Table I. Two significant clusters of semantic features

Cluster 1: centred on *prefaced*	Cluster 2: centred on *assumptive*
Questions are more often *prefaced*	Questions are more often *assumptive*
More often *related*	Less often *related*
More often *elaborated*	Less often *elaborated*
Answers are more often *responsive*	Answers are less often *responsive*
More often *adequate*	Less often *adequate*
More often *related*	Less often *related*
More often *elaborated*	Less often *elaborated*

The semantic features in each cluster have a 'natural' affinity with each other. The nucleus of clusters 1 and 2 in Table I are the features *prefaced* and *assumptive*, respectively: they form the basis for attracting or repelling the habitual occurrence of the other features. These clusters turn out to be statistically highly relevant in accounting for systematic variation in my data. The cluster in the left column is more likely to be found in the discourse of mothers from dominating families, while that in the right column is more likely to occur in the discourse of mothers from dominated families ($p < 0.0003$). Similar results were obtained by Williams (1999) in the context of joint book reading. Remarkably, when in my research young children's discourse is examined in terms of the same semantic features, an almost identical result is obtained ($p < 0.009$). Cluster 2 typical of the LAP dyads signifies that the mothers view the child as an extension of themselves, similar to them in essential ways, so that there exists an *interpersonal trust* between them; their children too display reciprocal regard, and a similar orientation toward their mother. Cluster 1, with its emphasis on individuation, on precision, and explicitly conveyed information, occurred more frequently in HAP mothers' discourse as well as in that of HAP children (for details, see Hasan, 1989). The expectations of discursive engagement that the two groups of children entertain, the principles for interactive practices that they internalise, are already being learnt at this early stage, and the learning varies systematically, in keeping with the predictions of Bernstein's code theory (1971, 1973, 1975).

I have gone into some detail about what children learn through the formative mode of the maternal discourse. The point seems worth making that neither group of mothers consciously sets out to teach by the formative mode what the children appear to be learning. It is in this sense that the formative mode is not a variety of pedagogic discourse. Bernstein points out:

> ... it is necessary to distinguish between pedagogic consequences and a pedagogic relation. All experiencing carries a pedagogic potential but all experiences are not pedagogically generated. (2000, p. 199)

Certainly, in employing the formative mode, the mothers had no pedagogic intention: in fact, even the word 'employ' overstates the case, for the mode is simply an expression of the mothers *being* themselves. What the mothers speak, their selection and organisation of meanings is a realisation of their social positioning, and 'the culturally determined device' for their social positioning is code, as Bernstein has pointed out (1990, p. 13). It is true that experience of the formative mode of discourse carries a pedagogic potential; but every experience does that, and all experience is utilised in the learning accomplished by the children. The relation between learning and teaching is not quite the same as that between buying and selling (Hasan, 1998): unlike buying and selling, learning and teaching are not necessarily the two sides of the same coin. But very often what we think of as learning is precisely that body of knowledge that is actively and consciously taught: the very word *knowledge* conjures up specialist domains where explicit concepts are the basic currency. Given this, one might wonder what, if any, significance can be attached to the learning by formative mode described above. I believe this learning is really the internalisation of the principles of the code that is *the* relevant code for the social subject. In closing the present paper, I want to present my arguments for this view.

First, if we examine a child learning how to mean (Halliday, 1975, 1993), it becomes obvious that the edifice of all learning is founded on interpersonal relations: in fact, during the pre-linguistic and proto-linguistic stage, all functions in the 'child tongue' are relational functions. There is no concept of information and certainly the informative function—that of telling someone something that might be new to them—does not surface until the child has entered the threshold of his/her mother tongue. Learning how to relate to persons is thus an earlier and essential condition for all other kinds of learning. As Vygotsky (1978, p. 57) claimed '... all higher [*mental*] functions [*in the child*] originate as actual relations between human individuals'.

Second, the boundaries between the formative and the informative modes are not impermeable: in fact, the very same string of words carries both implicational meanings and explicitly worded meanings. Clusters of the kind presented in Table I show quite clearly that the informative and formative modes intersperse in discourse: most of the semantic features that are 'logically' entailed by the implicational meanings of *assumptive* and *prefaced* are essentially informative in nature. The information to be given is, as it were, cut to suit the image of the other: its nature is predicated by the perceived relation.

This has a third consequence. The readiness to receive information, the very perception of what constitutes appropriate information, is fashioned through the specific experience of discourse, and this means through how the formative and the informative modes are interspersed in the discourse that children encounter everyday of their life. The school is where the business of learning is 'institutionalised' but again, as Vygotsky (1978, p. 84) pointed out, '... any learning the child encounters in school has a previous history'. Bernstein's message on this issue was more elaborated: he tried to show us what previous histories of discursive participation different groups of children bring to the school and how this history might impinge on learning in school given the nature of the official pedagogic systems. Part of the function of the child's previous history is precisely to help the child decide what is to be considered relevant by way of information, and how information is to be framed. The semiotic mediation of specialist concepts and knowledge structures calls for a particular kind of discursive experience, a particular form of consciousness, which may or may not have been accessible to all who come to schools to learn. We might claim justifiably that in official pedagogic sites the informative mode, an aspect of Bernstein's elaborated code, is the privileged mode but, in the experience of the growing child, formation and information are integrated: the former gives a specific shape to the latter. It seems appropriate to close the present highly condensed paper on code varieties and their relevance to learning with the words of Basil Bernstein himself:

> ... the particular form of a social relation regulates the options that speakers take up at both syntactic and lexical [*and semantic*, RH] levels ... different forms of social relations can generate very different speech systems or linguistic codes ... the different speech systems or codes create for their speakers different orders of relevance and relation. The experience of the speaker may then be transformed by what is made significant or relevant by different speech systems ... (1971, p. 144)

Acknowledgements

This research project consisting of several phases was funded by grants from the Australian Research Council and the Macquarie University Research Grants Scheme.

NOTES

[1] Conventions for the transcription of speech are as follows.

(4)	The following wording is message number 4 in this extract.
(?I wasn't)	segment unintelligible; enclosed is best guess on the basis of context and co-text.
**no **you hurt ...	wording paired by message—initial double star indicates speech overlap.
you didn't—	this message was left incomplete and/or interrupted by next speaker.
(?)	this segment was unintelligible; no clues to help interpretation.
(PETE CRIES)	situational information based on recorded information.

[2] For discussion on classification and framing see, especially, Bernstein (1990, 1996).

REFERENCES

BERNSTEIN, B. (1965) A sociolinguistic approach to social learning, in: J. GOLD (Ed.) *Penguin Survey of the Social Sciences* (Harmondsworth, Penguin) (reprinted in Bernstein (1971)).

BERNSTEIN, B. (1971) *Class, Codes and Control, Volume I: theoretical studies toward a sociology of language* (London, Routledge & Kegan Paul).

BERNSTEIN, B. (Ed.) (1973) *Class, Codes and Control, Volume II: applied studies towards a sociology of language* (London, Routledge & Kegan Paul).

BERNSTEIN, B. (1975) *Class, Codes and Control, Volume III: towards a theory of educational transmission* (London, Routledge & Kegan Paul).

BERNSTEIN, B. (1982) Codes, modalities and the processes of cultural reproduction, in: *Cultural and Economic Reproduction in Education: essays on class, ideology and the state* (London, Routledge & Kegan Paul).

BERNSTEIN, B. (1987) Social class, codes and communication, in: U. AMMON, K.J. MATTHIER & N. DITTMAR (Eds) *Sociolinguistics: an international handbook of the science of society* (Berlin, Mouton de Gruyter).

BERNSTEIN, B. (1990) *The Structuring of Pedagogic Discourse, Volume IV: class, codes and control* (London, Routledge).

BERNSTEIN, B. (1996) *Pedagogy, Symbolic Control and Identity: theory, research, critique* (London, Falmer Press).

BERNSTEIN, B. (2000) *Pedagogy, Symbolic Control and Identity: theory, research, critique*, revised edn (Lanham, Rowman & Littlefield).

BERNSTEIN, B. & COOK-GUMPERZ, J. (1973) *The Coding Grid in Socialisation and Social Control: a study of class differences in the language of maternal control* (London, Routledge & Kegan Paul).

BONCINELLI, E. (2001) Erasmus Lecture: brain and mind, *European Review*, 9, pp. 389–398.

CLORAN, C. (1999) Contexts for learning, in: F. CHRISTIE (Ed.) *Pedagogy and the Shaping of Consciousness: linguistic and social processes* (London, Cassell).

DEACON, T. (1997) *The Symbolic Species: the co-evolution of language and the human brain* (London, Penguin Books).

FIRTH, J.R. (1957) *Papers in General Linguistics 1934–1951* (London, Oxford University Press).

GREENFIELD, S. (2000) *The Human Brain: a guided tour* (London, Phoenix Paperback).

HALLIDAY, M.A.K. (1973a) Foreword, in: B. BERNSTEIN (Ed.) *Class, Codes and Control Volume 2: applied studies towards a sociology of language* (London, Routledge & Kegan Paul).

HALLIDAY, M.A.K. (1973b) Towards a sociological semantics, in: *Explorations in the Functions of Language* (London, Edward Arnold).

HALLIDAY, M.A.K. (1975) *Learning How to Mean: explorations in the development of language* (London, Edward Arnold).

HALLIDAY, M.A.K. (1993) Towards a language based theory of learning, *Linguistics and Education*, 5, pp. 93–116.

HALLIDAY, M.A.K & MATTHIESSEN, C.M.I.M. (1999) *Construing Experience through Meaning: a language-based approach to experience* (London, Cassell).

HASAN, R. (1973) Code, register and social dialect, in: B. BERNSTEIN (Ed.) *Class, Codes and Control, Volume II: applied studies towards a sociology of language* (London, Routledge & Kegan Paul).

HASAN, R. (1989) Semantic variation and sociolinguistics, *Australian Journal of Linguistics*, 9, pp. 221–275.

HASAN, R. (1992) Rationality in everyday talk: from process to system, in: J. SVARTVIK (Ed.) *Directions in Corpus Linguistics: Proceedings of Nobel Symposium 82* (Berlin, Mouton de Gruyter).

HASAN, R. (1998) Educating the language teacher: a social semiotic approach, in: B. ASKER (Ed.) *Teaching Language and Culture: building Hong Kong on education* (Hong Kong, Addison Wesley Longman).

HASAN, R. (1999) Society, language and the mind: the metadialogism of Basil Bernstein's theory, in: F. CHRISTIE (Ed.) *Pedagogy and the Shaping of Consciousness* (London, Cassell).

HASAN, R. (2000) The uses of talk, in: S. SARANGI & M. COULTHARD (Eds) *Discourse and Social Life* (London, Longman).

HASAN, R. (2001) The ontogenesis of decontextualised language: some achievements of classification and framing, in: A. MORAIS, I. NEVES, B. DAVIES & H. DANIELS (Eds) *Towards a Sociology of Pedagogy: the contribution of Basil Bernstein to research* (New York, Peter Lang).

HASAN, R. & CLORAN, C. (1990) A sociolinguistic study of everyday talk between mothers and children, in: M.A.K. HALLIDAY, J. GIBBONS & H. NICHOLAS (Eds) *Learning Keeping and Using Language, Volume 1* (Amsterdam, John Benjamins).

LABOV, W. (1969) The logic of non-standard English, *Georgetown Monographs on Language and Linguistics, Vol 22* (Washington, DC, Georgetown University Press).

TURNER, G.J. (1973) Social class and children's language of control at age five and seven, in: B. BERNSTEIN (Ed.) *Class, Codes and Control, Volume II: applied studies towards a sociology of language* (London, Routledge & Kegan Paul).

VYGOTSKY, L.S. (1978) *Mind in Society: the development of higher psychological processes* (Cambridge, MA, Harvard University Press).

WILLIAMS, G. (1999) The pedagogic device and the production of pedagogic discourse: a case example in early literacy education, in: F. CHRISTIE (Ed.) *Pedagogy and the Shaping of Consciousness: linguistic and social processes* (London, Cassell).

2 Pedagogic practices in the family socializing context and children's school achievement

Isabel P. Neves and Ana M. Morais

This paper describes a qualitative study about pedagogic practices in the family. The pedagogic code underlying family practices is characterized and related to specific social groups. Students' achievement is discussed in relation to family and school pedagogic practices. The analysis of family pedagogic practice was based on a model derived from Bernstein's theory. The model considers two main dimensions, the coding orientation and its specific realizations in both the instructional and regulative contexts. It provided indicators of the family discursive context and the form in which knowledges and values are transmitted. The model developed allowed a deep and delicate analysis of the family socializing context. The study showed that families differ in their coding orientation and pedagogic practices, and suggested that there are factors other than social groups to determine family's pedagogic practice. It also suggested that specific familial practices may explain children's differential achievement at school.

Introduction

This study is focused on the relations that characterize the socializing family context and it aims at analysing the extent to which these relations interfere on children's answer to school socialization contexts. Theoretically, the study is based on Bernstein's model of pedagogic discourse (Bernstein, 1990, 2000), which gives the possibility of establishing parallels between the pedagogic processes occurring in the family and in the school.

There are many studies centred on the family context. Most of them have a psychological or psycho-sociological basis (for example, Marjoribanks, 1979; Maccoby & Martin, 1983; Ochoa *et al.*, 1988) and describe family sets or parents' educational practices to find out reasons for specific children's behaviours in the school. The studies of a sociological character (for example, Walkerdine & Lucey, 1989) and, in particular, based on Bernstein's theory (for example, Hill & Varenne, 1981; Hasan & Cloran, 1990; Hasan, 2001; Williams, 2001) are specifically centred on social interactions that characterize family contexts to understand how social class or gender interfere on these interactions. The early research based on Bernstein's theory about the processes of family socialization explores the relation between social class and sociolinguistic codes (Bernstein, 1973; Cook-Gumperz, 1973) and is mainly focused on the coding orientation and on the modality of control that characterize the form of communication between mothers and children in the regulative context.

In our study, the analysis of the family takes into account both the regulative and the instructional dimensions of the family pedagogic code. We intend to develop a deeper and more detailed analysis of the family socializing context in order to get a better understanding of the relation usually pointed out between the social background of the children and their school achievement.

We shall start by presenting the model we constructed to analyse the family pedagogic code. This is followed by the methodology. In the analysis of the data, we present some examples of situations that led to the characterization of the family pedagogic code. We analyse the relation between family and school codes and children's achievement in science. Finally, we point out the most relevant results.

Theoretical framework

The pedagogic code in the family context

According to Bernstein, any given modality of pedagogic code is a realization of power and control relations in specific contexts of transmission–acquisition; namely, the instructional and regulative contexts. The modalities of pedagogic code in the school are different contextual realizations of the elaborated code in which the school is predicated. They are given by the formula $O^E/(C_{ie}{}^{\pm}F_{ie}{}^{\pm})$, in which O^E represents the school's elaborated orientation and C and F indicate the principles of classification and framing, whose strong or weak values (±) represent variations in the power and control relations at the level of the pedagogic contexts. The subscripts i and e refer to 'internal' relations (relations within the school context, e.g. the classroom) and to 'external' relations (relations between the school context and other contexts, e.g. the family), respectively. There is a variety of modalities of pedagogic practice representing specific realizations of the school's elaborated code, the consequence of different values of classification and framing. This variety arises also from the fact that the pedagogic discourse refers to a set of knowledges (instructional discourse) and norms of social conduct (regulative discourse), and that their transmission–acquisition is regulated in the instructional practice by discursive rules (selection, sequence, pacing, evaluation criteria) and in the regulative practice by hierarchical rules, which vary according to the control that the transmitter and the acquirer have in the pedagogic relation.

When we use in the analysis of the family socializing context the same conceptual framework used for the school context, the process of family socialization may be viewed as a specific modality of pedagogic code. However, since the code culturally acquired in the family may translate a restricted or elaborated orientation, the modalities of the family pedagogic code correspond to processes whose differences are present not only at the level of the specific form of contextual realization of meanings, but also at the level of the meanings themselves, particularistic or universalistic. Thus, the family's pedagogic codes may be represented by the earlier formula in which O^E is replaced by $O^{E/R}$ (family's 'elaborated' or 'restricted' orientation).

Model of analysis

The model contains the two dimensions of the code: the coding orientation and the realization of meanings in the family socializing context. The development of this model is part of another article (Morais & Neves, 1993), which presents in detail the theoretical assumptions, the objectives and the dimensions of analysis for its application to the study of the family. Space limitations led us to present here only the diagram containing the relations established by the model (Figure 1), with some references to their meaning for the study.

In this model, the family's pedagogic code is analysed at two levels which, although interlinked, are taken as separate components of the realization of the code at discursive and transmission levels. The discursive level, which includes both family instructional discourse (FID) and family regulative discourse (FRD), refers to the knowledges/activities and norms of social conduct present in the family. Through an indirect pedagogic practice (IPP), children, as spectators of the discursive universes of the families, learn (in a non-evaluative context) to value the meanings transmitted by parents' instructional and regulative discourses. The transmission level, which focuses on the realization of families' pedagogic discourses (i.e. on the instructional and regulative practices of families) refers to the process of transmission–acquisition used by parents in pedagogic interaction with their children. Through a direct pedagogic practice (DPP), children, as active participants in the learning process, acquire (in an evaluative context) specific skills and norms of social conduct that determine their answers in other learning contexts.

The model considers the contextual realization of meanings using the values of classification and framing that define the discursive and transmission components of the pedagogic code, and it also considers the coding orientation—that is, the meanings that are present in the family's discourses and practices. The analysis of this dimension of the code is made according to the particularistic/universalistic nature of meanings contained in the instructional and regulative discourses and according to the meanings transmitted through the instructional and regulative practices.

Methodology

Sample

The study refers to five families (five fathers and five mothers), distinct in social class (understood as a nominal concept) and race, and whose children had been shown to be particular cases within particular social groups, relatively to their science school

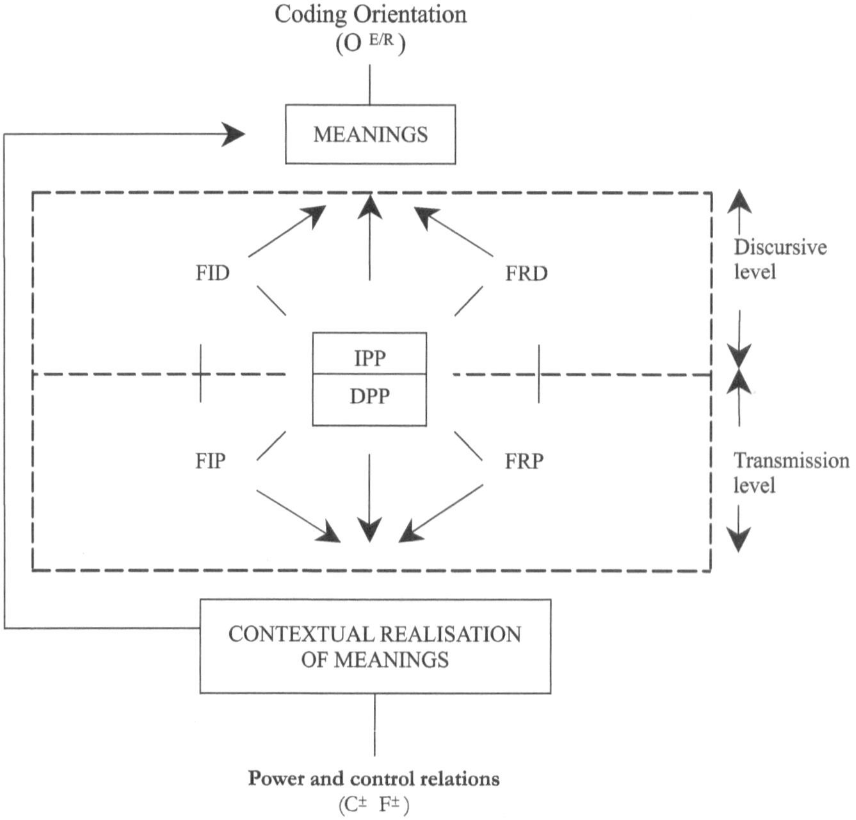

O E/R—Elaborated and restricted orientation

Figure 1. Model of analysis of the family's pedagogic code

achievement. These children, were part of two school classes of the fifth and sixth years of schooling (10^- to 12^+). Each school class was socially heterogeneous (social class, race, gender) and received in sciences, during two school academic years, one of two distinct modalities of pedagogic practice (P1 and P2).[1] These were implemented by the same teacher (female).

The pedagogic practices differed in terms of power and control relations between spaces, discourses and subjects. One of the practices (P_2) was characterized by strong framings at the level of the discursive rules (greater teacher's control over the selection, sequence, pacing and evaluation criteria) and the hierarchical rules (modalities of control fundamentally imperative or positional). The other practice (P_1) was characterized by weak framings (lesser teacher's control over the discursive rules and fundamentally interpersonal modes of control in the teacher–children communicative relations). The organization of spaces in the classroom was characterized in P_2 by a strong classification between teacher's and children's spaces and between children's spaces (particularly in terms of social class and school achievement), and in P_1 by a weak classification between spaces.

CHILD/ SCHOOL PRACTICE	RACE	SOCIAL CLASS	STUDENTS' ACHIEVEMENT (%)			SOCIAL GROUPS' ACHIEVEMENT (%)		
			SC	CC	Global	SC	CC	Global
Nuno *P2*	B	Low	57.0	25.0	41.0	43.1	21.1	32.1
Ana *P1*	B	Low	21.0	21.0	21.0			
Rui *P2*	W	Low	80.0	83.0	81.5	61.5	44.1	52.8
David *P1*	W	Low	53.0	23.0	38.0			
Sara *P1*	W	High	73.0	36.0	54.5	73.0	48.3	60.7

SC – Simple cognitive competences
CC – Complex cognitive competences

Figure 2. Selected children, according to gender, race, social class, school pedagogic practice and relative cognitive achievement in science

Given the importance attributed in the research to the general failure of the socially disadvantaged children, four families (two black and two white) were part of the lower social groups. The fifth family was selected among the highest social class.[2] Within the lower social groups, we selected two families whose children's cognitive achievement was above the average of his/her group and two families whose children's achievement was below the average. Two children were part of P_1 and two of P_2. In the highest social group, we studied a family whose child had shown low achievement, constituting a discrepant case within her group. This was a child from P_1.

The level of achievement refers to the mean obtained by children in the two science school tests done in the first term of the fifth year (the initial stage of the research). The tests were the same for all children and assessed two types of cognitive competencies, simple (SC) and complex (CC).[3]

Figure 2 presents the distribution of the children, according to the characteristics referred. It shows the achievement in sciences in SC and in CC, and also the global achievement, when both are joined together. Achievement was measured on a 0–100 scale.

Instrument of analysis

On the basis of the model already referred to (Figure 1), we defined the following dimensions of analysis to characterize the family's pedagogic codes:

(1) The knowledges/activities and norms of social conduct that are present in families' everyday lives.
(2) The principles adduced by parents as underlying the knowledges/activities and norms of social conduct they value.
(3) The form used by parents to transmit their knowledges and norms of social conduct and to explain tasks to children.
(4) The modality of social control used by parents in their communicative relations with children.
(5) The principles adduced by parents as underlying the ways they teach their children.

We constructed an instrument[4] that contained, for each dimension of analysis, some premises and a set of questions and objectives to orientate the empirical research. On the basis of these premises, questions and objectives, we constructed a guide[5] to orientate a semi-structured interview. We separated, in the interview's guide, the dimension designated by indirect pedagogic practice from the dimension designated by direct pedagogic practice. To obtain data about the indirect practice we introduced questions related to parents' occupations and free-time activities (television programmes, reading, outside leisure activities like cinema, football, trips) and related to child's school life. To obtain data about the direct pedagogic practice, the questions were centred on aspects related to the talk between father/mother and child (e.g. questions the child asks) and related to the child's control on his/her activities (school homework, help in home tasks and in father/mother's work and also free time occupation like reading, extra-school activities).

Data analysis

Figure 3 summarizes the fundamental characteristics of the pedagogic codes of the five families. The relations between the local pedagogic discourse (LPD) and the official pedagogic discourse (OPD) and the relations that characterize the family pedagogic practice (instructional and regulative) were translated, respectively, in a four-point scale for classification and a six-point scale for framing. Classification and framing scales were constructed in function of the situations analysed, and as such they should be taken in relative and not absolute terms. The figure also includes data related to the families' social background and to the school pedagogic codes children received in their science classes.

Let us first consider the *coding orientation* of the families. The interview's data suggested that Nuno's and Ana's parents tend to use preferably particularistic meanings, context dependent (O^R), whereas Rui's and Sara's parents tend to use universalistic meanings, relatively context independent (O^E). In the case of David's family, the father showed an elaborated orientation whereas the mother showed a restricted orientation. The following extracts of the interviews with Nuno's and Rui's mothers, related to the reason why they like to watch a given television serial and to the talk they have with their children about that serial, are examples that illustrate differences in coding orientation.

RACE	SOCIAL CLASS	CHILD/ SCHOOL PRACTICE	FAMILY	RELATION BETWEEN LPD/OPD	FAMILY'S PEDAGOGIC PRACTICE: INSTRUCTIONAL	FAMILY'S PEDAGOGIC PRACTICE: REGULATIVE	FAMILY CODING ORIENTATION	SCHOOL CODING ORIENTATION	SCHOOL PEDAGOGIC PRACTICE: INSTRUCTIONAL	SCHOOL PEDAGOGIC PRACTICE: REGULATIVE
BLACK	Low	Nuno *P2*	Father	Ce^{+}	Selection – Fi^{++} Criteria – Fi^{++}	Imperative and *positional* control (Fi^{++})	$_{O}{}^{R}$	$_{O}{}^{E}$	*P2* Selection – Fi^{++} Criteria – Fi^{++}	*P2* Imperative and *positional* control (Fi^{+})
			Mother	Ce^{--}	Selection – Fi^{+++} Criteria – Fi^{++}	*Imperative* control (Fi^{+++})	$_{O}{}^{R}$			
		Ana *P1*	Father	Ce^{-}	Selection – Fi^{++} Criteria – Fi^{++}	Imperative and *positional* control (Fi^{++})	$_{O}{}^{R}$	$_{O}{}^{E}$	*P1* Selection – Fi^{-} Criteria – Fi^{-}	*P1* *Interpersonal* control (Fi^{--})
			Mother	Ce^{--}	Selection – Fi^{+} Criteria – Fi^{++}	*Imperative* control (Fi^{+++})	$_{O}{}^{R}$			
WHITE	Low	Rui *P2*	Father	Ce^{++}	Selection – Fi^{-} Criteria – Fi^{+}	*Interpersonal* and positional control (Fi^{-})	$_{O}{}^{E}$	$_{O}{}^{E}$	*P2* Selection – Fi^{++} Criteria – Fi^{++}	*P2* Imperative and *positional* control (Fi^{+})
			Mother	Ce^{+}	Selection – Fi^{+} Criteria – Fi^{-}	*Positional* and interpersonal control (Fi^{+})	$_{O}{}^{E}$			
		David *P1*	Father	Ce^{+}	Selection – Fi^{++} Criteria – Fi^{++}	*Positional* control (Fi^{+})	$_{O}{}^{E}$	$_{O}{}^{E}$	*P1* Selection – Fi^{-} Criteria – Fi^{-}	*P1* *Interpersonal* control (Fi^{--})
			Mother	Ce^{-}	Selection – Fi^{++} Criteria – Fi^{++}	Imperative and *positional* control (Fi^{++})	$_{O}{}^{R}$			
	High	Sara *P1*	Father	Ce^{++}	Selection – Fi^{+} (LP) – Fi^{+} (OP) Criteria – Fi^{-} (LP) – Fi^{+} (OP)	*Positional* and interpersonal control (Fi^{+})	$_{O}{}^{E}$	$_{O}{}^{E}$	*P1* Selection – Fi^{-} Criteria – Fi^{-}	*P1* *Interpersonal* control (Fi^{--})
			Mother	Ce^{++}	Selection – Fi^{-} (LP) – Fi^{+} (OP) Criteria – Fi^{-} (LP) – Fi^{+} (OP)	*Interpersonal* control (Fi^{--})	$_{O}{}^{E}$			

LPD – Local pedagogic discourse
OPD – Official pedagogic discourse
LP – Local practice
OP – Oficial practice

Figure 3. Family and science classroom modalities of pedagogic code

Nuno's mother: I enjoy watching … things of Raquel, things the daughter does to her mother […]. I just ask Nuno what happened … He said 'everything went well and then Fátima went there to argue with her mother and after the mother does not want' … He says lots of things […].

Rui's mother: Because I find in it [the serial] … gives some ideas to … therefore one watches the serial and sometimes draws conclusions from it […]. Sometimes, in the moment something is happening, I say 'see, look at that example, she looks so intimate, it looks such a good thing … and she is false after all' […].

Nuno's mother refers to the serial emphasizing its immediate and local meaning, as the talk is focused on concrete situations that take place in the serial, whereas Rui's mother emphasizes specific general principles that can be drawn from the concrete situations of the serial.

If we now take the relation between the *local pedagogic discourse* and the *official pedagogic discourse*, the data show that in Sara's family and with Rui's father the official pedagogic discourse tend to be strongly embedded in their respective local pedagogic discourses, showing the high status given to the OPD (C^{++}). The relation between these discourses seems also to characterize the pedagogic code of Nuno's and David's fathers and of Rui's mother, although the embedding of the OPD in the LPD is smaller (C^{+}). In Ana's and Nuno's families, the official pedagogic discourse is totally absent of mothers' local pedagogic discourse, which means that the OPD is not embedded in their LPD (C^{--}). For Ana's father and David's mother, the OPD is relatively absent from their LPD (C^{-}).

The difference at the level of the relation between the LPD and the OPD reflects, in part, the degree of father's/mother's schooling. For example, the fact that Nuno's and Ana's mothers are illiterate is by itself a reason for their discourse to be characterized by commonsense knowledges and manual activities, without an OPD being present. On the contrary, parents who had access to the school show discursive patterns that reflect the higher status given to the OPD relative to the LPD. The difference between C^{+} and C^{++} translates, in the second case (C^{++}), the presence at home of subjects and activities usually characteristic of the official pedagogic discourse (e.g. reading, helping children with their school homework) and, in the first case (C^{+}), that presence but in a smaller degree (e.g. fathers/mothers give some help with children's school tasks or seek help from others and show some interest in academic subjects).

The analysis of the characteristics of the *instructional practice* suggests a trend in Nuno's, Ana's and David's families to value a didactic theory of instruction, essentially centred on the transmitter. Rui's and Sara's families show a relative similarity at the level of the transmission of everyday knowledge (local practice). The theory of instruction seems to be, for these families, more centred on the acquirer (i.e. more self-regulated), meaning that, in some aspects, it is given to the child greater control on his/her learning. This situation is particularly evident in the local pedagogic practice of Sara's mother whose selection and evaluation criteria are regulated by weak framings (F_i^{-}). It is interesting to note that, in Sara's family, where some difference seems to exist at the level of the theory of instruction underlying the learning of home tasks (local practice) and the learning of school tasks (official practice), the daughter has lesser control on the learning related to school tasks (selection and criteria regulated by strong framing, F_i^+); that is, there is, in this case, a trend for a theory of instruction to be more transmitter-centred.

The transcripts that follow are examples from interviews with David's and Sara's mothers and Rui's father, related to control over *selection* of home activities done by children:

> David's mother: [...] he likes painting [the house walls] very much but cannot be allowed to do so ... I don't let him [the son] paint.
>
> Sara's mother: She [the daughter] was still very little and I think it had some relation with her enjoying to play with water ... Thus one day ... she washed up a few things ... but mostly by the enjoyment of playing with water [...]. Now that she has grown up she asks for and enjoys [speaking about the daughter asking for do the washing].
>
> Rui's father: He [the son] tried to make an omelette his way ... we even thought it was good he had initiative ... Because I think he should also take initiatives [...].

Whereas David's mother answer illustrates a situation where the selection is explicitly controlled by the transmitter (F_i^{++}), Sara's mother and Rui's father answers show situations where the child's activities are selected in function of the acquirer (F_i^-).

Differences at the level of the *evaluation criteria* are exemplified by Rui's and Sara's fathers' texts, when talking of home tasks:

> Rui's father: I taught him ... the fork should be placed on this side, the knife on this, the napkin on this side outside the plate, the bread is placed in the saucer ... It must be laid in this way according to hotel service standards [speaking about the form he teaches the son to lay the table].
>
> Sara's father: [...] the way she [the daughter] tidies up [the toys] for me is not important ... The way she tidies up is something personal ...

Rui's father gives more emphasis to explicit evaluation criteria, defined by the transmitter (F_i^+), and Sara's father seems to legitimate implicit evaluation criteria (F_i^-).

The following example evidences differences shown by Sara's father of the control of evaluation criteria at the level of school tasks when compared with home tasks.

> Sara's father: For example ... sometimes she [the daughter] comes 'oh daddy give me a clue for an essay or see how it is' ... And I give! ... Or I change the form of a sentence [...].

In this case, the father intervenes directly, giving his criteria to the production of the text he considers adequate for an essay (F_i^+).

Finally let us consider the characteristics related with the *regulative practice*. The analysis suggested a general trend by all families studied to use positional modalities of control. However, whereas Nuno's, Ana's and David's families also used imperative modalities, Rui's and Sara's families also used interpersonal modalities of control. In general, we can say that the hierarchical rules that regulate the regulative practice of Nuno's, Ana's and David's families are characterized by strong framing values:

F_i^{+++} when the control is essentially imperative, F_i^{++} when the control, essentially positional, is associated to forms of imperative control, and F_i+ when the control is essentially positional. In any of these situations, the regulative practice of the family celebrates hierarchy, making explicit authority relations. The hierarchical rules that regulate the regulative practice of Rui's and Sara's families are regulated by weak framing values: F_i^{-} when the control, essentially interpersonal, is associated with forms of positional control, and F_i^{--} when the control is essentially personal. In the regulative practice of these families, the hierarchy, although present, is somehow implicit, the relations of authority being blurred through the frequent use of appeals of an interpersonal nature.

These differences are evidenced by the following examples:

Ana's mother:	Sometimes, afterwards, I reprimand her [the daughter] ... Says 'oh Ana do this, if you are not going to do this... you'll "levas porrada"'[6] [speaking about home tasks]. I beat her up and say she must pay more attention ... if I am not to beat her up again [speaking about school tasks].
Sara's mother:	No, no [she does not get angry with her daughter] ... I explain to her that if in fact somebody comes in it is a bit unnice to enter in the bedroom and not be neat ... But alright ... that's her problem ... if she likes that way ... 'Sara it's your bedroom, therefore if somebody comes it's you that after all will suffer the shame of the people who enter and see your room unneat... because if they go to mum's bedroom, the bedroom is neat' [speaking about home tasks]. [...] Usually I do not get angry with her ... Although she had a bad mark in the school test ... And afterwards of course I called her attention 'if you had studied a bit every day ... because you let many things to the end ... and then you are uncapable' [...]. If she has a good mark I praise her, that I liked ... I am pleased with her ... [speaking of school tasks].
Rui's father:	[...] Whenever you are everything must ... either studying, working must be done willingly. And if he was told to do, he must do ... he cannot disobey ... [speaking of home tasks]. [...] For I tell him that I ... daddy likes the fact that she has passed the year and has good results, that is good for him and I am pleased [speaking of school tasks].

Ana's mother uses orders and sometimes physical coercion, features that illustrate frequent modes of imperative control. Sara's mother emphasizes interpersonal relations in her regulative practice, as she appeals to the attributes of her daughter as a person and not to her attributes based on status of gender, age or parental relation. In the case of Rui's father, the use of positional appeals is evidenced by the transcript about home tasks, and the use of personal appeals is also evident in the same text and in the transcript about school tasks. The association of these distinct control modalities, showing greater emphasis in personal modes of control, led us to characterize the regulative practice of this father by weak framing, although less weak than in the case of Sara's mother.

According to the dimensions of analysis derived from the model, many other aspects of the primary socializing context were used to characterize the pedagogic code of the five families. An important aspect refers to the *norms of social conduct* to be followed at home, and so we obtained information about the attitudes/social norms present in the family's regulative discourse and practice. The following examples evidence differences at this level.

Rui's father: Sometimes the sister, the sister herself 'today it's you who lay the table' [...]. They agree ... it was agreed between ... I myself have already laid the table [...]. The school is like any occupation, be waiter, be doctor, be ... it is to be done willingly and at 100% ... It is what I tell them [...].

David's mother: I tell him [the son] that he should have done what I ordered [to do the bed]. [...] I tell him that he should have studied ... if I work, if I sacrifice myself and his father, he should also sacrifice himself [...].

Sara's father: Look this, during 10 years [referring to his adolescence] I did my bed everyday [...] No, it is not a division of tasks ... If she is the one [the daughter] who sleeps in her bed, why should not be her who does it? [...]. I ask her ... if she wants me to do her bed ... or if she wants me to study in her place or if she wants me to do her bedroom [...].

Whereas Rui's father seems to value attitudes of cooperation and responsibility, these being reasons to lead his son to do the tasks, David's mother and Sara's father show to value attitudes of obedience and respect.

If we analyse the relation of (dis)continuity between family's and school's pedagogic codes, we can discuss the extent to which children's differential achievement may be influenced by that relation.

In the case of Nuno's and Ana's families (black, lower working class), there is a discontinuity (more marked for Ana) between the family and the school pedagogic discourses. The official instructional discourse is not embedded in their mothers' local instructional discourse. If we consider both the family and the school pedagogic practices, it is Ana who initially finds herself, in the science classroom, in a situation of more marked discontinuity. Whereas for Nuno the theory of instruction and the communicative relations transmitter–acquirer, which characterize the science pedagogic practice he received, approximate to the characteristics of the family instructional and regulative contexts, for Ana the school pedagogic practice was opposite to her family pedagogic practice. Since Nuno had a fair achievement in simple cognitive competencies and had a better global achievement than Ana, we can give as an explanatory hypothesis for the differential achievement of these children the interactive relation of family and school pedagogic practices. The fact that both children failed in the complex cognitive competencies can be a consequence of the restricted orientation underlying the pedagogic code of their families.

David (white, working class), who receives the same science pedagogic practice as Ana, showed like her a low global cognitive achievement. However, the fact that David has access, through his father, to an elaborated orientation (the father participates actively in a trade union) and also the fact that the official instructional discourse is relatively embedded in the father's local instructional discourse can constitute reasons to justify his better achievement (fair in the simple competencies) relative to Ana. One can think that his failure in complex competencies is partly a consequence of the socializing process used by his mother, who has a restricted orientation.

When we compare Ana's, David's and Nuno's achievement, according to the distinctive characteristics of the respective family and school contexts, we can discuss the meaning of the school achievement of these lower-working-class children. The relative similarity of David's and Nuno's achievement suggests that the effect of the favourable characteristics of David's family context (particularly father's elaborated orientation) parallels the effect of the relation of continuity between the family and school pedagogic practices in Nuno's family. For Ana, the cumulative effect of the unfavourable characteristics of the family context (e.g. parents' restricted orientation) may justify her lowest achievement when compared with David and Nuno.

Rui's family departed from the pattern of primary socialization found in the other working-class families. His father (with only primary schooling) showed possession of some knowledge of English and Latin and he learned to play music. His interests (reading, television programmes) are particularly centred on the area of scientific and musical knowledge (classical music), and through his occupation (waiter in a restaurant of the high middle class) he has contact with the high social classes. Rui's mother (also with only primary schooling) joins her husband in part of his cultural activities (visits to museums, concerts) and she is a close friend of the family of a secondary school teacher (female) of whose baby she takes care. This is a family that values the pedagogic principles legitimized by the agents of symbolic control and seems to have a class consciousness fundamentally regulated by the values of education. The father's cultural interests and the communicative social relations that father and mother have with the middle class, particularly from the field of symbolic control, are aspects that can justify the characteristics of the pedagogic context of Rui's family and that may have contributed to the high achievement of their child. In this family, similarly to the higher social class family, the official pedagogic discourse is embedded in the local pedagogic discourse (particularly father's) and both father and mother showed an elaborated orientation. The father's fundamentally interpersonal form of control, tend to reproduce principles of social relations legitimized by the agents of symbolic control. However, since in the family's regulative context the child is more socialized by the mother (who uses mainly a positional control), it is possible to think that Rui's good achievement is also partly reflecting the relation of continuity between the regulative practices of mother and school. In the instructional context, the continuity at the level of the family and school discourses and practices may justify the good science achievement of this child. The great interest of the father for the area of scientific knowledge and the fact that he legitimizes a theory of instruction relatively centred on the transmitter, in which there are explicit evaluation criteria, led the son to acquire recognition and realization rules appropriated to the instructional context of a school practice with characteristics near to the family practice. For this child there is a double continuity between the family and school contexts, since he has access at home to the elaborated orientation of the school and he is also socialized in a modality of pedagogic code that is near to the form of realization of the elaborated code present in his science class.

Another interesting case is Sara's family who is part of the high middle social class. This family possess an elaborated orientation and, at home, modalities of control are mainly personal in the case of the mother and positional in the case of the father. We think that, at the level of the regulative context, the father's preference for a positional control (not only between him and his daughter but also between him and his wife) may be a consequence of a class consciousness essentially regulated by the relations of production (he directs a large industrial enterprise). Furthermore, in the regulative context of the family, there seems to exist a relation between father and daughter (as between father and mother) in which attitudes of obedience and respect are more valued than, for example, cooperation, suggesting that the child is socialized in forms of communication in which her social role is more atributed than acquired. Sara has, at home, the official pedagogic discourse embedded in the local pedagogic discourse. Her mother, who has more contact with her daughter, uses an instructional practice characterized by discursive rules of relatively strong framing, particularly at the level of the transmission of science knowledge. Her father showed also to value a theory of instruction relatively centred on the transmitter, with respect to the learning of school knowledge. In the particular case of science, he perceives the learning of this school subject as based on memorization.

Although submitted in the family to a process of socialization favourable to school success (elaborated orientation and official pedagogic discourse), there is for Sara a certain discontinuity between family and school instructional practices. If we consider the characteristics of her family's instructional practice (with respect to the official discourses), the data suggest that the success in science of Sara may be limited, to a certain extent, by that discontinuity. The fact that this child obtained a good global achievement in science shows how school success may be a function of the relation between social class and family socialization. However, her difficulties in developing complex competencies may reflect the lack of recognition and realization rules for the competencies required in the specific instructional practice of her science class. The fact that socio-affective dispositions required by the family and the fact that the family form of control were inconsistent and not always in accordance with the regulative context of her school practice may also explain Sara's low achievement.

Conclusions

We saw that, in general, there seems to exist a relation between social class and the general coding orientation of families. Although this confirmed the data of other studies (for example, Bernstein, 1973; Cook-Gumperz, 1973; Adlam *et al.*, 1977; Fontinhas *et al.*, 1995), the qualitative analysis of the family pedagogic context provided data that show the importance of mediating factors on that relation. For example, the active participation in social agencies[7] and the access to middle-class cultural contexts constitute sociological factors that may explain departing situations related to the coding orientation we found in some members of the working-class families.

Furthermore, the study suggests a relation pattern between the social group and the form of the realization of the code (restricted/elaborated) in the pedagogic context of transmission–acquisition of knowledge and norms of social conduct, which constitute the instructional and regulative discourses of the family. The data showed that, in the working-class families, the father/mother–child relations were regulated by strong values of framing and by a relation between discourses in which the official pedagogic discourse was excluded from the family discourses. In the middle-class family, the transmitter–acquirer relations were, in general, regulated by weak values of framing and by a relation between discourses in which the official pedagogic discourse was present in the family discourses. However, the data suggest situations that depart from the pattern referred to. The most discrepant case is Rui's family whose pedagogic code, particularly of the father, has characteristics closer to the middle-class family than to the other working-class families.

When we see that the children who received the science pedagogic practice of weak framings (Ana, David, Sara) had school results that, contrary to the children who received the practice of strong framings (Nuno, Rui), are below the mean achievement of the respective social groups, we could be led to think that the former pedagogic practice is less favourable than the latter to children's learning. However, we should not forget that the data refer only to five children, and that since they are centred on school science results obtained in the beginning of the research they may not yet show the influence of the school pedagogic practice. In fact, other data obtained during the broader research (Morais *et al.*, 1993) of which this study is part showed that, after two years of schooling (submitted to the same pedagogic practice in science), the children showed a differential evolution according to the school practice. If we consider the specific case of the working-class children object of this study, we saw that Ana and David improved their achievement whereas the opposite happened with Nuno. The comparison of the initial and final results of these three children raises the possibility of a specific school pedagogic practice, although with opposite characteristics of their families practices, having, in the long run, a beneficial effect on the learning of disadvantaged children. The fact that a school pedagogic practice characterized by general weak framings favours the exchange of ideas and experiences between children from different cultural universes and opens up interaction relations teacher–child and child–child that facilitate the acquisition of a higher positioning and of an elaborated orientation by the socially disadvantaged children, may constitute an explanatory hypothesis for the improvement on their achievement within that school pedagogic practice. On the contrary, a pedagogic practice characterized by strong framings, although it can be initially better for socially disadvantaged children (given the family practice in which they were primarily socialized), will reinforce the low positioning assumed by these children in the school and will also make more difficult their access to the school-elaborated orientation.

For middle-class children or working-class children who have access, through their parents, to an elaborated orientation, the school success seems not to be so problematic, since those children acquire easily the recognition and realization rules of a given practice.

The five cases studied do not certainly provide data for generalizations, either about the family pedagogic practices or about its relation with children's achievement in school. However, they showed clearly that families differ in their coding orientation and in their power and control relations (i.e. they differ in their pedagogic codes). They also showed that pedagogic codes are not necessarily a function of the social group of the family. This points out to the importance of analyses that are not limited to the simplistic and reductionist relation of school achievement and social group.

From the point of view of educational research, our study may contribute to get a better understanding of family factors that explain the general failure of socially disadvantaged children. While suggesting that there are fundamental differences within the working class that are reflected in children's primary socialization and that, in turn, reflect on their school achievement, the study can lead schools and teachers to understand how some children succeed and others fail. These considerations may reinforce the relevant role that the school/teacher can have in changing children's' differential achievement. Teacher's work in the classroom requires the awareness of factors that intervene in the child's primary socialization and also the understanding of the possibilities offered by specific school practices in creating conditions to reduce the gap between distinct groups of children. We believe that teachers' knowledge of primary socialization discourses and practices may give them a clear vision of the causes of success and failure of children from lower social backgrounds and enable teachers to act in a more explicit and efficient way in classroom contexts to improve these children's learning.

An important aspect of the study concerns the model constructed to analyse family pedagogic codes. This model opens up new ways to explore the meaning of differential achievement in terms of the family–school relation. This is possible by the strong conceptual structure and explanatory power of the theory on which our research is based. The explanatory power of Bernstein's internal language of description allowed us to use the same concepts in family and school contexts to broaden the relationships studied and conceptualize the results at a higher level. The application of the model in the analyses we carried out required an operationalization of its concepts, through a language of description that was adequate to each of the relations under analysis. This methodological aspect constitutes, in terms of the model's application, a fundamental dimension of the research, given the potentialities revealed in the analysis and interpretation of the results obtained.

Acknowledgments

The authors acknowledge JNICT and the Gulbenkian Foundation for the financing of the study. The authors are grateful to Professor Basil Bernstein for stimulating discussions.

Notes

1. Morais *et al.* (1993) give a detailed description of the pedagogic practices.
2. Lower social class refers to degrees 1 and 2 (academic qualifications not above primary schooling and manual occupations) within a scale of 1–6 (composite of father's and mother's occupations and academic qualifications). Higher social class refers to degree 6 (university degree or equivalent and high non-manual occupations).
3. Simple cognitive competencies refer to memorization and understanding of primary concepts at the lowest level. Complex cognitive competencies refer to the understanding of concepts at the highest level and the application of concepts to new situations (involving complex cognitive processes).
4. A detailed description of the instrument is presented in Morais and Neves (1993).
5. A detailed description of the interview's guide can be seen in Morais and Neves (1993).
6. Jargon used by the lower working class to refer to beating.
7. We considered that active work in agencies of challenge, opposition and resistance (e.g. unions, political parties) and in agencies of cultural reproduction (e.g. cultural and recreative associations) gives access of the lower working class to an elaborated orientation and to a distinct status in the social hierarchy regulated by the class structure.

References

Adlam, D., Turner, G. J. & Lineker, L. (1977) *Code in context* (London, Routledge & Kegan Paul).

Bernstein, B. (1973) *Class, codes and control: applied studies towards a sociology of language* (London, Routledge & Kegan Paul).

Bernstein, B. (1990) *Class, codes and control: the structuring of pedagogic discourse* (London, Routledge).

Bernstein, B. (2000) *Pedagogy, symbolic control and identity: theory, research, critique* (rev. edn) (London, Rowman & Littlefield).

Cook-Gumperz, J. (1973) *Social control and socialisation: a study of class differences in the language of maternal control* (London, Routledge & Kegan Paul).

Fontinhas, F., Morais, A. M. & Neves, I. P. (1995) Students' coding orientation and school socialising context in their relation with students' scientific achievement, *Journal of Research in Science Teaching,* 32(5), 445–462.

Hasan, R. (2001) The ontogenesis of decontextualised language: some achievements of classification and framing, in: A. Morais, I. Neves, B. Davies & H. Daniels (Eds) *Towards a sociology of pedagogy: the contribution of Basil Bernstein to research* (New York, Peter Lang).

Hasan, R. & Cloran, C. (1990) A sociolinguistic study of everyday talk between mothers and children, in: M. Halliday, J. Gibbons & N. Howard (Eds) *Learning, keeping and using language: Vol. I* (Amsterdam, Benjamins).

Hill, C. & Varenne, H. (1981) Family language and education: the sociolinguistic model of restricted and elaborated codes, *Social Science Information,* 20(1), 187–228.

Maccoby, E. & Martin, J. (1983) Socialization in the context of the family: parent–child interaction, in: P. Mussen (Ed.) *Handbook of child psychology* (New York, John Wiley).

Marjoribanks, K. (1979) Family environments, in: H. Walberg (Ed.) *Educational environments and effects: evaluation, policy and productivity* (Berkeley, CA, MacCutchan).

Morais, A. M. & Neves, I. (1993) Práticas pedagógicas e teorias de instrução no contexto de socialização familiar—um modelo de análise, in: A. M. Morais, I. P. Neves, A. Medeiros, D. Peneda, F. Fontinhas & H. Antunes (Eds) *Socialização primária e prática pedagógica, vol. 2: Análise de aprendizagens na família e na escola* (chapter XIV) (Lisbon, Gulbenkian Foundation).

Morais, A. M., Neves, I. P., Medeiros, A., Peneda, D., Fontinhas, F., & Antunes, H. (1993) *Socialização primária e prática pedagógica, vol. 2: Análise de aprendizagens na família e na escola* (Lisbon, Gulbenkian Foundation).

Ochoa, G., Sanchez, J. & Fuster, E. (1988) *Familia y educación: prácticas educativas de los padres y socialización de los hijos* (Barcelona, Editorial Labor).

Walkerdine, V. & Lucey, H. (1989) *Democracy in the kitchen: regulating mothers and socializing daughters* (London, Virago Press).

Williams, G. (2001) Literacy pedagogy prior to schooling: relations between social positioning and semantic variation, in: A. Morais, I. Neves, B. Davies & H. Daniels (Eds) *Towards a sociology of pedagogy: the contribution of Basil Bernstein to research* (New York, Peter Lang).

3 Literacy and Pedagogy in Flux

Constructing the object of study from a Bernsteinian perspective

Gemma Moss

ABSTRACT *This paper considers the principles of description that underpin Bernstein's theoretical language, and how these can be applied to empirical data. The particular case explored here is the relevance of the distinctions Bernstein draws between (i) invisible and visible pedagogies, and (ii) competence and performance pedagogies, for thinking about the literacy curriculum from a social practice perspective. The paper argues that it is the generative potential of Bernstein's theoretical language, and the supple and flexible ways in which the dichotomies he delineates can be used to map out changing boundary relations in a given field, which make his work so powerful.*

> It is misleading to confound content analysis with a language of description. Often content analysis is concerned with self announcing contents. I would rather say that principles of description construct what is to count as empirical relations and translate those relations into conceptual relations. (Bernstein, 1996, p. 136)

Introduction

This article explores the relationship between Bernstein's theoretical work and his work on literacy as a social practice. Steering by Bernstein's concept of languages of description, it will consider both the usefulness of Bernstein's theoretical formulations for thinking about empirical data on literacy, collected within the *literacy as social practice* tradition, and the way in which the empirical data itself can in turn speak back to Bernstein's theoretical formulations. The aim is to explore the value of such a dialogue.

Delineating the Literacy as Social Practice Tradition

Within education, *literacy as social practice* perspectives define themselves through their opposition to the predominant traditions of literacy study in psychology and psycholinguistics, which treat reading and writing as a set of universal cognitive skills that can be adequately specified in the abstract and then transported wholesale from one site to another. By contrast, *literacy as social practice* perspectives consider that reading and writing are fundamentally cultural activities, shaped by the social contexts in which they are enacted (Street, 1984). Both the competencies that readers or writers display and the evaluative criteria they use will vary according to the setting (Heap, 1990).

This insistence on the local and the context specific leads to a research emphasis on the close documentation of particular literacy events—those moments when reading or writing takes place. Analysis focuses on identifying and elucidating variation in literacy practices that such events embody. Variation in the way literacy gets done is seen as indicative of social variation, and the privileging of one form of literacy over another as always ideologically motivated. The tools employed to document literacy in this way have been developed primarily within anthropology and socio-linguistics and put a premium on describing reading and writing from the participants' perspective, rather than judging them against an abstract standard. Data may encompass transcripts of the spoken exchanges that constitute the literacy event (Baker, 1990), photographs that document its material and interpersonal setting (Moss, 2001a), as well as the texts that form the focus of the encounter (Barton & Ivanic, 1994). Researchers use these means to bring into relationship the range of social resources that participants deploy when they read or write. The event provides the telling case, the instantiation of literacy as a social practice, and the analytic vehicle by which the social structuring of literacy, its differentiation in this context, can be made visible (Mitchell, 1983). Differences within the field arise over how the social is conceptualised and invoked, and the analytic tools used for that task (Moss, 1999, 2001b).

Bernstein's theory and literacy as social practice perspectives do not compete to occupy the same terrain. Yet there are some suggestive points of contact. How can these best be exploited in order to establish a genuine dialogue between these fields? To answer this question I want to consider two possible moves: how Bernstein's theoretical language can be used to bring different elements of the empirical data on literacy into an analytic relationship; and how juxtaposing different elements in the data can react back on Bernstein's theoretical formulation.

Steering from Theory to the Data: applying Bernstein's categories to literacy events

Bernstein's theoretical formulation often proceeds through establishing sharply delineated and opposing dichotomies as key analytic terms: restricted/elaborated codes, instructional/regulative discourse, visible/invisible pedagogies, and horizontal/vertical discourses. These have been variously applied to the study of literacy and its place in the curriculum (Williams, 1995, 1999; Christie, 1999; Martin, 1999; Bourne, 2000; Kress, 2000; Moss, 2000, 2001b). In some quarters, peeling off such dichotomies from their secure anchorage in the wider theory looks like a dangerously reductive act [1]. However, taken on Bernstein's terms, such dichotomies have strong generative potential (Bernstein, 1996, pp. 126–127). On the one hand his conceptual language can be used to identify key polarities in the field, while at the same time providing a subtle and flexible means of bringing a range of different elements into the relationship.

> Dichotomies all can be generated on the basis of *boundary rules: things must be kept apart: things must be put together*. How things are put together depends upon the formulation of the organizing principle to generate a range of forms. We can

> ask further questions: In whose interests is the apartness of things? In whose interests is the putting together of things? These questions immediately raise the issue of the relation of power relations to boundaries: Whose power is maintained and relayed by whose boundaries? (Bernstein, 1996, p. 127; original emphasis)

It is at this level that I want to explore the relevance of Bernstein's theoretical language for the empirical study of literacy in its social context.

In the first instance, I turn to Judith Solsken's (1993) enquiry into the gender differentiation of literacy in the early years and the use she made of Bernstein's contrast between visible and invisible pedagogies to help track the shifting orientations to literacy that children adopted as they moved from home into their first year of schooling. Solsken characterised the literacy curriculum of the classroom where her case study was based as invisible pedagogy. In this classroom, wherever possible, reading and writing were integrated with activities that looked like play rather than work. To a great extent, children were free to choose which activities they participated in over the day, and to direct the form that participation took. In evaluating what children did, teachers prioritised meaning-making over technical accuracy. As Solsken succinctly comments 'Children's play in such pedagogies is their work' (Solsken, 1993, p. 61). She is very aware that such a pedagogy is not socially innocent, but rather can be closely allied with the interests of a fraction of the middle class. Yet despite the fact that the school predominantly served such a catchment, her research documents the tensions that surround such a pedagogical approach, both inside the classroom and at home, for the teacher, the parents and, most of all, for the children. The tensions are there, not so much because invisible pedagogies are inherently weakly defined, but because invisible pedagogies in the literacy arena are always to some extent stalked by their shadow other, visible pedagogies. Thus, while parents might welcome the play-centred approach to the school day, they worried over the apparent absence of explicit instruction in literacy skills, and the difficulty of assessing the progress their children were making. Meanwhile, the teacher herself operated in a school environment where others adopted a more visible pedagogy in their own classrooms, and in a system where her class would ultimately be faced with end-of-year standardised, skills-based literacy tests. The boundary line between visible and invisible pedagogies becomes a contested resource in this community.

Solsken's real interest is in how the children responded to all this. Tracking the contrast between work and play-based orientations to literacy in the settings of both home and school, she analyses the contradictory ways in which adults and older siblings often position her case-study children in relation to their reading and writing activity, and how, in turn, these children then position themselves, both conforming to and resisting what is on offer in the immediate environments of home and school. So, for instance, she highlights one boy who strongly resisted the work-based, proficiency-orientated notions of literacy he encountered at home from his mother and older sisters, which seemed to position him as less knowledgable than themselves. He then carried this distinction over into school, where he took at absolute face value the invitation to 'play' in the classroom, eschewing the literacy element to the activities he engaged with. He would not do 'hidden work'. By managing the tensions between visible and invisible pedagogies in this way, he wrong-footed almost all of the adults around him. Indeed, in the book as a whole, Solsken is able to demonstrate that gender holds a crucial part in how the tensions between work and play-based definitions of literacy are both produced and managed, not least because of women's ambiguous role in inducting young children into literacy.

For me, what is interesting about such an analysis is that it shows Bernstein's categories in dynamic relationship to each other, and to the data. The data are not consumed by the theory. The language on the one hand conceptually structures the field by bringing different elements in the scene into association with each other, establishing what goes together and what stays apart. But make the opposition between visible and invisible pedagogies clear and it at once throws into relief the ability of these two categories to interact, as they attempt to re-write each other. Solsken's empirical study tracks the specific conditions under which this happens in this case.

Changing Boundaries, Changing Language: categories in flux

Accept the dynamic relationship between categories and it becomes possible to look for changes in their realisation over time. Accordingly, I have used the contrast Bernstein draws between horizontal and vertical discourse to explore the fluctuating boundary relationships between home and school literacy practices, established in education in respect of media texts and their potential re-contextualisation into the curriculum content of Media Studies (Moss, 2000), and in relation to the kinds of claims the English curriculum makes about itself (Moss 1993, 2001b). Taking the long view shows that until recently, in the school context, the boundary lines between horizontal and vertical discourses were being increasingly down-played or blurred by significant fractions of the professional community. Yet as control over the curriculum changes, these boundary lines are now being actively re-instated by those external agencies who currently hold most responsibility for what actually happens in English classrooms (Moss, 2001b). Such an element of flux becomes amenable to study once one sees the categories as operating, not as hermetically sealed entities, but as always in active dialogue with each other. That dialogue changes over time.

In many respects, Bernstein's own work has developed in this light. Thus in the paper, 'Pedagogising Knowledge: studies in recontextualisation', Bernstein (1996, pp. 54–81) re-formulates the distinction between *invisible* and *visible* pedagogies by recasting them as *competence* and *performance* pedagogies. By changing the terminology, Bernstein simultaneously adjusts the scope of what the language can bring into relationship and does so in response to shifts in the wider scene, to which his paper alludes. Thus the paper re-traces the emergence of invisible pedagogies in the 1960s, considers their apparent dominance on the education scene during the subsequent decade, and then goes on to review the current trend towards their replacement by much more visible forms of pedagogy in many parts of the world. His own theoretical re-formulation focuses on the current terms in which the challenge to invisible pedagogies is being made brings into view the sponsors of the new forms of visible pedagogy that are replacing the old, and outlines what else alters in their wake. Competence and performance are neither co-terminous nor interchangeable with invisible and visible. Rather, 'invisible' and 'visible' are subsumed by them. They become modes of their expression.

The act of re-description in 'Pedagogising Knowledge: studies in recontextualisation' entails identifying both the underlying generative principles that characterise the change in pedagogic practices as well as the potential realisations that they give rise to in the new context. The formulation is in some senses provisional in so far as it is pitched at the way things stood at the point of writing, and things move on. Yet, Bernstein's account also stresses the necessity of understanding the evolving relationship between one form of pedagogic discourse and another, as the parts re-align themselves into a new whole. From my point of view, his paper represents an attempt to map out still emerging boundary lines. Empirical data has a crucial role to play in this process. Consequently, in the remainder of this article, I will use what has been happening to the literacy curriculum in the UK as a telling case which helps delineate the emergence of performance pedagogies as well as tracing their effects.

From Competence to Performance: the literacy curriculum as a telling case

The distinction Bernstein draws between competence and performance pedagogies is multi-faceted and his argument wide-ranging, in line with the scope of his theory as a whole. In turning to the literacy curriculum at this juncture, I do not expect to consider everything he brings into relationship here. Rather, I want to pursue one particular strand in the argument: how the evaluation of the curriculum shifts along with its changing specification, and the consequences this has for the relationship between teacher and taught. As empirical evidence of these changes I will contrast the sequence of official documents that have been used to define the English Curriculum in school and in Initial Teacher Training (ITT) since the introduction of the National Curriculum for English (DES/WO, 1989), before turning to student-produced texts that play an evaluative role under the current curriculum regime.

For Bernstein, competence and performance pedagogies operate with a different underlying social logic. They construct and assess the curriculum differently. Where competence-based models of pedagogy focus on the learner and the progress they make as they learn,

> a performance model of pedagogic practice and context places the emphasis upon a specific output of the acquirer, upon a particular text the acquirer is expected to construct, and upon the specialized skills necessary to the production of this specific output, text or product. (Bernstein, 1996, pp. 57–58)

In performance-based pedagogies, the text takes precedence over its author, and its contents can be objectified into the range of skills it is taken to represent. This is quite different from competence pedagogies, which consider the text as an expression of the author's development: text and author cannot be divorced, one from another. This has different regulative consequences. This contrast in underlying logic becomes clear when the structure of the initial National Curriculum document for English is compared with some of the more recent documents that lay down English curriculum content for primary schools and for ITT, such as the National Literacy Strategy (NLS) Framework document (DfEE, 1998a) and Circular 4/98 (DfEE, 1998b).

Conventional policy analysis draws little distinction between the imposition of the National Curriculum and the succession of further curricular interventions that have followed it. All are seen as equally centralising measures. Bernstein's analysis is more subtle, focusing attention more precisely on the form these curricular interventions take. And there are distinct contrasts. The form of the original National Curriculum for English (DES/WO, 1989) in many ways remains rooted in the historic convergence on the concept of competence, which Bernstein sees as so typical of pedagogic discourse in the 1960s and 1970s. In comparison, Circular 4/98 and the NLS Framework document look decidedly different.

In a number of ways, the first version of the National Curriculum for English defines its curriculum content through growth in pupil competence, specified in terms of what pupils can do. The document is centrally structured around the concept of 'more'. Pupils will become 'more' knowledgeable as their (linguistic/literary/literate) repertoire expands. The level descriptors for reading, writing, speaking and listening are all couched in these terms. Such descriptors become the bench mark against which pupils will be assessed. So at Level 2, pupils are expected to 'listen and respond to stories', at Level 3 to 'listen attentively to stories'. By Level 9 they are expected to 'make more knowledgable spoken and written responses to literature'. Similarly, in the Speaking and Listening levels, 'take an active part' is replaced by 'take a leading role'. No matter quite how it is couched, the 'more' clearly rests with the pupil. The curriculum itself is then constructed as a series of experiences that will enable this 'more' to happen. This is indicated by the phrases used to introduce key areas of curriculum content: 'pupils should be encouraged', 'pupils should be given increasing opportunities to', 'pupils should be shown', 'pupils need to be aware of', and so on. The level descriptors themselves are introduced by the phrase 'pupils should be able to'. References to teaching run like this: 'Teachers should encourage', 'teachers should recognise', 'teaching about language should draw attention to', 'teachers should help pupils', 'teachers should both create and respond' (DES/WO, 1989). The language maintains teachers in a relationship with the taught, in which they facilitate and enable the pupil, rather than directly deliver a given curriculum content. Lines of authority stay blurred.

The subsequent revisions to the National Curriculum progressively re-order these relationships, as they re-write the terms in which the curriculum is couched. The first governmental review of the National Curriculum in 1995 begins this process by re-wording the level descriptors. The introductory phrase 'pupils should be able to' disappears, while the writing descriptors shift the emphasis in assessment directly from the writer, to the product they produce: 'pupils should be able to ...' (DES/WO, 1989) becomes 'Pupils' writing is ...' (DfE/WO, 1995). The structure and wording of the National Literacy Strategy, introduced 2 years later, breaks more decisively with the structure of the English National Curriculum. No longer presented as a developmental sequence so much as a teaching programme, it uses the bald statement 'Pupils should be taught' to introduce the termly specification of the curriculum content that teachers in the primary sector are expected to cover. In effect, this move re-orders the central focus of curriculum regulation from what pupils learn to what teachers deliver. Both teachers and pupils become directly accountable to outside agencies.

Bernstein's formulation encourages close scrutiny of the precise mechanisms used to achieve the switch from competence to performance pedagogies. In relation to the English curriculum, I would argue that performance pedagogies emerge most clearly post the introduction of the NLS and Circular 4/98 (and its successor documents) to the primary sector and ITT, respectively. The transformation can be traced in the language of the regulatory documents for English, as they are revised, proliferated and are then brought into different kinds of association with each other. So, returning to the version of the National Curriculum for English issued post-NLS, mention of pupil learning has now shrunk down to hanging paragraphs in the margin of the main text, while the main imperatives that structure the specification of curriculum content have changed to 'teaching should ensure' and 'pupils should be taught to' (DfEE/QCA, 1999).

The response to the post-NLS curriculum from the professional community concerned with the teaching of English has been two-fold. Those most strongly committed to invisible pedagogies have focused in on the all too apparent loss of control. The way in which the government has seized the curricular initiative has been read as an unwarranted and unsanctioned paradigm shift, which breaks the normal rules of play [2]. By contrast, those who advocate explicit pedagogies welcome the change as a more honest pedagogic settlement, which by making explicit what is to be learnt stands a better chance of working, and working best in the interests of those who currently get least within the system (Bourne, 2000). As the new curriculum settlement unfolds over time, this professional disagreement seeks resolution at the level of the classroom through review of the extent to which the new pedagogy can be said to deliver better outcomes (Stainthorp, 2000; Fisher, 2002). Yet this is to cast the point of comparison too narrowly.

For Bernstein, neither visible nor invisible pedagogies are an absolute good, capable of being judged by their instrumental efficacy alone. Instead, he characterises them as opposing modalities of pedagogic practice, which either way still do their work in the field of symbolic control:

> [Pedagogic] practices are cultural relays of the distribution of power. Although visible and invisible pedagogies are apparently opposing types ... both carry social class assumptions. (Bernstein, 1990, p. 74)

What he identifies are the respective social costs and social investments of running with one, rather than the other; and the different social logics that lead different fractions of the social body to align themselves with one form of pedagogy over another. Raising the level of the argument from *visible/invisible* to *performance/competence* pedagogies allows him to bring into view the re-ordering of relations taking place in this much broader field.

Demonstration as Regulation: performance pedagogies in action

To understand more precisely what the shift in pedagogic discourse, and its accompanying curriculum regulation, signifies at this level, I turn now to Circular 4/98 and some student-produced texts associated with it. Introduced in the same year as NLS, with the necessary statutory weight to govern the content of teacher training programmes, Circular 4/98 for the first time defined what would-be English teachers should know in order to gain Qualified Teacher Status. In a series of tightly-worded injunctions, the document specifies that 'trainees must demonstrate', 'they must teach pupils to', 'providers must ensure', 'providers must audit'. I would argue that the language used here is symptomatic of the current round of performance pedagogies, not least because there is a double act of regulation going on: assessment of trainees and trainers/teachers and pupils is being elided, at every level of the system. Evidence of achievements of the one stand for evidence of compliance by the other. Both are equally subject to external validation, judged by the texts they are expected to produce, rather than the inner processes in which they are engaged. What difference does this make?

To examine how such a mode of assessment changes the pedagogic formation, I will take as my data a series of self-portraits that a PGCE cohort were asked to produce during one of their first course sessions. Occupying a single side of A4 paper, each text included a pictorial representation of their author and accompanying writing, in which students had been asked to list the relevant skills they brought to the course and their targets for the coming year. I collected them at the end of the course from noticeboards in the top corridor of the Education Department suite, where they had been pinned *en masse* shortly before an Ofsted inspection took place. From a *literacy as social practice* perspective, these texts have travelled from one setting to another, and can be associated with two rather different kinds of literacy event: the original event that shaped their construction; and the potential succession of literacy events to which they then became subject, once put on display in a public space. (I do not know if anyone actually stopped to read them, but their re-location from one space to another clearly had a function for those who undertook this task.)

At first sight, this might seem like a curious set of texts to choose to examine the impact of performance pedagogies, as they were produced almost incidentally to the course and were not subject to formal assessment. Yet this takes me back to the regulatory imperatives that now drive curriculum delivery in ITT: 'providers must ensure' as well as 'trainees must demonstrate'. In this regulatory context, any text can be used as evidence, not only of what students know, but also of what they have been asked to do. Both become relevant. Thus, the re-location of these texts to a public space during an Ofsted visit demonstrates that the course does indeed audit its students, almost regardless of the particular answers students gave. The task completed and massed into a different kind of display becomes evidence of the compliance of the trainers, as much as a comment on the students' competencies. This double role gives the texts themselves a new life, beyond their authors' intentions.

What of the students' take on the actual task? The students resolve the requirements of the task in the immediate context in which they complete it. That resolution is in part coloured by the time commitment they make to either the drawing or the writing side of the task, to the actual content of their text or the form of its display, as well as how they read what they have been asked to do. Some seemed to treat it as no more than an introductory activity, offering them a chance to say something about themselves to fellow members of the group. So one writes under skills: '1. Somewhat mad sense of humour 2. Reasonable pianist 3. Computing background'. Others assumed the need to demonstrate how they might meet the criteria to merit qualified teacher status. The answer 'I am very calm. I know lots about parts of speech, grammar!' draws on two very different such claims to entitlement.

In many of the texts, there is an ambivalence over how they should respond to what they have been asked to do. Do they tell the truth, or tell the version that fits the occasion? This ambivalence shows most clearly in their responses to the request to set targets. Some answer this section as if what they have written is a private declaration: '1. I must not panic (visibly!) 2. I WILL survive this year! 3. All subjects except Maths'. Others limit the threshold of the question to the immediate moment: '—to interact and learn the names of the people of the course—to keep work organised and up to date'. Others hedge their bets through adopting a more formal tone: 'Achieve the required standard in English. Try to get my mind around teaching theories—from knowing very little. Develop the acting skills required for teaching'. Some invert the proposition, like the student who included as one of her targets: 'To impruve(sic) my spelling' or the student who suggested 'Remove mullet!' (i.e. change hairstyle) as one of his. Some seem to side-step the whole affair like the student who only offered 'Learn to sing'. They agree only in their differences.

There is a wonderful photograph of a nineteenth-century primary classroom, which occasionally surfaces in history textbooks, in which serried ranks of pupils sit at their benches writing while a clutch of girls stand at the side of the classroom holding the individual letters that spell the word 'watched'. Propped up around the walls are a series of identical slate drawings of a sailing boat (Channel 4 Schools, 1996, p. 31). This is explicit pedagogy committed to tightly constrained reproduction. The children reproduce what the teacher has taught them to do. By contrast, the PGCE students' self-portraits are highly differentiated. They fulfill a different imperative. It seems to me that what the current round of performance pedagogy demands of the texts it creates is the ability to be endlessly recontextualised from one context of assessment to another. Indeed, the multi-functionality of the text, its ability to speak to more than one context about more than one thing, seems entirely symptomatic of these new times. The new system threatens the older forms of teacher autonomy, for the texts that students produce are used to judge them, also. Yet, paradoxically, it also seems to weaken the controls. For a gap opens up between what the students' texts can be taken as evidence for in relation to their authors, the ones who make the text, and in relation to their sponsors, who create the tasks. By the end of the year, long after the Ofsted inspection was over, some curious graffiti had crept on to the students' texts, which at first sight I mistook for teacher comment. A small tick had appeared next to the target 'Remove mullet', while on a different sheet the same hand seemed to have neatly written next to the target '—Manage tantrums', 'Please provide evidence'. The genre of assessment turned back against the assessors, knowingly highlighting the difference between the form of the text and its substance.

A Language of Description for Performance Pedagogies in New Times

Within the academic community there is a considerable degree of disquiet over the loss of autonomy that the new pedagogic concordat represents. This is almost always told as a story of deep loss, without always owning up to the real strengths and weaknesses of what went before. But the new pedagogic economy produces new affordances as well as new constraints. This is not to welcome new times as they stand uncritically, although my own preference is certainly for the kind of visible pedagogy I contributed to in my brief stint as a primary English PGCE tutor over the invisible pedagogy I was subject to during the duration of my own secondary English PGCE. (Bernstein would almost certainly be able to account for this choice in terms of my own social location.) Rather, it is to argue that we need to understand the underlying principles that both generate and connect a range of disparate surface phenomena into their motivated possibilities. The line Bernstein draws between competence and performance pedagogies in 'Pedagogising Knowledge: studies in recontextualisation' (Bernstein, 1996, pp. 54–81) is strong on the underlying principles that take one to one side of that boundary or the other. Yet, written prior to the election of New Labour to government, and the policies for education they have since pursued, his analysis is fine-tuned in line with the potential enactments of that earlier time. The landscape continues to shift. In the conclusion to his paper on 'Research and Languages of Description', Bernstein says:

> I have tried to sketch an approach which places, in the centre of research, the role of description, especially in the case of ongoing 'open' contexts, an approach which accords to the researched power of redescription … and opens the possibility of showing both the strengths and the limits of a theory. (1996, pp. 142–143)

We owe it to Bernstein to test out the strengths of his approach by renewing the dialogue between his language and empirical data that can throw light on performance pedagogies as they evolve in new times. In many ways, the literacy curriculum provides an ideal test case.

NOTES

[1] Given the mis-appropriation of the terms 'elaborated' and 'restricted' when they were mistakenly conflated with language variety in the early 1970s, there are good precedents for feeling cautious on this front.

[2] This point seemed more than proved when the theoretical underpinnings for the NLS were commissioned, written and then published, long after the NLS itself had already been implemented, by someone who had not been directly involved, and clearly therefore had not steered that process (Beard, 1999).

REFERENCES

BAKER, C. (1990) Literacy practices and social relations in classroom reading events, in: A. LUKE & C.D. BAKER (Eds) *Towards a Critical Sociology of Reading: papers of the 12th World Congress of Reading* (Amsterdam, John Benjamins).

BARTON, D. & IVANIC, R. (Eds) (1994) *Writing in the Community* (London, Sage).

BEARD, R. (1999) *The National Literacy Strategy: review of research and other related evidence* (London, Department for Education and Employment).

BERNSTEIN, B. (1990) *Class, Codes and Control, Volume IV: the structuring of pedagogic discourse* (London, Routledge).

BERNSTEIN, B. (1996) *Pedagogy, Symbolic Control and Identity* (London, Taylor & Francis).

BOURNE, J. (2000) New imaginings of reading for a new moral order: a review of the production, transmission and acquisition of a new pedagogic culture in the UK, *Linguistics and Education*, 11, pp. 31–45.

CHANNEL 4 SCHOOLS (1996) *Television and Resources for Primary and Secondary Schools* (Warwick, Channel 4).

CHRISTIE, F. (1999) The pedagogic device and the teaching of English, in: F. CHRISTIE (Ed.) *Pedagogy and the Shaping of Consciousness: linguistic and social processes* (London, Cassell).

DES/WO (1989) *English for ages 5 to 16* (London, HMSO).

DFE/WO (1995) *English in the National Curriculum* (London, HMSO).

DFEE (1998a) *The National Literacy Strategy: framework for teaching* (London, Department for Education and Employment).

DFEE (1998b) *Teaching: High Status, High Standards. Requirements for Courses of Initial Teacher Training* (London, Department for Education and Employment).

DFEE/QCA (1999) *The National Curriculum for England: English* (London, HMSO).

FISHER, R. (2002) *Inside the Literacy Hour* (London, Routledge)

HEAP, J. (1990) A situated perspective on what counts as reading, in: A. LUKE & C.D. BAKER (Eds) *Towards a Critical Sociology of Reading: papers of the 12th World Congress of Reading* (Amsterdam, John Benjamins).

KRESS, G., JEWITT, C. & TSATSARELIS, C. (2000) Knowledge, identity and pedagogy: pedagogic discourse and the representational environments of education in late modernity, *Linguistics and Education*, 11, pp. 7–30.

MARTIN, J. (1999) Mentoring semogenesis: 'genre-based' literacy pedagogy, in: F. CHRISTIE (Ed.) *Pedagogy and the Shaping of Consciousness: linguistic and social processes* (London, Cassell).

MITCHELL, J.C. (1983) Case and situation analysis, *Sociological Review*, 31, pp. 187–211.

MOSS, G. (1993) Girls tell the teen romance, in: D. BUCKINGHAM (Ed.) *Reading Audiences: young people and the media* (Manchester, Manchester University Press).

MOSS, G. (1999) Texts in context: mapping out the gender differentiation of the reading curriculum, *Pedagogy, Culture and Society*, 7, pp. 507–522.

MOSS, G. (2000) Informal literacies and pedagogic discourse, *Linguistics and Education*, 11, pp. 47–64.

MOSS, G. (2001a) Seeing with the camera: analysing children's photographs of literacy in the home, *Journal of Research in Reading*, 24, pp. 279–292.

MOSS, G. (2001b) On literacy and the social organisation of knowledge inside and outside school, *Language and Education*, 15, pp. 146–161.

SOLSKEN, J. (1993) *Literacy, Gender and Work in Families and in School* (Norwood, NJ, Ablex).

STAINTHORP, R. (2000) The National Literacy Strategy and individual differences, *Journal of Research in Reading*, 23, pp. 299–307.

STREET, B. (1984) *Literacy in Theory and Practice* (Cambridge, Cambridge University Press).

WILLIAMS, G. (1995) Children entering literate worlds: perspectives from the study of textual practices, in: F. CHRISTIE & R. MISSON (Eds) *Literacy and Schooling* (London, Routledge).

WILLIAMS, G. (1999) The pedagogic device and the production of pedagogic discourse: a case example in early education, in: F. CHRISTIE (Ed.) *Pedagogy and the Shaping of Consciousness: linguistic and social processes* (London, Cassell).

4 Explorations in policy enactment

Feminist thought experiments with Basil Bernstein's code theory

Parlo Singh, Barbara Pini and Kathryn Glasswell

ABSTRACT
This paper builds on feminist elaborations of Bernstein's code theory to engage in a series of thought experiments with interview data produced during a co-inquiry design-based research intervention project. It presents three accounts of thinking/writing with data. Our purpose in presenting three different accounts of interview data is to demonstrate the relation between theory and empirical data. In the first two accounts, interview data are interpreted and performed through the lens of theory. By contrast, in the third account attention is paid to the ways in which care is practised not only in terms of policy enactment, but also research enactment. Empirical data are not moulded to fit generalisable theoretical frameworks. Rather, empirical data push back on theoretical concepts in a collaborative thought experiment.

Introduction

Our aim in this paper is to engage in a series of thought experiments with concepts such as policy discourses, policy actors, gendered work, and policy enactment. We articulate these concepts with feminist elaborations of Bernstein's work on code theory, pedagogic discourse, recontextualisation, institutional identities, and affect. These thought experiments are articulated in three different accounts of interview data (see also Taylor 2013). In the first account, interview data are interpreted as a discourse about education policies and categorised along a continuum from welfarism to managerialism. The aim is to explore Gewirtz and Ball's (2000) work on gendered discourses of school leadership policies and test the proposition that schools are increasingly dominated by masculinist discourses of market managerialism. The categorisation of interview data has been guided by Bernstein's (2000) work on the ways in which the power and control relations that shape schooling are relayed through changes in pedagogic discourses. The second account draws on feminist elaborations of Bernstein's code theory and policy recontextualisation. The aim is to explore the positioning of women in the occupational structure of the teaching workforce and speculate on how this positioning may affect their work as policy actors engaged in processes of policy interpretation (decoding) and translation (recoding). The earlier feminist work on Bernstein's code theory focused on the structural positioning of women in the workforce, and how this positioning impacted on what work women did, how they did this work, and how this work re/produced gendered relations (Arnot 1995; Chisholm 1995; Delamont 1995). The third account draws on recent feminist elaborations of Bernstein's sociological work, particularly his work on code theory and affect, to explore the relational dynamics of policy enactment (Ivinson 2014; Lapping 2011). Recent feminist scholarship has revisited and redeveloped the sociological work of Basil Bernstein, particularly his earlier work on restricted codes and affect (Ivinson 2014) and later work on pedagogic discourses and recontextualisation (Lapping 2011). This body of scholarship explores the relational processes of affect and social/institutional identities.

By presenting these three accounts, we demonstrate how theoretical tools attune researchers to pay attention to particular practices. We are not proposing that the three accounts are different perspectives on a singular reference point or a particular practice. Rather, we ask how might theoretical concepts developed by others be used, adapted, and changed in the specific practices of our own research work (Mol 2014). In so doing, we foreground 'our ontological, epistemological and ethical responsibilities as producers of knowledge' (Taylor 2013, 690). We propose that attention to the types of theoretical sensitivity articulated by recent feminist elaborations of Bernstein's sociology *matters* in the way that they set up interactions between researchers and researched (Ivinson and Renold 2013). Such theoretical sensitivity treats research objects, including interview data, as recalcitrant with the capacity to push back and contribute to collaborative thinking, rather than as passive objects moulded to fit generalisable theoretical frameworks (Mol 2014; Taylor 2013).

Prior to detailing the accounts of interview data, we describe the data-driven education reform policies that emerged in Australia at the time of the research project. We also describe the components of the research partnership project and present a sketch of the schools participating in the project. In addition, we provide details on how, when, and where the interview data for the research partnership project were generated.

National partnership policies, research partnerships

One of the key policy platforms of the Rudd Labor government elected nationally in Australia in November 2007 was articulated in the policy document *The Australian Economy Needs an Education Revolution* (Rudd and Smith 2007). The platform encompassed the *Smarter Schools National Partnerships Program* (DETE 2010), which included the Smarter Schools National Partnership for Low Socio-economic Status School Communities (henceforth, National Partnership), a project directed at addressing socio-economic inequality in education (DETE 2012). Such a goal was to be realised via the scheme's 'six priority reform areas': the introduction of incentives to attract high-performance principals and teachers; the adoption of performance management for principals; the strengthening of school accountability; the initiation of greater flexibility in school operational arrangements; the provision of innovative and tailored learning opportunities; and the extension of schools' external partnerships (Australian Government 2011; DETE 2010).

Our concern in this paper is with the enactment of these education reform policies in a cluster of primary schools, all servicing high-poverty communities, and participating in a university–school partnership project. In accordance with national policy reform agendas, all schools in the partnership project were led by principals on five-year contracts with increased pay and ongoing appointment tied to a series of performance criteria. These criteria included factors such as staff and student retention, student enrolment, number of suspensions, and student academic performance. Through the latter, the National Partnership scheme reinforced another key dimension of the broader 'education revolution' of the Labor Government, that is, the 2008 introduction of national assessment (ACARA 2012b). This is manifest in the National Assessment Program – Literacy and Numeracy (NAPLAN) tests for students in Years 3, 5, 7, and 9 (aged 8, 10, 12, and 14 years). While individual students are provided with results, levels of achievement by school are also aggregated and posted on the government website My School (ACARA 2012a, 2012b) and extensively discussed in the media.

In this paper, we draw on the data generated through interviews with nine primary school principals[1] who partnered with us[2] to improve literacy learning attainment for students attending their schools. The majority of the schools had enrolments of between 450 and 600 students. All the schools had a considerable number of students who used English as an Additional Language or Dialect (EAL/D). In two of the schools, over 30% of the student population were categorised as EAL/D users. The number of single-parent families at all the schools was very high with figures of at least a quarter of the population. Moreover, the percentage of students categorised as experiencing learning difficulties was high in the cluster of schools.

The school–university partnership research project emerged in response to a sense of urgency in the school district to collectively and collaboratively address the extremely low test score results of students on NAPLAN, particularly in the literacy area of reading. The aim of the partnership project was to engage district administrators, school leaders, and classroom teachers in a collaborative inquiry model of research. This research model involved regular intensive engagements with classroom teachers over a three-year period to collectively diagnose student learning difficulties, co-design instructional innovations, and evaluate the effectiveness of such innovations on students' learning outcomes. At the end of the co-inquiry research phase, another team of researchers generated data through interviews, focus groups, and field notes from district administrators, school leaders, and classroom teachers participating in the partnership project.

Data generation: interviews

In this paper, we focus on one set of data, namely interview data produced with a cohort of primary school principals, collected from the second phase of the research partnership project. The participants were generous in providing interview data based on the trust established in the research partnership project over a period of three years. Interviews were approximately one hour in length, although many of the participants spoke for a longer period and then gave the researchers a guided tour of the school facilities. Interviews covered implications of and views about educational policy, particularly national testing and the National Partnership scheme, schooling for social justice, curriculum and pedagogic interventions, the specific context of the school, and community–school relations. A second round of interviews focused more specifically on leadership, with questions on background to leadership, experiences of leadership, leadership challenges and successes, future leadership plans, and advice for potential leadership aspirants.

Policy enactment: account 1

In our first attempt to make meaning of the interview data, we turned to the literature on policy as discourse and specifically the gendered coding of discourses of leadership and marketisation (see Blackmore 2010, 2013; Power 2006). According to Ball (1990, 17–18):

> ... Discourses are [not only] about what can be said, and thought, but also about who can speak, when, where and with authority. Discourses embody meaning and social relationships, they constitute both subjectivity and power relations. ... Thus, the possibilities for meaning, for definition, are pre-empted through the social and institutional position from which discourse comes. Words and propositions will change their meaning according to their use and the positions held by those who use them.

We coded the interview data in the first instance for examples of (i) managerialist discourses characterised by competitive principles, or to schooling as an essentially rational system, subject to the principles of business, and (ii) welfarist discourses characterised by notions of nurturing and care, comfort and therapy, and aspirations and emotions. These coding categories were derived from the work of Gewirtz and Ball (2000) who described the narrowing and changing options in relation to policy about school leadership, and noted a shift in discourse from that of 'welfarism' to 'new managerialism'. While acknowledging that, in fact, multiple discourses of leadership exist and indeed typically overlap, they used these as broad typologies to examine a case study of changing school heads. The authors outlined the leadership styles articulated by two principals, 'Ms English' and 'Mr Jones', both working at an inner London comprehensive school when Tony Blair's 'New Labour' was only beginning to mark the educational policy landscape. The former defined her leadership in terms of a public-sector ethos, an emphasis on social justice, and a commitment to consultation and cooperation. Meanwhile, Mr Jones readily embraced the emergent emphasis on business values and practices in education citing the importance of competition, technical rationality, instrumentalism, and competition as defining his leadership. Gewirtz and Ball (2000, 265) concluded by identifying 'the beginnings of a discursive shift discernible' away from 'welfarism' to 'managerialism'. It is, as they note in passing, reflective of a movement away from a 'more feminine' style of headship to a mode that is 'somewhat masculinist' (see also Blackmore 2013). What Gewirtz and Ball (2000, 265) describe as 'somewhat masculinist' managerialist policies have introduced a new set of discourses around school leadership, including new discourses around leader identity, roles, and responsibilities aligned to market and business principles. O'Reilly and Reed (2010, 961) identify two strands of managerialism: (i) entrepreneurship, which prioritises devolved authority and service innovation within competitively designed environments; and (ii) culture management, which prioritises the alignment of the beliefs and values of managers with those of policy-makers. Moreover, managerialist policies have introduced sets of business principles which policy actors holding leadership positions are expected to deploy in schools such as 'setting targets, monitoring and holding children and the workforce responsible for outcomes' (Gunter 2013, 204).

While there were clear-cut examples of both managerial and welfarist discourses as interviewees talked about a range of school factors such as the students and the wider community, the teachers, and the uses they made of student achievement data, there was also evidence of the two discourses being woven together as the participants welfare ⟷ balanced/negotiated ⟷ managerial

Figure 1. Welfare-managerial discourse continuum.

accounted for their practices. To visualise this variation, the extracts were placed in a continuum from ones that drew primarily on the welfare discourse, through ones that acknowledged both/negotiated across welfare and managerial concerns, to ones that drew primarily on the managerialist discourse. The continuum is depicted in Figure 1.

Data extracts positioned on the welfare end of the continuum contained phrases often associated with feminine qualities such as 'interpersonal relationships', 'respecting all views', and 'accountability as extremely supportive and very human'. On the managerial end of the continuum, we placed interview data extracts which contained phrases such as 'performance driven', 'healthy competition', 'non-negotiable data-driven goals', and 'business breakthrough models'.

Overall, the leadership discourses produced in the research project were most reflective of Gewirtz and Ball's (2000) notion of welfarism. However, this was not unequivocal. For example, the school principals talked proudly of the 'wraparound' support given by the schools in addressing student and familial housing, clothing, food, and mental health. At the same time, they cautioned that social disadvantage should not be used as an excuse for poor student learning achievement. Rather, it was important to build a 'no-excuses culture' in the schools to ensure a focus on continuous learning improvement. In another illustration of ambivalence and tensions around discourses of welfarism and managerialism, this cohort of principals expressed a much more critical view of the shift to data regimes in educational leadership, joking that it was now at a stage where as a principal 'you can't put a sentence without that word in it'. Nevertheless, school principals concurred that the 'world had changed' and greater accountability was a requirement and necessity in education. At the same time, these principals raised concerns about the 'competitive potential of data'. They acknowledged negative media headlines about their schools and the ways in which the politics of reputation affected morale and did not necessarily speak to the work being undertaken by teachers. Overall, the cohort of principals endorsed the philosophy of the audit culture in schools, but distanced themselves from the instrumentalist and disembodied forms of managerialist, edu-business styles of leadership.

Tellingly, the principals expressed wariness about simply 'collecting' or 'displaying' data and claimed that what was important to improving student outcomes were sensitive conversations about test results and supporting teachers in making a difference to student learning outcomes. Summing up a vision of leadership and the impact of the research partnership project in a data-driven performance regime, one school principal stated:

> Looking back it's been a catalyst for change across the whole school and I guess it gave us that *extra layer of support* in bringing about a whole new culture in the school where we had *agility and strategic use of student data* to inform what we're doing with the kids. That was something that we were desperately wanting to do but *felt inadequate* and unequipped to do. I think a lot of school leadership teams felt the same way and probably still do.
>
> The benefits of this project in helping us, walking us through *how to gather good quality data, process it well, have high quality conversations* about that data with our staff has been transformational.

> I think that the history of the project here at the school is probably similar also to some other schools in the sense that it was a *little bit uncomfortable* at first. It was certainly for our staff not widely or unanimously applauded at first but, as people became used to *having these sort of conversations*, actually looking at real stuff and *having to problem solve that together* they began to and have increasingly enjoyed that sort of work. That's been for me, big picture, the big thing, not just about our reading data but the culture of the school. (Emphasis added)

In contrast to the combative, competitive, masculinist styles of leadership evident in discourses of managerialism and edu-business, the principals (both male and female) used feminine language of feelings and emotions expressing their own and teachers' concerns about entering into a partnership project, the support experienced through the partnership, and the quality of the conversations around student data. The principals saw their role as providing teachers with the tools, including research tools to generate good quality school-based data, and to use these data to inform the design of learning innovations. Pedagogy and curriculum were important, and they were to be designed by teachers on the basis of school-based data, rather than the monolith of NAPLAN. There was no individualist teacher naming and shaming strategy based on student performance data in these conceptualisations of leadership. Rather, the cohort of principals emphasised relational leadership and the importance of nurturing and building confidence and capacity in the teaching staff so that learning problems were addressed collectively on the basis of high-quality school-generated data, and the design of innovative pedagogies. Moreover, this collective strategy within schools and between schools and the university partner was constructed as an institutional defence against the fear factor of NAPLAN.

Policy enactment: account 2

Our first attempt at narrating the data produced few surprises. The simplification of interview data into two categories, albeit along a continuum, simply did not do justice to the complex ways in which official policies on data-driven education reform were being interpreted or translated in these schools.

We turned our attention to thinking about policy enactment as recontextualisation, that is, principals as policy actors engaged in processes of interpreting (decoding) and translating (recoding) official government policies into school-level policies and practices (see Singh, Heimans, and Glasswell 2014; Singh, Thomas, and Harris 2013). According to Ball et al. (2011), official state policies are enacted in schooling practices through complex meaning-making processes which involve both interpretation and translation. The term interpretation suggests 'an initial reading, a making sense of policy – what does this text mean to us? What do we have to do? Do we have to do anything? It is a political and substantive reading – a "decoding"' (Ball et al. 2011, 619). Interpretation is regulated by the particularities of specific contexts, such as student performance on high-stakes testing, student attendance levels, parental satisfaction with the local school, and teachers' sense of professional agency. The data generated, interpreted, and decoded by school leaders in these specific contexts regulate which aspects of policy texts are privileged and/or 'filtered out'. The second process, translation, according to Ball et al. (2011), is the process of 'recoding' policy, that is, selectively appropriating and organising policy discourses to enact specific schooling practices.

Processes of policy recontextualisation take place in different arenas of state education bureaucracies, including central and district education departments, and specific schools and classrooms. A number of feminist scholars (Arnot 1995; Chisholm 1995; Delamont 1995) have argued that positions within the education recontextualising field are increasingly occupied by women. This is because work undertaken in this field is central to symbolic control, and women's work has traditionally been about regulating and reproducing moral order. As Chisholm (1995, 35) argued, women are not likely to reach particularly controlling occupational positions within the field of symbolic control. Rather, they are likely to be clustered in the occupations Bernstein (2001) described as 'repairers' (e.g. social workers and counsellors), 'reproducers' (teachers), and 'executors' (administrators). Women's role in policy interpretation and translation is regulated firstly by their positioning within the occupational structure, that is, location predominantly in the field of recontextualisation rather than in the field of production of official state policies (Singh 2014, 2015). In other words, the occupational positioning of women in state education bureaucracies is gender coded, and this positioning regulates what is thinkable and possible about women's policy work. On this point, Jill Blackmore (1996, 345) argued:

> A new core-periphery model of the labour market is emerging with the hollowing out of middle management and devolution to self- managing schools. The effect has been in Victoria of the re-masculinisation of the centre or core where financial management and policy maintain a strong steering capacity for the state, and a flexible peripheral labour market of increasingly feminised, casualised and deprofessionalised teaching force as central wages awards are replaced by individual contracts in the deregulated market ...

In this restructured feminised teaching workforce, women are being encouraged to take up leadership positions as school principals and expected to take on the 'emotional management work of education in handling the stress and low morale within the profession' (Blackmore 1996, 345). In the Queensland context, approximately 60% of the Education Queensland workforce in leadership/management positions are women, and hold one of the following positions: Head of Curriculum (HoC), Head of Department (HoD), Deputy Principal, or Principal (Department of Education and Training 2010, 111, 2011, 126). In addition, over 80% of primary school teachers are women, a figure that has stayed relatively static since 2011 (Australian Bureau of Statistics 2012).

So the first point we want to make is that the research partnership project was dominated by women's work. The research leadership team comprised mainly women engaged in hands-on work in schools over a long period of time. The school leadership team comprised largely women, taking up roles as principals, deputy principals, HoCs, and teacher mentors. In addition, the classroom teachers responsible for effecting improvements in student learning outcomes were predominantly women. And yet in our initial categorisation of the data, we missed this very obvious point. We had not written about the gendered division of labour involved in education reform policy recontextualisation.

We began to think about the possibilities of gendered work in policy recontextualisation, that is, policy interpretation and translation. Rather than categorise discourses in a binary gendered form (masculine vs. feminine), we wondered about the gendered decoding and recoding of official state policies into schooling practices. Recontextualisation refers to the spatial-temporal movement of policy discourses from sites of production to sites of reproduction. Bernstein's (1990) concept of pedagogic discourse is useful for thinking about the 'what and how' of policy text movement. The term pedagogic discourse does not refer to a specific discourse, but rather to the power and control principles (coding principles) structuring education policy discourses. Power relations refer to the strength of symbolic boundaries, for example, the strength of the insulation or classification around what is thinkable and possible about women's policy and leadership work. Control relations refer to the principles of communication which reproduce, contest, challenge, and change power relations and symbolic boundaries. 'Control is double-faced for it carries both the power of reproduction and the potential for its change' (Bernstein 2000, 5).

Education reform policies seek to steer from a distance and control what goes on inside schools through explicit and implicit regulatory devices or technologies, such as data-driven accountability regimes. However, as Bernstein (2000) has suggested the pedagogic device, in this case, centrally mandated data-driven accountability policies, cannot control what they set out to control. Rather the distribution of power relations through the device, that is, devolved power through a steering from the centre strategy, creates potential sites of challenge and opposition. So women positioned in the education bureaucracy to enact education reform policies wield considerable power to challenge, oppose, resist, and subvert such policies.

Opening up conversations, managing and containing staff anxieties

All of the primary school principals expressed a strong commitment to inclusion and collaboration along with valuing difference and diversity. Asked to identify what makes a good leader in education, for example, one principal stated:

> I think I would say to any principal coming into this area, be aware that there are a lot of *different* perspectives that people will bring that you need to *respect* .... Get the staff to *see (difference)* as a *strength not as a threat* and to work through those types of things together. (emphasis added)

Others talked of openness to staff and parental involvement in a wide range of areas from curriculum to budgeting. It was not surprising then to hear most principals talk about data as a school-wide issue and performance concerns as something to be addressed collaboratively and in dialogue with policy, rather than as a technical, managerial implementation of policy. The following explanation provided by a principal about how the whole school engaged with negative NAPLAN data illustrates the collaborative approach adopted across the schools.

> ... we try to say in all our meetings that we share this data. This is a big problem. It's not one teacher's problem. We have to all work on it together. If we can't work on it together we're lost.

The cohort of school leaders stressed the need for 'dialogue' about data and 'information sharing' between administrators and teachers and across the teaching staff. Further to their emphasis on collaboration and inclusion, all principals expounded the importance of establishing strong and positive relationships with staff and leveraging the capital from these relationships to focus on performance. One principal described this as a 'strengths-based model' of leadership. Another outlined ways in which staff were 'valued', for example, by asking them to present at a professional development seminar or by publicly acknowledging their contributions in staff meetings. In continuing the conversation above, for example, the principal argued that staff had to hear 'the hard stuff', but that if it is presented in the absence of a relationship of trust, it will be 'threatening'. In an equivalent observation, another principal suggested:

> I know from experience with staff that ... the way that I can get the best out of them is to be super positive and point out 'Okay, what can we do with this?' Not to say, 'You've done a bad job' ... You've got to have lots and lots of positive conversations. Then you're ready for the negative conversation .... If the only time you hear from the boss is something to rap you on the knuckles, what sort of relationship do you have?

In seeking to develop relationships with staff and in further describing their leadership style, it was common for principals to refer to their own background in the classroom. One principal talked about discourses of leadership, and a desire to demonstrate and share classroom knowledge with staff. This principal, like some of the other primary school leaders, taught one class a week using this as an opportunity to connect with students and to work alongside teachers. In another case, a principal talked about visiting every classroom each day of the school week as a means of remaining connected to teachers.

Importantly, as would be expected given that they were appointed as National Partnership principals, the majority of the school leaders endorsed a focus on accountability and performance, but in a qualified way. For example, they expressed sympathy for the pressures their staff were under. They reminded us of the incredible challenges of their student cohort. Exemplifying this was the declaration from one of the longest serving principals who said, 'I've been teaching since 1960 so I've seen an awful lot of different contexts throughout that time and I have never seen anything as complex as this'.

All of the school leaders talked endlessly of how they managed staff anxieties and stress related to the policy culture of data-driven performance management regimes. For example, one cautioned the need to focus not only 'on the colour of those damn boxes',[3] but also on anecdotal stories of individual student improvement. Adding to this, another explained that working as a leader in an environment of high-stakes testing required reminding teachers of their expertise and not becoming a servant to data. This principal said: 'I talk to them about having faith in their own professional judgements. That everything doesn't have to be a test. A simple comment is enough'.

Thus, of the nine principals interviewed, the majority were circumspect about the efficacy of nationally collected data as an objective measure of teacher performance, despite endorsing the need for accountability. However, only one was overtly critical of the way 'policy as numbers' (Lingard, Creagh, and Vass 2012, 315) had manifest in schools in terms of standardised national testing. This principal opined, 'NAPLAN's been the hugest waste of money' and the only reason it was imposed on staff and students was because s/he was compelled to do so. For this principal, leadership required 'protecting' the staff: 'I'm here for my staff and I'd do anything to protect them and keep them as skilled as they can'.

There was little evidence of the heroic leadership style of New Public Management discourses, that is, 'the celebration of the new macho individual ... fundamental to the new morally ascendant position ... of survival of the imposed systems' (Davies 2003, 96; Kulz 2015) of data-driven audit, accountability, and performativity. Rather, discourses of leadership were largely about the containment of staff anxieties about new performativity practices, in order to comply with state policy directives.[4] While the school leaders endorsed principles of managerialism such as accountability measures and performance audits, this was not embedded in the type of 'rugged individualism' that is usually associated with corporatisation. Instead they advocated some of the tenets of caring leadership discourses, stressing cooperation, self-reflection, and care, and thus easing the enactment of edu-business policies in high-poverty schooling contexts.

Major education reforms were steered by the Federal government through policy directives tied explicitly to funding and linked to performance outcomes as measured by a National testing system. However, this steering from a distance policy work was enacted predominantly by women in primary school leadership positions. As evidenced by the interview talk, much of this work is emotional, sharing, caring work, traditionally taken up by women as paid and unpaid work. Women leaders, school principals, took on the role of managing classroom teachers' anxieties in stressful work environments exacerbated by high-stakes data-driven performativity regimes.

Policy enactment: account 3

Something still continued to trouble us about the ways in which we articulated concepts with interview data to present accounts of the research partnership project. In the second account, we tried to make visible what seemed to have become invisible in a number of accounts about policy enactment. We placed front and centre women's positioning in the occupational field of teaching and their role as policy actors. We foregrounded the central role that women play as primary school leaders and classroom teachers in enacting policies. And in so doing, we examined the ways in which women, in their accounts of their own leadership practices, talked about negotiating the tensions and ambiguities around implementing data-driven accountability regimes through communication principles of support, co-operating, caring, and nurturing. But in the process of re-presenting the interview data in this way, we were erasing our own entanglement as researchers in schooling practices (see Singh, Heimans, and Glasswell 2014). Yet the research team had managed to attract significant research funds to work closely with school leaders and classroom teachers in a co-inquiry, design-based intervention project for three years. Why did we erase ourselves from the account? What type of account of the principals as policy actors were we trying to produce, and for what purposes, and what effects?

We again turned to Bernstein's work on policy recontextualisation. In the second account of interview data, we drew on code theory, particularly as it has been articulated by feminists exploring the gendered dimensions of women's work in schooling. However, we had not explicitly engaged with the work of feminists developing Bernstein's concepts of pedagogic discourse, recontextualisation, affect, and institutional identities (see Ivinson 2014; Ivinson and Renold 2013; Lapping 2011). We turned to this work to assist us to think and write differently about the data.

Practising care in enacting policies

It is hard to write about care and the ways that care might be expressed through communication codes, given that care can be evoked by a look, a gesture, a series of paintings, a feeling of calmness, or a wall filled with student and teacher photographs (Bernstein 2000; Heimans, Singh, and Glasswell 2015; Mol 2014). But the interview talk of all the principals reminded us repeatedly of care for the other. Bernstein (1975, 1990) speculated that 'girls in working-class families ... are more likely to develop better verbal skills than boys. This is because girls are often forced to mediate verbally, not physically; hence they develop [capacities to] ... negotiate the perspective of the other' (Danzig 1995, 159). We wondered whether 'the specific history of the place and the gendered legacies' (Ivinson and Renold 2013, 705) of growing up poor affected policy enactment practices. All seven female primary principals had worked in schools serving high-poverty communities for most of their careers. Many of them had entered teaching from working-class families themselves and held strong convictions about the difference that education could make in the lives of students from disadvantaged communities. This conviction was shared by members of the research team, who also had entered primary teaching and then university teacher education positions from working-class families. In what follows, we focus on one interview undertaken with Mrs White (Principal) and Mrs Smith (Deputy Principal) at Wynville Primary because it provides rich data to think with and about the complexities of policy enactment.

The foyer outside the Principal's office was beautifully furnished. The curtains draping the windows, the cushions snuggled on the sofa, the plants placed carefully in vibrant pots, and the colourful rugs hugging the concrete floor, all added to the liveliness of the place. This was a place we felt welcomed into, a place where we felt the vitality of learning. We found out later that Mrs White and the leadership team had spent a lot of time selecting, arranging, and rearranging the furnishings to create a welcoming effect. We noticed that the walls of the foyer were adorned with photographs of the principal and school staff, taken over successive years. Women were everywhere – in the photographs, at the school reception, handling the phone calls from parents, and dealing with distressed children.

There were two researchers engaged in the interview with the Principal, Mrs White, and the Deputy Principal, Mrs Smith. We asked for an hour to do the interview. We were given almost two hours for the interview and then shown around the classrooms and grounds of the school. The Principal was eager to share her experiences of engagement in the research partnership project, and eager to think out loud about the questions from the interview schedule.

Strong boundaries: acceptable and non-acceptable behaviour

Mrs White started the interview by talking about the challenges she faced in taking up the principal role. She admitted openly to having her 'share of doubts' about whether she could make a difference to the learning attainment of students. Mrs White felt that when she first arrived at the school, many of the teachers were in survival mode because the 'behaviour of the kids was appalling'. She suggested that the school was full of 'very high-grade teachers' who were 'just managing', 'just coping' in dealing with 'high incidence behaviour', which included students 'hitting teachers', 'spitting on teachers', 'swearing at teachers', 'throwing things', 'getting on the roof', 'getting into trees', 'port racks', 'anything they could climb into'.

The Deputy Principal, Mrs Smith, attributed the behaviour management issues to a constant 'change in leadership' and no 'consistency in leadership' over a 10-year period of time at the school prior to Mrs White's appointment. Several past principals had seen the leadership role as a stepping off point to a more senior leadership role. By contrast, in her interview for the principal role, Mrs White made a commitment to stay at the school for five years, that is, the duration of the contract under the National Partnerships Project.

Mrs White described her first year as the 'year from hell' and felt that her experiences of trying to bring about change were 'incredibly traumatic'. She took a stance on acceptable behaviour, arguing that individuals who behaved badly were affecting the learning of other students. Also, she felt that she 'couldn't live with her staff being treated the way they were being treated'. In her words, she had 'to draw the line in the sand and say, you will not do these things'. The consequences for what was deemed 'bad behaviour' were suspensions and exclusions. Not all the teachers or the parents accepted the leadership stance taken on acceptable student behaviour. Indeed, a group of parents were so resentful of this stance that they exercised an 'incredible impact of aggression bordering on violence'. Moreover, many of the staff kept sliding on the issue, weakening the boundaries and making excuses for the students because of their 'tough background'.

Could Bernstein's gendered code theory assist in thinking about this interview talk? We represented Bernstein's (2000) distinction of different modalities of communication code as in Figure 2.

Classification rules refer to the strength of power relations realised in boundary insulation and are represented on an *x*-axis from strong to weak. Framing rules refer to the strength of the control relations realised in the interactional frames and are represented on the y-axis as strong to weak.

So what happens when we put the diagram alongside the interview data and think about caring practices? A female principal with a largely female teaching staff asserts strong boundaries (power relations) around acceptable and non-acceptable parent and student behaviour in the school. These strong boundaries are maintained by strong relations of control with the principal suspending and excluding students who refuse to accept the new rules of school conduct. The response from some parents is aggressive behaviour as they challenge the principal's authority. The response from some of the teachers is to weaken the interactional frames, and accept behaviour that does not meet the new codes of conduct.

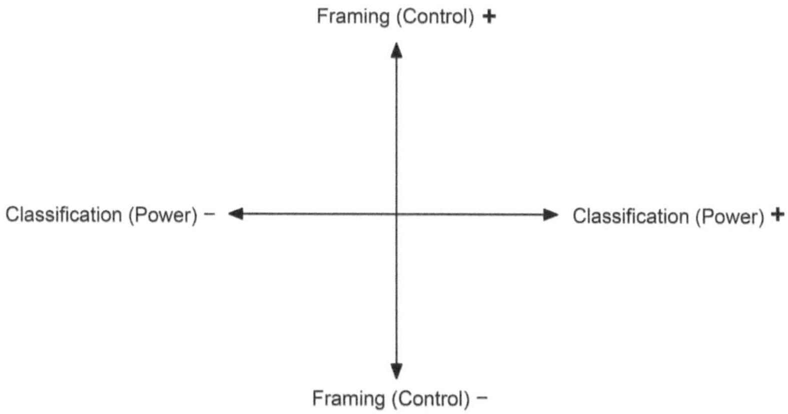

Figure 2. Modalities of communication code.

We listened to Mrs White recount her painful struggles and wondered about the gendered dimensions of the resistance to change? What orientations to meaning were evoked by these coding principles? Why were the responses from some parents so aggressive, bordering on violence? Why did some teachers continually weaken the interactional frames?

Rather than thinking about context as the backdrop to the practices taking place in the school (see Ball, Maguire, and Braun 2012), we thought about context as generated through the shifting power and control principles structuring the communication codes. In other words, the communication codes became the context, a shifting, fluid, dynamic, always emergent context (see Ivinson 2014). In defining acceptable behaviour in the school through strong principles of classification and framing (+C, +F), Mrs White exerted her authority as principal and school leader.

The D word: deficit and poverty

Mrs White talked about how parents discussed their feelings of helplessness and inadequacy, wanting to do more for their children, but not knowing how. She described the effects of poverty, unemployment, drug abuse, time in prison, and domestic violence on families. She encouraged parents to come into the school and meet with her if they had any concerns. Parents did not need to make an appointment, but could come to the school administration office anytime. She felt that many parents had bad experiences with schooling themselves and needed to be encouraged to walk through the front gates. While the boundaries around acceptable behaviour in the school remained strong, the interactional frames were weakened to encourage parents to walk into the school grounds, to talk to the school leaders and teachers, to voice their concerns, and to share in the education of their children.

Mrs White thought out loud about poverty and the experiences of living in poverty for the students and parents serviced by the school. She recalled a conversation with another research team working in her school on the topic of poverty. We (the interviewers) felt the pain and anger of that encounter as Mrs White spoke of being criticised for adopting a supposedly deficit model of poverty. During our interview, it seemed that Mrs White was reliving those feelings of pain. But rather than allowing herself to be simply silenced, become mute, she thought and practised out a different response (see also Lapping 2011; Renold and Ivinson 2014). She said: 'I thought … poverty is a deficit bloody life. I'll stick you in the bloody car and take you down to Central Road,[5] and see what it's like'. She had justified her decision to open the school up to multiple research teams claiming 'we're not in a position to turn away anybody. This school needs all the help it can get'. But the encounter with another research team had left her feeling that she needed to defend her professional position. Her defence was justified in the following way: 'That's not me being awful about my parents, that's me *understanding*' (emphasis added).

What was this understanding/ knowing based on? Firstly, it was based on embodied experiences of living and growing up in a working-class family herself 'where money was always an issue' and the family 'lived on a shoestring'. Mrs White contrasted her experiences of growing up poor with what she understood to be the experiences of families serviced by the school. 'It was different from here though … We weren't text poor in the same way as I see children here.' She recalled that her father had worked two jobs, and her mother took up cleaning work to support the family. In contrast, many of the students attending the school were from single-parent families, with few experiences of paid full-time work. Mrs White produced a textual account of her experiences of being poor and learning to understand poverty in the local community. Secondly, it was based on positioning this textual account in the current context of leading a school servicing a high-poverty community. Thirdly, it was based on reflecting on her personal text of 'growing up poor', the con-text of poverty in the current school, and recontextualising these accounts to bring about change.

Moore (2004, 20) wrote about the co-inquiry process of research interviews as enabling participants to think/feel differently about their own professional identities. He described the research interview as potentially generating a space for participants to move dynamically from text → con-text → recon-textualisation. So Mrs White was not simply re/presenting an account of schooling, and nor were we simply re/presenting an account of a research interview (see also Lapping 2011). Rather, the interview performed an account or produced what Mol (2014) describes as relational realities, not only through the relationships between researchers and researched, but also through the various instruments and artefacts introduced into the school through the research partnership project over three years (Heimans, Singh, and Glasswell 2015).

Mrs White talked about working closely with her teacher aide who lived in the local area, had worked at the school for a long time, and was not afraid of giving negative feedback. So Mrs White positioned herself as one with the people in the high-poverty community, she understood what it meant to be poor, she had lived as working class. She talked about her dress code. At times she wore inexpensive clothes purchased from supermarket chain stores, not because she wanted to dress down to fit into the local community, but because she was comfortable wearing inexpensive and expensive clothes. Mrs White recounted a story of a student who said she wanted to be a teacher, because her teacher dressed nicely, painted her nails, and went on holidays to different places. She moved in and out of different dress codes, staying connected to the teaching staff and teacher aides, and also standing apart, wearing clothes that might suggest other ways of being and becoming (see also Ivinson 2014).

Mrs White talked about the moral code that had been forged between the leadership team and a group of parents who came to support her leadership. She spoke about the way parents performed parenting roles to save face. For example, many parents claimed that they read regularly to their children, but many of them were illiterate themselves, and had not managed to successfully complete schooling. She was adamant that she wanted to co-create positive schooling experiences not only for the students, but also for their parents. She talked about how she tried to get to know about poverty, not only through reading literature, but also by visiting parents in their homes, talking regularly to the teacher aides, and adopting an open-door policy so parents came into the school and spoke about their concerns.

In this account, we have tried to pay close attention not only to the interview data, but also to our field notes of being engaged and affected by our work in these schools over three years. Instead of superimposing a theoretical lens on the data and reading the data through this lens, we have paid attention to how care was practised not only in the schools, but also in the research partnership project, including the research interview and the production of this research account (Heimans, Singh, and Glasswell 2015; Mazzei

2013). In this third account, we examined the ways in which the research partnership project, including the interviews, interfered in schooling practices, and thus contributed to the performance of relational realities.

Discussion

This paper is a thought experiment about the enactment of policies around education reform. We articulated three accounts of thinking with Bernstein's code theory and the interview talk generated by two researchers and primary school leaders (principals and deputy principals). As we used the tool of code theory, we came to realise that this tool is not neutral, nor does it provide us with a god's eye view on what was really going on in these schools. Rather, any tool 'co-produces the thinker' (Stengers 2005, 191). In addition, we began to question our attachment to the tool of code theory, to the way feminist scholars have appropriated and made use of this tool, and how we could use our attachment to this tool 'to feel and think, to be able or to become able' (Stengers 2005, 191) to practise research differently.

In articulating the first account, we took Bernstein's notion of discursive boundaries, boundary maintenance, and boundary change to explore discourses of welfarism and managerialism in the interview talk. We devised a classification scheme to distinguish between welfare and managerial leadership discourses and then categorised data extracts from each interview along a continuum from welfarism to managerialism. Our aim was to take up Stephen Ball's (2015) notion of policy as a discourse and explore the dominant discourses in education reform policies in Australia. The systematic analysis of data led us to concur with colleagues that the world of schools had changed and was dominated by managerialist discourses around data-driven performativity and accountability. In the schools participating in the research partnership project, these discourses were embedded in a regulative discourse of welfarism. In other words, the fear factors of managerialist discourses were counteracted through welfarist discourses of care, co-operation, and relational trust. Our detailed data analysis produced no new surprises!

In articulating the second account, we reviewed the feminist take up of Bernstein's work on code theory and examined the positioning of women in the occupational structure of the educational bureaucracy, in the leadership practices of schools, and in research partnership teams. We drew on the notion of policy enactment as processes of interpretation and translation, that is, the systematic decoding and recoding of policy texts by policy actors (Ball, Maguire, and Braun 2012). And then we juxtaposed Bernstein's (2000) concept of recontextualisation alongside these concepts to think about the way policy texts are selectively appropriated, delocated, and relocated by policy actors positioned within different arenas of the educational bureaucracy. We concluded that women were increasingly given responsibility in a devolved education bureaucracy of implementing policy discourses of managerialism, audit, and accountability. Women tended to do the hard, emotional work of policy enactment by leaning towards welfarist, feminine discourses of leadership. Again, few new surprises! We could, however, point out the silences in the policy research literature around the gendered forms of policy work.

In articulating the third account, we realised that we had erased ourselves from the interview research practices, and so we attempted to insert ourselves back into these practices. We were also conscious of the care with which schooling practices and research practices were enacted, and wondered how we could think about care, communication codes, and the interview data simultaneously. Our aim was not to think about care as some kind of heroic practice (Kulz 2015), or to think about the work of school leaders and researchers as saving poor people, the victimised other. Rather, we wanted to think with care about research practices, the communication codes of these practices, and the feelings and emotions that were evoked in these practices. School context was not a backdrop to the enactment of education reform policies, a place where policy actors (principals) interpreted and translated policies. Rather, school contexts emerged, policy actors (school leaders, researchers, data walls, and interview schedules) came into being, as policies were enacted.

Our point in articulating these three accounts of interview data was to demonstrate how theoretical tools attune researchers to pay attention to particular practices. We have not suggested that the three accounts articulate different viewpoints on a singular practice (research interview, schooling, and policy enactment). Rather, through this thought experiment exercise, we aimed to demonstrate how theoretical concepts developed by others might be appropriated, used, and modified in the specific practices of our own research work (Bernstein 2000; Mol 2014).

Notes

1. Twelve schools participated in the project, three high schools and nine primary schools, and seven of the nine primary school principals were female. In this paper, we pay particular attention to the practices of the female principals as they all had long experiences of working in high-poverty communities.
2. The research team comprised two chief investigators (Authors 1 and 3), two partner investigators, six school-based researchers, and three research assistants (all with doctoral qualifications). Only two members of the research team were male, a Partner Investigator and a Research Assistant.
3. Reference to the gradient of colours from red to green, with dark red signally significantly below average learning outcomes, and dark green signally significantly high in learning outcomes.
4. These contradictory and ambivalent responses to managerialist discourses of data-driven accountability and performativity have also been covered in recent reports prepared by professional associations and teachers' unions (see Canvass Report 2013; Queensland Teachers Union 2015).
5. An area well known for high levels of unemployment, drug use, violence, and public housing.

Disclosure statement

No potential conflict of interest was reported by the authors.

Funding

This work was supported by the Australian Research Council Linkage scheme [grant number LP0990585].

References

ABS (Australian Bureau of Statistics). 2012. "In-school staff (FTE) 1997–2011." Schools, Australia, 2011, Cat. No. 4221.0, Canberra: ABS.

ACARA (Australian Curriculum Assessment and Reporting Authority). 2012a. *My School*. Melbourne: Australian Curriculum Assessment and Reporting Authority. http://www.myschool.edu.au/.

ACARA (Australian Curriculum Assessment and Reporting Authority). 2012b. *NAPLAN. National Assessment Program Literacy and Numeracy*. Melbourne: Australian Government. http://www.naplan.edu.au/.

Arnot, M. 1995. "Bernstein's Theory of Educational Codes and Feminist Theories of Education: A Personal View." In *Knowledge and Pedagogy. The Sociology of Basil Bernstein*, edited by A. Sadovnik, 297–321. Norwood, NJ: Ablex Publishing Corporation.

Australian Government. 2011. "Smarter Schools National Partnership for Low Socio-economic Status School Communities." *Fast Facts*. http://smarterschools.gov.au/.

Ball, S. 1990. *Politics and Policy Making in Education. Explorations in Policy Sociology*. London: Routledge.

Ball, S. J. 2015. "Subjectivity as a Site of Struggle: Refusing Neoliberalism?" British Journal of Sociology of Education iFirst: 1–18. doi:10.1080/01425692.2015.1044072.

Ball, S., M. Maguire, and A. Braun. 2012. *How Schools Do Policy: Policy Enactments in Secondary Schools*. New York: Routledge.

Ball, S. J., M. Maguire, A. Braun, and K. Hoskins. 2011. "Policy Actors: Doing Policy Work in Schools." *Discourse: Studies in the Cultural Politics of Education* 32 (4): 625–639. doi:10.1080/01596306.2011.601565

Bernstein, B. 1975. *Class, Codes and Control: Towards A Theory of Educational Transmission. Vol III*. London: Routledge.

Bernstein, B. 1990. *The Structuring of Pedagogic Discourse*. London: Routledge.

Bernstein, B. 2000. Pedagogy, Symbolic Control and Identity. 2nd ed. Lanham: Rowan & Littlefield.

Bernstein, B. 2001. "Symbolic Control: Issues of Empirical Description of Agencies and Agents." *International Journal of Social Research Methodology* 4 (1): 21–33. doi:10.1080/13645570118017.

Blackmore, J. 1996. "Doing 'Emotional Labour' in the Education Market Place: Stories from the Field of Women in Management." *Discourse: Studies in the Cultural Politics of Education* 17 (3): 337–349. doi:10.1080/0159630960170304.

Blackmore, J. 2010. "Preparing Leaders to Work with Emotions in Culturally Diverse Educational Communities." *Journal of Educational Administration* 48 (5): 642–658.

Blackmore, J. 2013. "A Feminist Critical Perspective on Educational Leadership." *International Journal of Leadership in Education: Theory and Practice* 16 (2): 139–154. doi:10.1080/13603124.2012.754057.

Canvass Strategic Opinion Research. 2013. "Primary Principals Perspectives on NAPLAN Testing and Assessment." http://www.appa.asn.au/wp-content/uploads/2015/08/Primary-Principals-Perspectives-NAPLAN.pdf.

Chisholm, L. 1995. "Cultural Semantics: Occupations and Gender Discourse." In *Discourse and Reproduction. Essays in Honor of Basil Bernstein*, edited by P. Atkinson, B. Davies, and S. Delamont, 25–50. Cresskill, NJ: Hampton Press.

Danzig, A. 1995. "Applications and Distortions of Basil Bernstein's Code Theory." In *Knowledge and Pedagogy. The Sociology of Basil Bernstein*, edited by A. Sadnovik, 145–170. Norwood, NJ: Ablex Publishing Corporation.

Davies, B. 2003. "Death to Critique and Dissent? The Policies and Practices of New Managerialism and of 'Evidence-based Practice.'" *Gender and Education* 15 (1): 91–103. doi:10.1080/0954025032000042167.

Delamont, S. 1995. "Bernstein and the Analysis of Gender Inequality: Considerations and Applications." In *Knowledge and Pedagogy*, edited by A. Sadnovik, 323–336. Norwood, NJ: Ablex Publishing Corporation.

DET (Department of Education and Training). 2010. *Annual Report 2009–2010*. Brisbane: Queensland Government.

DET (Department of Education and Training). 2011. *Annual Report 2010–11*. Brisbane: Queensland Government.

DETE (Department of Education Training and Employment). 2010. *Smart Schools National Partnership. Queensland Annual Report for 2009*. http://education.qld.gov.au/nationalpartnerships/three-form-initiatives.html.

DETE (Department of Education Training and Employment). 2012. *Low Socio-economic Status School Communities National Partnerships*. Brisbane: Queensland Government. http://education.qld.gov.au/nationalpartnerships/low-ses/index.html.

Gewirtz, S., and S. Ball. 2000. "From 'Welfarism' to 'New Managerialism': Shifting Discourses of School Headship in the Education Marketplace." *Discourse: Studies in the Cultural Politics of Education* 21 (3): 253–268.

Gunter, H. 2013. "Researching and Conceptualising the Field." *Educational Administration and History* 45 (2): 201–212. doi:10.1080/00220620.2013.768967.

Heimans, S., P. Singh, and K. Glasswell. 2015. "Doing Education Policy Enactment Research in a Minor Key." *Discourse: Studies in the Cultural Politics of Education* 1–12. http://www.tandfonline.com/doi/pdf/10.1080/01596306.2015.1074428.

Ivinson, G. 2014. "Pedagogy of improvised choreography and dance: Restricted codes revisited – developing pedagogies for the Corporeal Device." 8th International Basil Bernstein Symposium, A. Escandón, July 2014. Nanzan University, Nagoya Campus, Nagoya, Japan.

Ivinson, G., and E. Renold. 2013. "'Valleys' Girls: Re-theorising Bodies and Agency in a Semi-rural Post-Industrial Locale." *Gender and Education* 25 (6): 704–721.

Kulz, C. 2015. "Heroic Heads, Mobility Mythologies and the Power of Ambiguity." *British Journal of Sociology of Education*. doi:10.1080/01425692.2015.1044071.

Lapping, C. 2011. *Psychoanalysis in Social Research. Shifting Theories and Reframing Concepts*. London: Routledge.

Lingard, B., S. Creagh, and G. Vass. 2012. "Education Policy as Numbers: Data Categories and Two Australian Cases of Misrecognition." *Journal of Education Policy* 27 (3): 315–333.

Mazzei, L. A. 2013. "Materialist Mappings of Knowing in Being: Researchers Constituted in the Production of Knowledge." *Gender and Education* 25 (6): 776–785.

Mol, A. 2014. "Relative Realities, Theoretical Sensitivities. Forum for Social Sciences and Philosophy, Techno-scientific worlds in social sciences." In J. Zahle. Department of Philosophy, Department of Media, Cognition and Communication, University of Copenhagen. https://vimeo.com/108273539.

Moore, A. 2004. *The Good Teacher. Dominant Discourses in Teaching and Teacher Education*. Oxon: Routledge.

O'Reilly, D., and M. Reed. 2010. "Leaderism: An Evolution of Managerialism in UK Public Service Reform." *Public Administration* 88 (4): 960–978.

Power, S. 2006. "Markets and Misogyny: Educational Research on Educational Choice." *British Journal of Educational Studies* 54 (2): 175–188. doi:10.1111/j.1467-8527.2006.00340.x.

Queensland Teachers Union. 2015. *The Purpose and Use of Data in Queensland Schools QTU Position Statement*. Brisbane: QTU.

Renold, E., and G. Ivinson. 2014. "Horse-girl Assemblages: Towards a Post-human Cartography of Girls' Desire in an Ex-Mining Valleys Community." *Discourse: Studies in the Cultural Politics of Education* 35 (3): 361–376.

Rudd, K., and K. Smith. 2007. *The Australian Economy Needs an Education Revolution*. Australian Labour Party.

Singh, P. 2014. "Performativity and Pedagogising Knowledge: Globalising Educational Policy Formation, Dissemination and Enactment." *Journal of Education Policy*. doi:10.1080/02680939.2014.961968.

Singh, P. 2015. "Pedagogic Governance: 'Theorising With/After Bernstein.'" *British Journal of Sociology of Education*. doi:10.1080/01425692.2015.1081052.

Singh, P., S. Heimans, and K. Glasswell. 2014. "Policy Enactment, Context and Performativity: Ontological Politics and Researching Australian National Partnership Policies." *Journal of Education Policy*. doi:10.1080/02680939.2014.891763.

Singh, P., S. Thomas, and J. Harris. 2013. "Recontextualising Policy Discourses: A Bernsteinian Perspective on Policy Interpretation, Translation, Enactment." *Journal of Education Policy* 28 (4): 465–480. doi:10.1080/02680939.2013.770554.

Stengers, I. 2005. "Introductory Notes on an Ecology of Practices." *Cultural Studies Review* 11 (1): 183–196. http://www.tandfonline.com/eprint/Mrbka8hNRFZTZZ935RXq/full.

Taylor, C. A. 2013. "Objects, Bodies and Space: Gender and Embodied Practices of Mattering in the Classroom." *Gender and Education* 25 (6): 688–703.

5 Britton and Bernstein on Vygotsky

Divergent views on mind and language in the pedagogic context

Moira Inghilleri

ABSTRACT In recent influential work in language and social cognition relevant to pedagogical contexts, references to Basil Bernstein's work are notably absent, despite renewed recognition of the significance of his continued contribution to theories of classroom practices, sociolinguistics and the sociology of education. This article discusses several historical and ideological factors that have contributed to this lacuna. It reconsiders the organisation of the intellectual field of English education in Britain during the 1970s within which Bernstein's theorising about language took place. Within that field, it pays particular attention to the divergent readings of Vygotsky by James Britton and Bernstein with respect to power and the discursive regulation of 'legitimate' meanings in the pedagogic context. Finally, it considers the relevance in the post-Vygotskian field of social cognition of Bernstein's early attention to the relationship between social/institutional factors and individual functioning.

Introduction

In a number of recent influential contributions to sociolinguistic research relevant to educational contexts, the social dimension of language and cognition has been foregrounded in an attempt to re-establish a role of the mind in relation to the world and to social practices (Gee, 1990, 1992, 1999; Wertsch, 1991, 1998; Wertsch et al, 1995b; Light & Butterworth, 1992; John-Steiner et al, 1994). Two recent volumes entitled *Genres and Institutions: social processes in the workplace and school* (Christie & Martin, 1997) and *Pedagogy and the Shaping of Consciousness* (Christie, 1999) present classroom-based studies of mathematics, science and English teaching which attempt to bring together systemic-functional linguistic theory and Bernstein's theory of pedagogic discourse in considering how language features in a theory of human consciousness.

Common to all of these works is the claim that the patterns of meaning which shape, maintain and/or extend the boundaries both of individual 'thought worlds' and the social/symbolic order are formed and reformed through language in context. In some of these works, emphasis is placed on the divergent and sometimes conflicting sets of principles found across diverse social and cultural contexts which govern individual behaviour and which can and do position individuals unequally with respect to the acquisition of material and symbolic resources.

Amongst the work cited above, however, the Hallidayan approaches to language study (see Cope & Kalantzis, 1993; Painter, 1999) are alone in explicitly linking their work to the sociological theory of Basil Bernstein, despite recent recognition of the enduring significance of Bernstein's contribution to the sociology of education and sociolinguistics (see Atkinson, 1985; Atkinson et al, 1995; Sadnovik, 1995). Bernstein's work has been re-evaluated in the light of contemporary research and theory in the fields of linguistics, sociology and education within both structuralist and post-structuralist frameworks. However, in the area of language and social cognition, including that which Mercer has labeled 'neo-Vygotskian theory' (Mercer, 1994) – an area of interest which featured significantly in Bernstein's earlier work – references to Bernstein's work are notably absent even where his influence is self-evidently present (though see Daniels, 1994).

Two familiar factors have contributed to this omission: first, the organisation of the intellectual field of English education in which Bernstein's early theorising about language took place and in which James Britton, perhaps inevitably, predominated in influence over English language studies, and second, the political positioning of Bernstein's research through its association with deficit models of language acquisition and socialisation (see Inghilleri, 1996). However, more pertinently for the contemporary context, it is in the detail of Britton and Bernstein's relationship to Vygotsky's ideas that the relevance of Bernstein's theoretical work to post-Vygotskian approaches becomes apparent.

'Equality of Outcome' and the Intelligence Debate

During the post-war period in the United Kingdom one of the principal motives for the change in focus on language and communication had been, of course, the question of equality of outcome in education for students from divergent socio-cultural and socio-economic backgrounds. This concern over language and equality of outcome, moreover, merged with another debate already taking place in the United Kingdom regarding the relationship between social class and intelligence or cognitive ability. The 'intelligence' debate in the United Kingdom centred around the question of whether intelligence was innate and inherited or whether it was principally determined by and/or affected by the environment. The principal figure representing the former view was famously the psychologist Sir Cyril Burt, who conducted numerous well-publicised empirical studies which he offered as evidence for the belief that heredity and not environment was the major factor determining varying levels of intelligence within and between different social classes. Although Burt admitted the environment as a minor factor in shaping or constraining cognitive development, the general findings of his research were that the major component of intelligence (which he defined as an innate, general, cognitive mental capacity) was connected to an individual's genetic constitution, that this was biologically inheritable, and that it was the differential distribution of genotypes that accounted for lower performances on general intelligence tests amongst the working-class population (Burt, 1937, 1943, 1955).[1]

An alternative line of investigation emerged in the 1950s which challenged Burt's and others' privileging of heredity over environment as the explanation for students' educational success or failure. More sociological in orientation, it arose out of research in the area of post-war social mobility (see Glass, 1954) and was interested in the role of education in affecting more 'subtle' forms of social selection following its restructuring (see Himmelweit, 1954; Floud, 1956). This research called attention to social factors contributing to educational inequality, such as family size and home conditions, as well as psychological issues, for example the kinds of motivation and aspirations that working-class students and their families had with respect to their education, or that teachers encouraged in their working-class students. Although the research did not go so far as to claim that the material and 'cultural' features of the home environment should be regarded as social determinants of intelligence (Floud, 1956, pp. 143-144; Halsey, 1958), in underlining the importance of environmental and behavioural factors, research of this kind began successfully to challenge the widely held view that innate ability was the sole relevant factor in educational outcome.

It was from within this same tradition that the work of Basil Bernstein emerged in the 1950s. His work went further, however, both in challenging Burt's assumptions about cognition and in relating the features of the home environment to educational attainment (see Bernstein, 1958, 1961). Bernstein suggested that the distinctive, socially-derived modes of cognitive functions (e.g. perception and reasoning) that obtained between social classes developed through and were sustained by the medium of language:

> It is proposed that forms of spoken language in the process of their learning, elicit, reinforce, and generalise distinct types of relationships with the environment and thus create particular dimensions of significance. Speech marks out what is relevant – affectively,

> cognitively and socially – and experience is transformed by that which is made relevant. (Bernstein, 1961, pp. 288-289)

Bernstein's focus on language offered a more penetrating interpretation than previous sociological studies for the relationship of the environment to measurements of intelligence. According to his theory, unequal outcomes on IQ tests of verbal ability between social classes, for example, could not be explained solely through some general innate factor, nor seen simply as outcomes of problems of assimilation or attitude. They were, instead, a consequence of the distinctive forms of language which students acquired through socialisation within a particular family and/or class background. Bernstein thus foregrounded language as the key to environmental influences on cognitive performance. It was, he claimed, the principal means by which individual and social attitudes and behaviours were formed and made manifest.

These early formulations of Bernstein's theory served two important functions. They contributed to the aim of work in the sociology of education to highlight how social factors intruded on educational processes and they provided sociological, linguistic and psychological insights into the function of language in the learning process.

The Intellectual Field of English Education

By the 1970s, the renewed interest in language in the field of education was informed by several related areas of theoretical interest. At the centre of English teaching during this time was a focus on the role of language in cognitive and emotional development, due in large part to the influences of James Britton and Harold Rosen, both of whom were at the University of London Institute of Education, which provided an important institutional site for the dissemination of new ideas to the teaching profession (Britton, 1967, 1970a, 1970b; Barnes et al, 1969). Bernstein's investigations into language and social class were by then also well-known through the development of his sociolinguistic code theory at the Sociological Research Unit located at the Institute and the related empirical research that began to emerge during this period (see Lawton, 1968; Bernstein, 1973).

Meanwhile, also developing during this period was the new, interdisciplinary field of sociolinguistics, as work in the area of language and culture came to be known. In Britain, sociolinguistics came to the aid of the 'language paradigm' [2] of English as a school subject, especially through its contribution to several important interrelated themes: the notion of linguistic relativity; the relationship between language, culture and thought; and the question of the viability and/or desirability of 'cross-cultural' and 'cross-lingual' communication.

While each of the above elements in theoretical development must be viewed as independent of the others, together they generated the intellectual field of English education in the 1960s and 1970s and the shape of the conceptual/political framework from which the language paradigm was constructed.

The Fateful Split between Competence and Performance

Amongst the participants to the language debates, Britton and Bernstein both credit Langer, Cassirer, Sapir and Vygotsky with being important influences on the formation of their ideas (Britton, 1970b, 1987; Bernstein, 1971, 1993). Both Britton and Bernstein viewed language as a form of symbolic behaviour, as the medium by which ideas and beliefs as well as images and sensory data were transformed into verbal concepts. As Langer expressed it, 'Language is conception and conception is the frame of perception' (Langer, 1957, p. 126). Also evident in their writings is Sapir's notion of the heuristic function of language: the capacity of language to interpenetrate with experience. Language, suggested Sapir, not only represented experience, it also discovered and interpreted meanings for its speakers that they had not derived from first-hand experiences (Sapir, 1949, pp. 1-44). But although both Britton and Bernstein may have shared the view of language as both a symboliser and moderator of experience, their interpretations of the significance of this view with regard to education differed considerably.

Britton emphasised the creative and interpretative function of language in his work, seeing it as fundamental to students' cognitive and emotional development. In his influential book *Language and Learning* (Britton, 1970b), for example, he endorsed the idea that through talk and personal writing, students developed their natural capacities to extrapolate from personal experiences and construct patterned, mental models of the larger environment in which they lived and which were necessary for abstract, higher-order thinking. Britton and the followers of the 'personal growth' model focused almost exclusively on the cognitive and affective modes of representation which projected onto experience and were transformed into (and by) language. Their concern was to develop the innate potential that all children shared for making sense or meaning out of their environments. The emphasis was on the creativity and imagination that individuals demonstrated in constructing, categorising and classifying their way towards an experienced world view.

Although Britton acknowledged a social and cultural dimension to modes of representation in this early work (Britton, 1970b, pp. 19,116), his developmental model effectively *detached the social from the affective and cognitive domains*. The social became, in essence, the 'world' or the 'environment' within which experiences happened; it was presented as autonomous and real, as something 'out there' within which experiences occurred. This positioning of the social as active yet apart in Britton involved a choice on his part to remain focused on what for him was most meaningful and relevant: the relationship between 'structures of feelings' and symbolic forms. However, it can also be traced to the 'cognitive revolution' in psychology in the 1950s, when interest shifted from behaviourist-inspired observations of overt responses to environmental stimuli to cognitive-oriented explorations of the unobservable mental processes that guided actions. One important result in education of this new interest in the workings of the mind was the influence of Chomskian linguistics which formalised the Saussurean theoretical split between 'competence' (what an individual knew 'inside') and 'performance' (what an individual did 'outside') (Chomsky, 1965, pp. 3-4; Bruner, 1986). One of the implications of this was that, in terms of a child's cognitive development, it was permissible, even desirable, to view the mind independently of the social world. Hence, while culture happened outside the child's mind, cognitive and emotional development occurred inside.

But what had been introduced as a theoretical split within linguistics between competence and performance was recontextualised within the intellectual field of English education to universalise, and in effect, de-socialise, innate (linguistic/cognitive) competencies. Competence was championed over performance as proof of all children's universal – understood as equal – potential for developing essential competencies (Chomsky, 1964; Piaget, 1971; Hymes, 1972). Competence became viewed as, not genetically or socially, but rather mentally governed by an internal logic of the mind, and the development of various competencies was understood to occur naturally across stages of growth through similar mental operations and with similar results for all children.[3]

Against the geneticist account of innateness, Britton supported the view that all children could and did acquire the same capacity to represent both particular and universal aspects of experience because all were innately endowed with this capacity. From this, however, Britton and the personal growth model also assumed that meanings were the same for all children because of this shared capacity and because the 'world' in which meanings were generated was the same. In removing 'competence' from any social or cultural sources (and thus rescuing it from the geneticist account, which paradoxically needed the social world to sustain its position), Britton and the personal growth model were left with the 'world' as the unifying source for the patterning of meanings and their linguistic (or non-linguistic) representations. In this account, however, although the mind was released from geneticist interpretations of innateness, there was no mechanism for differentiating between the mind's capacity for meaning-making and the actual meanings which were produced (Britton, 1970b *passim*).

Bernstein's work *did* raise the questions which Chomsky and developmental cognitive psychology left to one side. Bernstein attempted to demonstrate how the mind interacted with the social and cultural to generate both different orderings of meanings and different forms of language. For Bernstein, however much creativity and imagination entered into this process, it nevertheless was both generative of and generated by the social in all its forms.

For Bernstein, the importance of Sapir's heuristic view of language was not primarily, as it was for Britton, its suggestion that language had the power to discover meanings for its speakers. What was important for Bernstein was that Sapir revealed language as a shaper – for better or for worse – of our experiences in and of possible worlds. Sapir himself would not have agreed with Britton's posing of an objective 'world' within which the merger of experience and language occurred, freely and naturally, through the mind. The connection between language and culture was made by both Sapir and Bernstein in terms of constraint; the possibilities of language's discoveries were necessarily limited by the culture and *vice versa*. Sapir, for example, makes the following point in his account of the heuristic function of language which Britton omits:

> Language is at one and the same time helping and retarding us in our exploration of experience, and the details of these processes of help and hindrance are deposited in the subtler meanings of different cultures. (Sapir, 1949, p. 8)

Bernstein, moving beyond Sapir, argued that linguistic and cognitive development was subject to the influences of power and discursive regulation found within distinctive cultures, social groups and social structures. Bernstein, unlike Chomsky, sought to locate competence (reattached to performance) within the restraints of power relations and their resulting differential unequal positionings. Bernstein insisted on the idea of competence as simultaneously cognitively inscribed and socially constituted. This problematised the popular view that all children were 'equally', because innately, competent by making competence a social rather than merely a cognitive aspect of the mind. The fact that the perception of the environment was patterned along sociological and cultural lines meant that the acquisition of different orders of meaning was not necessarily equivalent or equal. Different perceptions and interpretations which students held of their worlds as well as the forms of language which these generated could be limiting or innovating, constraining or creative, depending on the social circumstances surrounding their production and/or reception.

Britton's Vygotsky/Bernstein's Vygotsky

The attention given to Vygotsky by Britton and Bernstein was a natural extension of their interest in the ideas of Langer and Sapir discussed above, although their take-up of Vygotsky was distinctive. Vygotsky, like

Sapir, emphasised the interpenetration of language and the environment, but went further by actually describing how classifications of experiences were brought about in and by language. For Britton, Vygotsky contributed first a psychological and later a social dimension to his interest in the relationship between language, the environment and the development of thinking in children (Britton, 1970b, 1987). Vygotsky presented language as a regulatory device that assisted children in sorting and ordering their experiences of the world, enabling them to develop new forms of thought and more complex forms of behaviour. For Britton, Vygotsky's suggestion that a child's monologic use of language ('speech for oneself') served as a form of self-orientation with respect to the environment, assisting the internalisation of experiences (Vygotsky, 1962), supported the promotion of language for learning. In terms of the personal growth model, Vygotsky's observation that speech for oneself evolved into 'inner speech' revealed how the transformation from language to thought was accomplished.

In later writings (Britton, 1985, 1987), Britton focused more on Vygotsky's (and Luria's) articulation of the social nature of cognition, and how sociocultural conditions generated tools or 'auxiliary symbols' for learning in individuals which influenced new forms of behaviour (see Luria & Vygotsky, 1992, pp. 114-117). Britton interpreted this idea of the importance of the social conditions of learning as meaning that a child's consciousness was shaped in interaction with others in Vygotsky's 'zone of proximal development'.[4] In the liberal discourse of the personal growth model, however, 'social' simply came to mean 'interactive', and the zone of proximal development was interpreted as a site of benign interactive processes. It constituted the discursive space in which a child's consciousness met a more mature adult consciousness, enabling the child to internalise gradually various forms of shared social behaviour. The zone was perceived as the 'cognitive world' in which both particularistic and universal meanings originated and took shape for the child. The adult mediated these 'shared' meanings both by encouraging the expression of individual consciousness and by 'lending' consciousness to the child, helping the child become a member of a particular 'culture' or 'community' (Britton, 1987). For Britton, such communities were microcosms of the 'world'; they too were autonomous, objective environments within which interactive (social) learning took place:

> Taking community in a micro sense, it is likely that we all live in a number of communities. As teachers, we are responsible for one of those – the classroom. It is clear we have a choice: we can operate so as to make that as rich an interactive learning community as we can, or we may continue to treat it as a captive audience for whatever instruction we choose to offer. (Britton, 1987, p. 26)

In their reading of Vygotsky, Britton and the followers of the personal growth model continued to assume that the generation and patterning of meanings that occurred in interaction were transferable from the 'world' onto micro contexts such as the school and the family. Hence the source of students' and their adult mediators' meanings was never investigated beyond the immediate environment (e.g. school-based knowledge) or the individuals themselves. Neither was the asymmetry of the relationship between teacher and student within the zone addressed; rather interactive learning was assumed to rid the classroom of the issue of the imbalance of power. Vygotsky was essentially recontextualised into a pedagogic theory that offered a rationalisation for language-based, interactive learning in the classroom. The zone demonstrated how children acquired the ability to regulate and refine their individual behaviour through language interactively with adults and/or peers, while the individual child remained the sole creator and innovator of his or her own meanings.

For Bernstein, in contrast, Vygotsky's zone of proximal development would not simply be viewed as a neutral (or potentially neutral) site for the creation or exchange of mutually interpretable meanings. While Britton might have assumed that the presence of nurturing adults (teachers, parents, etc.) was all that was necessary to ensure successful interactive communication, Bernstein emphasised the diverse cultural sources (and resources) of both the meaning-makers and the meanings that were made (Bernstein, 1971, pp. 123, 176; 1972, pp. 135-151; 1996, p. 147; and see Atkinson, 1985, p. 14). Bernstein's understanding of consciousness as sociologically and culturally patterned would suggest that within the zone, conflict and/or strategic negotiation over meaning would naturally occur.

Furthermore, for Bernstein, the zone would be the cognitive representation of a social world, and hence the meanings as well as the 'tools' that were employed or made available within it – the social context of learning – would be subject to the uneven social regulation and distribution of the content and framing of the knowledge to be acquired and/or transmitted. The regulation of experiences by language was mediated by adults transmitting what, Bernstein argued, were the 'codes' or organising principles of the social world(s) in which they themselves were located (Bernstein, 1975, pp. 85-156; 1990; 1996, pp. 17-38). Hence, adults were not simply enablers or facilitators but potentially shapers or, to greater and lesser extents, determiners of children's consciousness, for within the zone of proximal development, it was possible for an adult socialiser to bring meanings (and the rules for their articulation) that were not shared by the child and *vice versa*.

Like Vygotsky, Bernstein perceived that words and meanings constituted and were constitutive of the historical and cultural basis of individual minds. Bernstein, however, raised the issue of the external (and internal) constraints on the generation and ratification of 'legitimate' meanings in both micro and macro communicative contexts. For Bernstein, the fact that language was grounded in culture meant that it was necessarily subject to the influences of power and discursive regulation. Britton's Vygotsky, however, remained outside Bernstein's view of culture as a site of contestation over meanings. For Britton, the zone of proximal development became a site of social and discursive freedom, a cognitive space where the 'shared' meanings of a culture were discovered, articulated and made valid. Britton effectively neutralised social/cultural linguistic communication by suggesting that meanings were universally available in the 'world', discovered rather than tacitly acquired, and openly exchanged and negotiated in interaction with others.

In the end, English education looked towards Britton and the personal growth model to define its agenda for the 1970s. Bernstein's conclusion that the educational process produced socially uneven products, due in part to different sets of sociolinguistic codes operating between students and schools, was not acceptable (or expressible) within the terms of the model. Instead, what was foregrounded was that, at the individual cognitive level, all students, regardless of class/cultural background, were equally, because innately, competent. The model sought to activate the role of the learner (the reader, the writer, etc.), focusing on the process of acquisition rather than on the (disparate) products that resulted.

While there was much gained from this developmental approach, the tendency within the personal growth model to separate innate potential or competence and actual performance did much to obscure and/or deny the role of class and culture in language and learning.[5] In the end, the personal growth model established a definition of culture in English education as 'environmental', something 'out there' in the world, distinct from Bernstein's conception of culture as 'social', something simultaneously 'in here' in the mind. The notion of cognition as a social activity was loosely interpreted as shared behaviour and learning in interaction with others, both of which assumed similarity and equality of input as well as output, regardless of social/linguistic background. By developing the view in education of the social world as detached from the cognitive one – however much it appeared to honour difference over deficit – the crucial issue of meaning was eliminated from discussion, and with it serious consideration of the external/visible social processes at work on the internal/invisible development and structuring of human consciousness.

Contemporary Accounts of Social Cognition

Contemporary approaches to the relationship between mind, language and the social continue to draw on Vygotsky and his concern with social mediation and the internalization of the social context of learning. Wertsch and other researchers (see Wertsch et al, 1995b) employ methods adapted from Vygotsky's notion of mediation – including semiotic mediation – as a key to understanding human action. They argue strongly that mediational means 'provide the link or bridge between concrete actions carried out by individuals and groups, on the one hand, and cultural, institutional and historical settings on the other' (Wertsch et al, 1995, p. 21). And like Bernstein, they view mediation in terms of both empowerment *and* constraint:

> We can never 'speak from nowhere', given that we can speak (or more broadly, act) only by invoking mediational means that are available in the 'cultural tool kit' provided by the sociocultural setting in which we operate ... this does not mean that we are mechanistically determined by, or are mere puppets of, the mediational means we employ, but it does mean that constraints of some kind always exist. (Wertsch et al, 1995a, p. 25)

With a similar focus on the social nature of meaning, Gee argues that 'any human action is meaningful and recognisable only within some Discourse' (Gee, 1992, p. 110). He suggests the notion of Discourse(s) as semiotic 'apprenticeships' or social practices through which social members are enculturated into ways of speaking, thinking and interacting. Discourses are embedded in a variety of social institutions, including the family and schools, and subconsciously acquired by individuals through exposure and practice:

> Discourses are mastered through acquisition, not learning. That is, Discourses are not mastered by overt instruction [...] but by enculturation ('apprenticeship') into social practices through scaffolded and supported interaction with people who have already mastered the Discourse. (Gee, 1992, p. 114)

Gee is more explicit than Wertsch in analysing the potential *limitations* of a Discourse for its members in terms of social and ideological determinants, noting when and where the mastery of a particular Discourse (or lack thereof) creates differential access to political power and/or social goods, including school-based knowledge. For Gee, the inherent ideological nature of Discourses thus implicates them in questions of social and cultural inclusion and exclusion, as well as in whether or under what conditions an individual or group is able to reflect on, criticize or change the status of a Discourse operating within and through social institutions, including educational settings.

In raising such questions regarding the interrelationship between language, the social and the constitution of the subject, the potential remains for issues to be raised about social, psychological or even biological determinism. Delpit's recent cautions with regard to Gee's work on Discourse, for example, echo similar critiques made of Bernstein's work in an earlier period when she writes:

> Gee's argument suggests a dangerous kind of determinism as flagrant as that espoused by the geneticists: instead of being locked into 'your place' by your genes, you are now locked hopelessly into a lower-class status by your Discourse. (Delpit, 1995, p. 154)

There is a reading of their respective positions, however (see Gee, 1990, pp. 164-193), that suggests a dynamic rather than a static account of this relationship. Underlying the view that patterns of meaning and their linguistic realisations or Discourses originate in the social structure (where 'thought worlds' collide) is the idea that language has a social/material as well as a social/symbolic base. What is refracted and reflected through language is the social/symbolic order and individuals' relationship to it. Where this relationship remains dynamic, albeit subject to constraint, individuals are always potentially aware of their and others' social/linguistic behaviour. In dialogic encounters (whether intra- or inter-individual, or intra- or inter-cultural) individuals can and do perceive the role that divergent or conflicting values play in both sustaining and altering 'cultured' meanings. This suggests the possibility, at least, of the transcendence of social/linguistic constraints or the development of strategies to counter such constraints, not the maintenance of social/linguistic orderliness. Moreover, it assumes a social world where creativity and constraint with respect to cognition have to be and can be taken together without contradiction.

Despite the controversial entanglements of Bernstein's ideas in the development of twentieth-century sociolinguistics, his conceptualisation through Vygotsky of the relationship between the individual and the social has nonetheless generated relevant theoretical and methodological tools to account for the influence of social/historical factors beyond face-to-face interaction.[6] Further and more explicit critical dialogue between contemporary post-Vygotskian approaches and Bernstein's contributions to the question of individual and group consciousness formation may result in important insights germane to the complex of issues involved in the interrelationship of the macro and micro variables involved in this process.

Notes

[1] Although this research has since been discredited (see Kamin, 1974; Eysenck & Kamin, 1981), it remains relevant to the present discussion beyond its historical significance, insofar as in establishing the idea of a

genetically derived 'innate', universal, general intelligence, it contributed to the confusion that would later appear in the deficit/difference debate between a genetically derived and a socially derived cognitive inheritance. Bernstein's identification of different cognitive capacities between working-class and middle-class students, for example, was conflated by many with the geneticists' claim for different innate capacities. The result was that the meaning of the terms in the context of academic and educational debates over competence became practically indistinguishable.

[2] This phrase refers to the frequently observed 'paradigm shift' in English teaching in which language and linguistics became the focus of teachers' and researchers' attention by the 1960s and 1970s (see Inglis, 1971; Shayer, 1972; Mathieson, 1975; Abbs, 1980; Allen, 1980; Ball, 1982; Burgess & Martin, 1990).

[3] The social was only reinstated in order to account for observable differences in individual performances, but the reasons given for socially constituted differences were always external not internal to the individual child. Explanations were initially sought from research in the sociology of education for its insights into the material and cultural conditions that contributed to unequal attainment amongst students. Later, the 'new sociology of education' emerged and the problem was seen more in ideological terms, as originating in social institutions (see Young, 1971).

[4] Britton's increased attention to the importance of the interactive element of language and learning was no doubt part of the general shift from sole focus on intra-individual to interest in inter-individual learning that was brought about by a revision of Chomsky within education in the 1970s (Moon, 1988, pp. 173-174).

[5] For an informed account of the strengths and weaknesses of the personal growth model and its relationship to the development of the English curriculum, see Burgess (1985, 1988, 1993).

[6] On the theoretical and methodological importance of Bernstein's work in social science research, see the various contributions in *International Journal of Social Research Methodology: theory and practice,* 2001, 4(1).

References

Abbs, P. (1980) The Reconstruction of English as Art, *Tract,* 31, pp. 4-31.

Allen, D. (1980) *English Teaching Since 1965: how much growth*? London: Heinemann Educational.

Atkinson, P. (1985) *Language, Structure and Function: an introduction to the sociology of Basil Bernstein.* London: Methuen.

Atkinson, P., Davies, B. & Delamont, S. (Eds) (1994) *Discourse and Reproduction: essays in honor of Basil Bernstein.* Cresskill, NJ: Hampton Press.

Ball, S.J. (1982) Competition and Conflict in the Teaching of English: a socio-historical analysis, *Journal of Curriculum Studies,* 14(1), pp. 1-28.

Barnes, D., Britton, J. & Rosen, H. (1969) *Language, the Learner and the School.* Harmondsworth: Penguin.

Bernstein, B. (1958) Some Sociological Determinants of Perception: an inquiry into sub-cultural differences, *British Journal of Sociology,* 9, pp. 159-174.

Bernstein, B. (1961) Social Class and Linguistic Development: a theory of social learning, in A.H. Halsey, J. Floud & C.A. Anderson (Eds) *Education, Economy and Society*. London: Collier Macmillan.

Bernstein, B. (1971) *Class, Codes and Control,* Volume 1. London: Routledge and Kegan Paul.

Bernstein, B. (1972) A Critique of the Concept of Compensatory Education, in C. Cazden, V. John & D. Hymes (Eds), *Functions of Language in the Classroom.* New York: Teachers College Press.

Bernstein, B. (1973) *Class, Codes and Control,* Volume 2. London: Routledge and Kegan Paul.

Bernstein, B. (1975) *Class, Codes and Control,* Volume 3. London: Routledge and Kegan Paul.

Bernstein, B. (1990) *The Structuring of Pedagogic Discourse: class, codes and control,* Volume 4. London: Routledge.

Bernstein, B. (1993) Foreword, in H. Daniels (Ed.) *Charting the Agenda: educational activity after Vygotsky*. London: Routledge.

Bernstein, B. (1996) *Pedagogy, Symbolic Control and Identity: theory, research and critique*. London: Taylor and Francis.

Britton, J. (1967) *Talking and Writing*. London: Methuen.

Britton, J. (1970) *Language and Learning*. Harmondsworth: Penguin Books.

Britton, J. (1970a) Their Language and Our Teaching, *English in Education,* 4(2), pp. 5-13.

Britton, J. (1985) Research Currents: second thoughts on learning, *Language Arts,* 62(1), pp. 72-77.

Britton, J. (1987) Vygotsky's Contribution to Pedagogical Theory, *English in Education,* 21(3), pp. 22-26.

Bruner, J. (1986) *Actual Minds, Possible Worlds*. Cambridge, MA: Harvard University Press.

Burgess, T. (1985) The Question of English, in J. Miller & M. Meek (Eds) *Changing English: essays for Harold Rosen*. London: Heinemann.

Burgess, T. (1988) On Difference: cultural and linguistic diversity and English teaching, in M. Lightfoot & N. Martin (Eds) *The Word for Teaching is Learning: essays for James Britton*. London: Heinemann Educational & Boynton/Cook.

Burgess, T. (1993) Returning History: literacy, difference, and English teaching in the post-war period, in B. Green (Ed.) *The Insistence of the Letter: literacy studies and curriculum theorizing*. London: Falmer Press.

Burgess, T. & Martin, N. (1990) Teaching English in England, 1945-1986: politics and practice, in J. Britten, R.E. Shafer & K. Watson (Eds) *Teaching and Learning English Worldwide*. Clevedon: Multilingual Matters.

Burt, C. (1937) *The Backward Child*. London: University of London Press.

Burt, C. (1943) Ability and Income, *British Journal of Educational Psychology*, 13, pp. 83-98.

Burt, C. (1955) Evidence for the Concept of Intelligence, *British Journal of Educational Psychology*, 25, pp. 158-177.

Chomsky, N. (1964) Current Issues in Linguistic Theory, in J.A. Fodor & J.J. Katz (Eds) *Readings in the Philosophy of Language: the structure of language*. Englewood, NJ: Prentice-Hall.

Chomsky, N. (1965) *Aspects of a Theory of Syntax*. Cambridge, MA: MIT Press.

Christie, F. (Ed.) (1999) *Pedagogy and the Shaping of Consciousness: linguistic and social processes*. London: Cassell.

Christie, F. & Martin, J.R. (Eds) (1997) *Genres and Institutions: social processes in the workplace and school*. London: Cassell.

Cope, B. & Kalantzis, M. (Eds) (1993) *The Powers of Literacy: a genre approach to teaching writing*. London: Falmer Press.

Daniels, H. (1994) *Charting the Agenda: educational activity after Vygotsky*. London: Routledge.

Delpit, L. (1995) *Other People's Children: cultural conflict in the classroom*. New York: The New Press.

Eysenck, H.J. & Kamin, L. (1981) *Intelligence: the battle for the mind – J. Eysenck versus Leon Kamin*. London: Macmillan.

Floud, J.E. (Ed.) (1956) *Social Class and Educational Opportunity*. London: Heinemann.

Gee, J.P. (1990) *Social Linguistics and Literacies: ideology in discourse*. London: Falmer Press.

Gee, J.P. (1992) *The Social Mind*. New York: Bergin and Garvey.

Gee, J.P. (1999) *Introduction to Discourse Analysis*. London: Routledge.

Glass, D.V. (Ed.) (1954) *Social Mobility in Britain*. London: Routledge and Kegan Paul.

Halsey, R.H. (1958) Genetics, Social Structure and Intelligence, *British Journal of Sociology*, 10, pp. 15-28.

Himmelweit, H. (1954) Social Status and Secondary Education since the 1944 Act, in D.V. Glass (Ed.) *Social Mobility in Britain*. London: Routledge & Kegan Paul.

Hymes, D. (1972) On Communicative Competence, in J.B. Pride & J. Holmes (Eds) *Sociolinguistics*. Harmondsworth: Penguin Books.

Inghilleri, M. (1996) Language, Culture and the Quest for Commensurability. PhD Dissertation. London: University of London.

Inglis, F. (1971) How to Do Things with Words: a critique of language studies, *English in Education*, 5(2), pp. 74-84.

John-Steiner, V., Panofsky, C.P. & Smith, L.W. (Eds) (1994) *Sociocultural Approaches to Language and Literacy: an interactionist perspective*. Cambridge: Cambridge University Press.

Kamin, L. (1974) *The Science and Politics of I. Q.* Potomac, MD: Lawrence Erlbaum.

Langer, S. (1957) *Philosophy in a New Key*, 3rd edition. Cambridge, MA: Harvard University Press.

Lawton, D. (1968) *Social Class, Language and Education*. London: Routledge and Kegan Paul.

Light, P. & Butterworth, G. (Eds) (1992) *Context and Cognition*. London: Harvester Wheatsheaf.

Luria, A.R. & Vygotsky, L.S. (1992) *Ape, Primitive Man and Child: essays in the history of behavior*. London: Harvester Wheatsheaf.

Mathieson, M. (1975) *The Preachers of Culture*. London: George Allen & Unwin.

Mercer, N. (1994) Neo-Vygotskian Theory and Classroom Education, in B. Stierer & J. Maybin (Eds) *Language, Literacy and Learning in Educational Practice*. Clevedon: Multilingual Matters.

Moon, C. (1988) Reading: where are we now? in M. Meek & C. Molls (Eds) *Languge and Literacy in the Primary School*. London: Falmer Press.

Painter, C. (1999) *Learning through Language in Early Childhood*. London: Continuum.

Piaget, J. (1971) *Structuralism*. London: Routledge and Kegan Paul.

Sadnovik, A. (Ed.) (1995) *Knowledge and Pedagogy: the sociology of Basil Bernstein*. Norwood, NJ: Ablex.

Sapir, E. (1949) Language, in D. Mandelbaum (Ed.) *Edward Sapir, Culture Language and Personality: selected essays*. Berkeley: University of California Press.

Shayer, D. (1972) *The Teaching of English in Schools, 1900-1970*. London: Routledge.

Vygotsky, L. (1962) *Thought and Language*. Cambridge, MA: MIT Press.

Wertsch, J. (1998) *Mind as Action*. Oxford: Oxford University Press.

Wertsch, J., del Rio, P. & Alvarez, A. (1995a) Sociocultural Studies: history, action and mediation, in J. Wertsch, P. del Rio & A. Alvarez, *Sociocultural Studies of Mind*. Cambridge: Cambridge University Press.

Wertsch, J., del Rio, P. & Alvarez, A. (1995b) *Sociocultural Studies of Mind*. Cambridge: Cambridge University Press.

Wertsch, J.V. (1991) *Voices of the Mind: a sociocultural approach to mediated action*. Cambridge, MA: Harvard University Press.

Young, M.F.D. (Ed.) (1971) *Knowledge and Control*. London: Collier Macmillan.

6 Pedagogic discourse and sex education

Myths, science and subversion

Gabrielle Ivinson

This paper elaborates possibilities and limitations for sex education in schools by mapping the consequence of introducing the topic 'sex' within a range of scientific and informal discursive settings. The organising and regulating structures of the school maintain the boundaries between common-sense and scientific discourses. Bernstein made a distinction between vertical discourse and horizontal discourses. Vertical discourses characterise scientific discourses that are coherent, explicit and systematically principled structures. Horizontal discourses characterise common-sense discourses that are local, segmented and context-dependent. The implications for teaching sex education through vertical discourses such as science, English and art as opposed to personal and social education, which is a horizontal discourse, are discussed. Yet, all discourses are unstable, and the notion of a 'tipping point' is introduced to demonstrate the potential for sex education when vertical discourses collapse.

Introduction

The topic 'sex' can be associated with birth and death, separation and union, and masculinity and femininity. The term 'sex' carries an almost limitless symbolic potential yet, once framed within a discourse, the network of meanings associated with it is brought into alignment. Therefore the structure of the discourse within which the term 'sex' is framed provides the key to how it is understood. This paper focuses on the structure of discourses as a key to investigate the potential for sex education within elements of the curriculum. Insights from Moscovici's work on common-sense knowledge and Bernstein's work on pedagogic discourse are used to argue that one potential source of sex *education* lies in juxtaposing discourses that frame 'sex' in different ways.

The term 'sex' can be seen to cover at least the following five strands:

- the sex act performed between people or auto-erotic sex acts;
- the anatomy and physiology of reproduction;
- forms of social identification and recognition such as heterosexual, les, bi, gay;

- eroticism; and
- aspects of morality such as family values and gender relations.

Schools are modernist institutions (Epstein *et al.*, 2003) that privilege scientific knowledge above common-sense knowledge. The curriculum can be viewed as a collection of scientific or specialist discourses (cf. Bernstein, 1990, 1996, 1999) and therefore, within schools, teachers frame the topic 'sex' within scientific discourses. Sex education often aims to limit and curtail young people's sexual thoughts, practices and desires rather than expand their imaginative repertoires. Yet, the term 'sex' has its own subversive potential. It is an unruly topic because it invokes the body. As Grosz (1995, p. 214, cited in Gard, 2003, p. 107) states:

> There is an instability at the very heart of sex and bodies, the fact that the body is what it is capable of doing, and what any body is capable of doing is well beyond the tolerance of any culture.

The topic 'sex' represents the ever-present 'irrational' that teachers fear can erupt into disorder and chaos. Understanding how this subversive potential can be exploited for the purposes of sex education requires a detailed consideration of the structure of discourses.

Science and myths

One requirement of sex *education* is to provide young people with information about biological and social functions. Such education is crucial to help prevent sexually transmitted disease, sexual oppression and social injustice experienced by minority, non-heterosexual groups. The need to reduce risk-taking in the sexual behaviour of adolescents (for example, Cleland & McKay, 1992; Warwick *et al.*, 2003) is acute. The problem that sex educators face is that young people often fail to see the relevance of information provided in school to their own lives and find it difficult to apply it to their sexual practices. We confront issues in our lives through common-sense rather than scientific discourses.

As modernist institutions, schools privilege the movement of ideas from the common-sense realm to the scientific realm, and not a movement in the opposite direction. Yet, sex education requires two-way traffic between scientific and common-sense discourses so that students can be encouraged to bring knowledge from the scientific realm to bear on everyday situations (Whitty *et al.*, 1994a, b). First, schools need to understand and legitimate common-sense knowledge and, second, they have to find ways to encourage two-way traffic between common-sense and scientific discourses.

Researchers within the field of sex education recognise that students come to school already equipped with social representations of sex as part of their local cultures (Renold, 2000, 2001; Duveen, 2001; Elliot, 2003; Epstein *et al.*, 2003). Common sense involves myths, beliefs and superstitions. Myths about sex circulate in peer groups as hearsay, rumour and bravado. One of the roles of sex education is to disrupt these commonly held myths in order to make alternative ways of thinking available. One way to challenge sexual myths is to confront common sense with scientific discourses. But schools can only do this if they understand more about the structure of common-sense discourse and its role in everyday life. Moscovici's work provides considerable insight by characterising common-sense and scientific knowledge as two universes each obeying a different logic.

Two universes: two systems of thought

Distinctions between realms such as the sacred and the profane, the public and the private, the moral and the amoral have a long history. Scientific and common-sense knowledge are often viewed as an opposition between abstract and concrete thinking (cf. Dowling, 1998). This distinction implies a hierarchy in which abstract thinking is privileged above concrete thinking. Moscovici's (1961 [1976], 1981, 2001) theory of social representations is a study of common-sense knowledge that seeks to reverse this hierarchy. According to this approach, the scientific realm provides a reservoir of terms, vocabulary and resources that people appropriated when they need to make sense of new or unfamiliar situations in everyday life. Moscovici argues that, in this respect, science has replaced religion as the realm in which ideas are invented or reinvented.

Moscovici based the division between common-sense and scientific knowledge on Lévy-Bruhl's (1925/1926) distinction between pre-logical and logic thought, and conceptualised this as two universes: a 'consensual' universe and a 'reified' universe, which he explained in the following way:

> In the consensual universe society is a visible, continuous, creation, permeated with meaning and purpose, possessing a human voice, in accord with human existence and both acting and reacting like a human being. In other words, man [*sic*] is, here, the measure of all things. In the reified universe, society is transformed into a system of solid, basic unvarying entities which are indifferent to individuality and lack identity. The society ignores itself and its creations which it sees only as isolated objects, such as persons, ideas, environments and activities. The various sciences that are concerned with such objects, can, as it were, impose their authority on the thought and experience of each individual and decide, in each case, what is true and what is not. All things are the measure of man. (Moscovici, 1984, p. 20)

In the reified universe, the scientific method, including the law of non-contradiction, and its 'truths' dominate. People are reduced to reified objects or data and human desires and meanings are killed off (cf. Devereux, 1967). Therefore, we cannot recognise ourselves in and through scientific discourses, because within these discourses 'society ignores itself and its creations'. This is precisely what research examining sex education has found. Young people do not recognise themselves in or through the scientific discourses of the curriculum and view such knowledge as 'irrelevant' to their lives.

Within the consensual universe, society has a 'human voice'. People recognise and anchor themselves in the world as they comment, make judgements and gossip in pubs, cafés and homes. In schools this takes place within peer groups at leisure times, between lessons and within lessons when the framing of scientific discourses is loosened. In this process of making sense, we appropriate terms, ideas and concepts from scientific discourses for our own everyday purposes. Moscovici's seminal text, *La Psychoanalyse son image et son publique* (1961 [1976]) described how groups in contemporary society appropriated terms from the scientific realm of psychoanalysis to differentiate types of anxiety. For example, terms such as 'neurosis', 'phobia' and 'panic attack' entered common-sense use only within the past 50 years. Moscovici demonstrated how different social groups such as Catholics and Marxists selectively excluded aspects of psychoanalytical discourse (such as libido) that did not fit with their dominant system of thought. This means that as scientific terms are drawn into common-sense discourses they are transformed and moulded to fit the everyday needs of specific groups. In relation to sex education, we can see that young people express commonly held ideas about sex, its social significance and symbolic meanings within peer-group conversations in ways that make sense to them and that allow them to be recognised, validated and to achieve social status. If one way of being validated is through stories of sexual exploits or through not using condoms, then these stories will continue to be used as a way to achieve social recognition.

It is a feature of common-sense discourses that they do not obey the law of non-contradiction. Ideas align, attract and repel each other according to a different logic. Mauss (1950) characterised this as somewhere between magic and religion, and Durkheim said it involved 'negative acts' with 'the function of preventing mixture and unwanted contact' (Durkheim, 1976, cited in Jodelet, 1991, p. 265). Many of the ways in which ideas are kept apart within common-sense discourse relate to societies' fears and anxieties about contagion, prohibition and impurity. This patterning of ideas constitutes the moral order of society. The initial reasons for the ritualistic maintenance of boundaries between pure and impure, good and evil, masculine and feminine have become lost in the mists of time. Yet such boundaries are continuously re-invoked when fears and uncertainties arise. We use disease, for example, as a common metaphor for social disorder. 'Feelings about evil are projected onto a disease. And the disease (so enriched with meaning) is projected onto the world' (Sontag, 1978, p. 63). The fear that AIDS can be transmitted through saliva or sweat can be traced back to 'the nightmare belief in the transmission of syphilis through bodily fluids' that accompanied fears surrounding sexual liberation in the nineteenth century (Jodelet, 1991, p. 301). The patterning and alignment of ideas within common sense can be partially mapped through historical or genealogical research (cf. Foucault, 1972). Yet, such research is not easy because associations between ideas get hidden and condensed (Heider, 1958). Unlike scientific ideas, the norms, beliefs and myths that make up common sense are not shaped by the relatively visible structures of institutions. Yet, it is common sense and not scientific discourse that provides people with resources to make sense, to reflect on their lives and to be recognised by others. Without common-sense discourses, people would be alienated from their own societies.

Ideas from the reified universe become absorbed into the consensual universe and vice versa through dynamic processes that take place in everyday conversations.

Ideas from one realm are appropriated and used in the other. It has been recognised that science is not free from the influence of common sense (cf. Latour, 1993). However, common-sense discourses are structured differently to scientific discourses and pedagogic discourse operates at the boundary between them. Teachers aim to induct learners into scientific discourses. The skill of teaching is to start from a topic that students can meaningfully connect with and reframe it within a scientific discourse. This process of recontextualisation shifts thinking into a different symbolic realm. Bernstein described the distinction between common-sense and scientific discourse as one between horizontal and vertical discourses (Bernstein, 1996, 1999). Within the next section the structure of scientific discourse is considered in more detail.

Vertical and horizontal discourses

The curriculum is composed of a collection of scientific discourses. In Bernstein's earlier work, subjects such as science and art were conceptualised as 'contents'. Later, influenced by Foucault, he re-conceptualised subjects as discourses. This shift emphasised that subjects are dynamic: active constructions and reconstructions that are formed between teachers and students in every day practice. Therefore the slippage and movement of ideas as they are framed within different discourses becomes central to the process of learning. In his last essay, 'Vertical and Horizontal Discourse', Bernstein (1999) clarified his position on the relation between concrete and abstract thinking. He linked concrete thinking with horizontal discourses, which he described as:

> ... likely to be oral, local, context dependent and specific, tacit, multi-layered, and contradictory across but not within contexts... the crucial feature is that it is segmentally organised. (Bernstein, 1999, p. 159)

Horizontal discourses are context specific and therefore 'contradictory across but not within contexts' (Bernstein, 1999, p. 159). He also made a distinction between discourses and the knowledge structures that underlie discourse. Bernstein referred to the knowledge structures that underlie horizontal discourse as:

> contextually specific and context depended, embedded in on-going practices, usually with strong affective loading and directed towards specific immediate goals, highly relevant to the acquirer in the context of his/her life. (1999, p. 161)

Although Bernstein's aim was to characterise what Jean Lave and others have called situated knowledge, it is also possible to recognise features such as 'relevance' and 'the context of his/her life' that apply to common-sense discourses.

In contrast, the curriculum can be viewed as a collection of vertical discourses that relate, although not directly, to disciplines such as science, art and the humanities. Bernstein's work on vertical discourse provides a way to differentiate between scientific discourses. He defined two forms of knowledge underlying vertical discourses: hierarchical knowledge structures and horizontal knowledge structures. Horizontal knowledge structures consist of a series of segments that:

> form a series of specialist languages with specialised modes of interrogation, specialist criteria for the production and circulation of texts e.g. in humanities and social sciences. (Bernstein, 1999, p. 159)

The humanities and social sciences have horizontal knowledge structures, and in English literature the segments are the languages of criticism. In sociology the segments are 'functionalism, post-structuralism, post–modernism, Marxism, etc' (Bernstein, 1999, p. 162). In contrast, science is a vertical discourse with a hierarchical knowledge structure because it:

> attempts to create very general propositions and theories, which integrate knowledge at lower levels, and in this way shows underlying uniformities across an expanding range of apparently different phenomena. (Bernstein, 1999, p. 162)

Acquiring vertical discourses involves learning principles. Principles are 'procedures… linked to other procedures hierarchically—it is an ongoing process in extended time' (Bernstein, 1999, p. 161). Bernstein differentiated horizontal knowledge structures further into those with strong and weak grammars. Those with strong grammars make the rules for acquiring the languages of the discipline relatively explicit. An example of this is mathematics, which is a vertical discourse with a horizontal knowledge structure and which consists of a series of segments, such as algebra, arithmetic and calculus. Disciplines with weak grammars, such as sociology and English, have less explicit rules for acquiring its various languages. Overall, the rules by which ideas are aligned within vertical discourses are relatively explicit and publicly available. The rules reside in communities of scholars in universities and colleges, in academic journals and other texts. Because the knowledge related to vertical discourse is institutionalised, there are more signposts available for tracking structure and content in comparison with horizontal discourses.

Bringing together insights from Bernstein and Moscovici, it could be argued that social representations underlie horizontal discourses just as hierarchical and horizontal knowledge structures underlie vertical discourses. Although commonsense beliefs are not strictly speaking irrational, they align through association, condensation and sedimentation. Social representations have deep historical roots and their fused structures endow them with a force that makes them seem *natural*. Ideas that circulate in the consensual universe obey a *different logic* to ideas that circulate in the reified universe. Understanding the structure of the ideas that underlie common sense makes it easier to see why rumours, myths and superstitions about sex are ubiquitous and resistant to rational argument. However, education is dependent on there being discourses that are differently structured and that can disrupt and challenge each other. The following section considers the potential of a range of scientific discourses for sex education.

Sex education and scientific discourses

Sex *education* lies in the potential for disrupting the inner logic of common-sense discourses in order to challenge sexual myths in the interest of sexual health, social justice and sexual equality. One way to achieve this is to juxtapose scientific with common-sense discourses about sex. Given that lessons in school are usually framed within scientific discourses, it ought to be possible to introduce aspects of the topic 'sex' in most subjects. The argument presented so far emphasises that people cannot recognised themselves in and through scientific discourses because they are structured in ways that expel personal meanings. People do not make sense of their lives using the laws of scientific rationality. This does not mean that people are irrational. It means that in everyday life we employ a different logic: the logic of the moral order or of the consensual universe. Therefore successful sex education requires that personal as well as scientific meanings are recognised. The following section considers the possibilities and limitation of achieving this in a range of subjects starting with science. Examples given in the next section are drawn from classroom observations carried out in a range of secondary schools, mainly in year nine classes (students aged 13/14). The incidents arose in lessons observed while tracking cohorts of students across a range of curriculum subjects. The observational focus was on students undertaking activities set by teachers with specific attention paid to how teachers introduced activities to classes.[1]

Science

Scientific discourses are arguable the furthest removed from common-sense discourses. Sex as a topic can be framed within discourses of biology, physiology, chemistry and anatomy. Science is governed by an internal logic that privileges objectivity, distance and linearity, which *destroy* (cf. Bernstein, 1999, p. 158) subjective views, personal experiences and individual expression. This appears to be a most unlikely discourse for introducing aspects of sex that might be useful to students in their everyday lives. Yet scientific discourses carry information that can directly challenge common sense myths about sex.

Common-sense ideas, for example, about how AIDS/HIV can be transmitted are caught up with ideas about moral purity and fears about sexual practices that break with the moral order maintained for example by patriarchy. Yet, disease is impersonal; it ignores people and their subjective experiences. Scientific discourses can deal, for example, with the mechanics of a condom as a barrier to the spread of disease. The juxtaposition of scientific discourse with common-sense discourse can be used to disrupt and disturb chains of associations that form the inner logic of commonly held myths about the spread of sexually transmitted disease, contamination and beliefs about *who* is prone and not prone to such disease. In this case, scientific discourses can usefully be used to *destroy* such myths.

However, the limitation of teaching about sex using scientific discourses is that students are highly likely to view this knowledge as irrelevant in their personal lives. For example, Elliot (2003) recently discussed how the vagina was presented within school textbooks. She argued that 'when exclusively examined as part of the reproductive process' the vagina was disconnected from any notions about sexual experiences either pleasurable or painful. Thus girls are not able to recognise themselves within textbook discourses, and in addition male/female penetrative copulation is restricted to 'a narrow non-pleasurable heterosexist conception of sexuality' (Diorio & Munro, 2000, cited in Elliott, 2003). Elliott (2003, p. 135) suggests that this 'misleading universal representations separates the body from the rest of the person, their emotions their intellect, their spirit' and, in doing so, it denies young women the opportunity to explore and understand their bodies in any way other than reproductive and heterosexual. However, opportunities do arise to integrate horizontal and vertical discourse in the science lesson.

In lessons there are moments when students inject anecdotes from their own experiences into classroom discourse. For example, in one biology lesson as part of the national curriculum science syllabus entitled 'Life processes and the organisation of livening things', a male teacher in a year nine (students aged 13/14 years) lesson was using a worksheet entitled' Keeping the Body in a Steady State'. The syllabus stated that 'They [students] should consider how hormones can be used to control and promote fertility'. A girl interrupted by calling out:

> What are hormone tablets? My aunt May said you get things growing in and out that you don't want. (Year nine girl, co-education class)

The class collapsed into laughter and the male teacher was thrown off course as the pedagogic discourse dissolved. In this case, the teacher failed to recognise the pedagogic potential of the girl's intervention and interpreted it as a subversive act, which in part it was. Even so, he could have followed up her funny comment to make a point about subjective experiences of drugs, hormones and bodily regulation. Instead, he disciplined the girl for interrupting as a bid to regain control.

English

English can be described as a vertical discourse with a horizontal knowledge structure and a weak grammar. Discourses in literature connect to personal quests for meaning and therefore can be used to *expand* available ways of imagining sexual life without necessarily challenging beliefs and myths about sex. Romance, love, passion, sexual intrigue, marriage, jealousy and sexual betrayal are found within both contemporary and classical texts. Literature can be used to signal historical changes in social norms relating to, for example, marriage, non-heterosexual sexual identities and lifestyles, and to address social and political aspects of human relationships. Reading authors such as D.H. Lawrence can open up sexual landscapes that take young people beyond their local cultures. Thus, literature has the potential to subvert and challenge contemporary sexual norms.

However, the subversive power of literature is often not realised within the classroom. One reason for this may relate to its weak grammar, which means it can be colonised by conservative influences (cf. Peim, 2004). Peim argues that in schools in England and Wales, English is 'structured around a normative model of language privileging standard English while failing to define it' (2004, p. 7). The texts that make up English literature in the United Kingdom are tightly controlled and any radical intrusions from post-structuralism or critical literacy have been successfully fended off (cf. Peim, 2004). English constitutes a 'narrow concept of textuality referred to as literature and gives nodding recognition to literature from other cultures' (Peim, 2004, p. 7). Peim suggests that success in English requires 'an already acquired cultural capital' that fulfils the demand for a 'personal response'. Thus, 'getting it right' in English can be both a class and a gender issue. The following example is taken from Ivinson and Murphy (2003).

In a year nine lesson on creative writing, Adam and Tom started to experiment with the romance genre after listening to extracts that girls had read out in the English lesson. Adam said that his story started off as a way of taking the 'mickey' out of Tom, who during the lesson had tried writing an 'erotic type thing'.

> Yeah cause I—it started out with me hearing Tom Bank's I think and he was trying to write an erotic type thing you know, one of those, and I started taking the mickey out of him and I just thought I came up with like a sort of comedy/romance type thing, with him getting ready for his girlfriend to come round 'cos he was baby-sitting at his home and his girlfriend was coming round and it was about him and checking himself in the mirror and making himself look smart and buttoning up his top buttons. He said he was going to play scrabble with her, she walked through the door, he could not find the scrabble set. She asked where the scrabble set was—he was like, 'What scrabble set?' and stuff like that so it was me basically really just taking the mickey out of Tom. (Year nine boy, co-educational class)

Normally, Adam did not enjoy writing, yet in this lesson he said that he was 'actually getting into it'. While he was writing the teacher came and read what he had written. Adam confided to us that his writing was 'starting to get a bit rough'. Instead of pursuing his interest and helping Adam to employ appropriate writing techniques that would have allowed him to explore emotion and desire, the teacher said 'Make sure it doesn't get into an X-rated sort of thing'. The scenario described by Adam related to his experience of dating and had great pedagogic potential, yet, after his teacher's comment, Adam abandoned his exploration of romance and started writing a war story.

Art

Art is also a vertical discourse with a horizontal knowledge structure and a weak grammar. Art comprises segments such as classical art, fine art, modern art, abstract art, cubism, expressionism, and so forth. The mode of transmission is tacit as with other craft pedagogies (cf. Lave, 1988; Gamble, 2002) and knowledge is acquired through showing and modelling followed by repeated practice. Creativity in the curriculum is associated with individuality and autonomous meaning-making and requires the expression of feelings through images and artefacts. Students learn to interpret images and artefacts, their own and others, as expressions of human emotion and meaning. Art objects can be used as mediating tools to facilitate discussion about love, romance, eroticism and beauty as well as fear, violence, oppression and destruction. In this way, art discourses allow students to recognise and reflect upon personal emotions and desires.

The limitations of teaching about emotions, and specifically sexual emotions, through art derive from its weak grammar and tacit mode of instruction. The art that students encounter in lessons is often governed by the school of art that was privileged in the teacher training college attended by the teacher. In the United Kingdom, this is often modern, abstract art. The required cultural capital needed to recognise the weak grammar of modern art is likely to be available to only a minority of students. School art is in danger of mis-recognising students' experiences and therefore limiting potential for self-expression and autonomous meaning making. The following example is taken from an art lesson in all boys' class with a male teacher (Ivinson & Murphy, forthcoming).

In one all-boys art class the male teacher had instructed boys to imitate the style of a famous artist who specialised in jazz scenes depicting male figures. The focus of the lesson was on the use of tones. Students were required to mix flesh colours and to restrict paintings to the use of yellow, grey and black. On inspecting the boys' paintings we noticed that hardly any boys had used pink paint for flesh and instead had chosen black or dark brown. Throughout the lesson an undercurrent of homophobic discourse was audible. Boys regularly accused each other of being 'queer'. This talk rose to a crescendo at the point when the teacher demonstrated how to mix flesh-coloured paint, which in effect was pink. Probably to avoid trouble, the teacher did not insist that the boys mix pink paint. He let them off the hook. Mixing pink paint and drawing male figures challenged the maintenance of masculine identities. In order to defend themselves the boys indulged in 'negative acts' that involved othering: accusing other boys of being queer. The boys at this point needed some support to break with the common-sense myths about masculinity being carried by the peer group. Yet, instead of providing this, the teacher colluded with the boys in their football banter, referring a number of times to shared football trips.

Tales of football activities were appropriated to support the teacher's masculine as opposed to art identity. Although it would have been challenging, the teacher could have confront the boys with their anxieties about drawing male figures and 'pink' flesh by invoking male artists and drawing attention to the diverse subjects and colours legitimated by art discourses. Instead, the teacher colluded in the collapse of the art discourse, and joined the boys in maintaining a narrow, hegemonic version of masculinity that was being use as a defence within the uncertain gender territory of the art activity. The male art teacher was responding to a threat to his gender identity. The example demonstrates the power of common-sense ideas to take hold of a situation and the difficulty teachers can experience in maintaining a scientific discourse when they perceive that they too are being judged by the norms of the consensual universe.

Physical education

In contrast to art and literature, physical education (PE) is a vertical discourse with a horizontal knowledge structure that has a strong grammar. The rules for taking part in sport are explicit, yet the mode of transmission is tacit. Teaching about sex in PE revolves around the body, in terms of movement, exercise, health and hygiene.

There is a growing *rapprochement* between the scientific discourses of physiology, health psychology and sport. In the United Kingdom a GCSE in PE that integrates personal, practical and scientific knowledge has been available since the early 1990s. Unlike English, school PE has absorbed the vertical discourse of sport science. Sport is about disciplining the body, yet a body connected to the mind. Sex education potentially involves exploring of the connection between physical and mental life. Yet, a limitation to teaching about sex through PE is furnished by the tacit mode of transmission that makes it difficult to *articulate* relations between mind and body.

PE purports to expand the recreational options of children and young people, yet it has become a discipline restricted to sport. There is no such thing as *raw* physical experience: experiences are mediated by available discourses. Therefore, in schools students' experiences of their bodies are framed by the discourse of sport, which excludes other discourses such as those that describe erotic pleasure and displeasure. Kirk argues that the emphasis on sport in PE is a hangover from the games ethic of the late-nineteenth-century English private schools (Kirk, 1998, 1999). Therefore a wide range of bodily possibilities are neglected in schools. Kirk argues that sport draws on a discursive association with institutional (male) heterosexuality for its legitimacy and that this excludes or marginalises female forms. Gard (2003, p. 105) points out that 'contemporary theories of the body and embodiment are yet to make a substantial impact on educational research and particularly PE', which remains an overtly rational and scientist vision of physical activity (McKay *et al.*, 1990; Macdonald, 1993; Pronger, 1995).

In a co-educational school in which girls and boys were taught in separate classes we spoke to girls about PE (Ivinson & Murphy, forthcoming). They said they had requested and won the case for football to be included in the year nine curriculum. Their motivation was that they did not want to be excluded from a sport that they knew was held in high esteem by boys. Boys and girls took PE in separate classes. When we accompanied the girls onto the field one wet and windy morning they were unenthusiastic and had to be cajoled by the female teacher to take part. Their teacher said that few of them went on to play football after year nine. In the school, the high status attached to masculine activities dominated, leaving the girls with few discursive resources to value and so request activities that would have allowed them to celebrate movement in ways that they genuinely enjoyed such as dance. Schools can develop local cultures that do not support hegemonic masculinity and a narrow range of sport, yet to do so PE departments need to create structures that legitimate, value and celebrate a wider range of physical activities.

Personal, social and health education

Personal, social and health education (PSHE) can be categorised as a horizontal discourse because it has no agreed disciplinary base and as such there is no recognisable boundary between PSHE and common-sense discourse. PSHE lessons provide a space in which students can potentially voice anxieties, curiosities and commonly held ideas about sex. Potentially, teachers can gain insights into the sexual myths that circulate in peer group culture and challenge them, yet this rarely happens in schools.

The following vignette is from a co-educational school that taught boys and girls in separate classes (Ivinson & Murphy, forthcoming). A sex education lesson was taking place within a PSHE class. The female teacher described a pub scenario to the boys. She asked them to imagine going to the bar with a new girlfriend.

> You both get up to pay for drinks. Imagine that as she goes to pay, the girl's handbag falls open and you see that she has a packet of condoms with her. Would you feel pressurised to have sex with her? (Female teacher, year nine boys' class)

Her intention was to make the boys think about this scenario from a personal perspective and to encourage them to be assertive. As she continued, her pedagogic discourse painted a picture of adolescent girls as marauding and predatory. She positioned boys as victims, using comments such as 'do you really want to do it' and 'what would happen if you started and then found you could not get it up'. By drawing on an inappropriate discourse of male impotence, she used shock tactics to scare the boys. Had it been available, boys could have countered her description using a scientific discourse to point out that male impotence is predominantly found in older and not younger men. In PSHE, common-sense discourses can be used to invoke fear because they are the discourses that we use to recognise ourselves and to make sense. In PSHE, teachers are free to impose moral positions without any check from scientific discourses that might prompt them to reflect on common-sense views.

Summary: scientific discourses and sex education

The degree of insulation between scientific discourses and common-sense discourses provides opportunities for sex education. The further the structure of the scientific discourse is from the structure of the common-sense discourse, the greater the power it has to disrupt, challenge and upset myths and beliefs about sex. However, this very distance also creates limitations. The greater the difference between scientific and common-sense discourse, the less likely it is that students will connect knowledge gained in lessons to everyday life. On the other hand, teaching about sex through literature and art has the potential to expand students' sexual repertories and encourage them to imaging alternative sexual futures and practices to those encountered in local cultures. The boundary between PSHE and common sense is weak creating a pressing need for PSHE teachers to examine their own social representations of sex to avoid imposing unexamined moral views on students.

Tipping points and slippage

Vertical discourses suppress embodied knowledge, evacuate subjectivity and deny emotions. They limit, in different ways, the horizons for students' subjective re-signification. However, the more a scientific discourse suppresses emotion, embodied knowledge and subjective experiences, the greater the potential for subversion. All discourses, even scientific discourses, shift and change, are inherently unstable and contain contradictory as well as coherent elements (Moscovici, 1981; Latour, 1993). Classrooms are sites where 'play', contestation and resistance as well as compliance are visibly at work (Luke, 1995; Singh, 2002). The potential for subverting scientific discourses is ever present. Tipping points can be defined as moments when students introduce unruly topics such as bodies or sex into classroom discourse. Teachers often fear these moments because they puncture the vertical discourse and threaten chaos. In these moments, teachers can feel personally under attack. As the pedagogic discourse is subverted, as in the example for the science lesson given above, teachers have a choice; they can either abandon the pedagogic role and join students in a shared moment of hilarity, or retain their distance and show disapproval. Such interjections from students are a common feature of everyday classroom life and teachers can either exploit them for their pedagogic potential or over-ride them. Recovery from such situations depends greatly on the teacher's skill, authority and relationship with the class. If managed with expertise, tipping points can provide cathartic moments because they are based on an unspoken recognition of sexual taboo. Students become aware of their teacher's vulnerability and are often relieved to have a moment of shared humanity with them. Skilled teachers are able to abandon the pedagogic role momentarily and as they recover they can juxtapose a vertical discourse alongside common-sense discourse allowing the topic of sex to be recognised in a new way. However, it takes confidence to exploit these moments and teachers need to be supported by a tolerant school culture and a strong sense of professional autonomy.

Concluding remarks

Bernstein's analysis of the pedagogic device describes instructional discourse as embedded within regulative discourse, where regulative discourse relates to the moral order of the school. Vertical discourses have the potential to disrupt common-sense myths about sex and make them available for critical inspection. Teachers do not teach the principles of vertical discourses maintained by communities of scholars; rather they change and adapt them for the purposes of schooling. Schools are positioned to fulfil political and social functions that become manifest in the moral order to the school. Bernstein (1974) has spoken about the importance of analysing the degree of insulation between schools and other social contexts. This becomes particularly important when thinking about sex education. If there is no insulation between the institution and the social world beyond the school, then instructional discourse collapses back into regulative discourse. In such cases the moral order of the school comes to mirror the moral order of society in general. It has been argued that effective sex education relies on the juxtaposition of discourses with different structures. In this sense the boundary between schools and everyday life is essential for education. Modernists institutions have a role to play; they disrupt the spread of archaic beliefs.

This raises the question about what kind of internal cultures schools need to foster in order to make sex education possible. By staying close to the grammar of scientific discourses, teachers can confront issues arising in the lesson that relate to sex; for example, aesthetics including eroticism in art, alternative ways of living and relating such as Romanticism encountered in literature, bodily pleasure and pain in PE and physiological knowledge of the vagina in science. These possibilities rely on teachers knowing their subjects in depth and on school cultures that privilege instructional discourse above regulative discourse (i.e. where the primary intention is not to control but to educate). Such culture can be fostered if there is a shared understand that the *raison d'être* for regulative rituals and discourses is the pursuit of knowledge.

In the United Kingdom, teachers have experienced a loss of autonomy through increasingly centralised government control over education. Loss of autonomy decreases the possibility that teacher will choose to exploiting the subversive potential of scientific discourses. Teachers have become susceptible to, for example, common-sense discourses about the feminising of the curriculum that some say has led to boys' underachievement. Pedagogic interventions to alleviate such perceived problems are often based on deeply entrenched myths about gender and sexuality. Teachers need autonomy and a strong sense of the subversive potential of disciplinary knowledge to challenge such myths. As Kehily (2002) points out, the present climate of increasing regulation and surveillance through national testing is making students' sexual cultures even more resistant to the intervention of adults and the curriculum. While scientific discourses do not fulfil all the requirements of sex education, they are usually a better resource than common-sense discourses that collude with and perpetuate myths about sexuality as with the art and PSHE teachers described above. In an ideal world sex would cease to be a taboo topic, and education about sex would be truly cross-curricula. Yet, as we pointed out when health education was introduced as a cross-curricular theme in the national curriculum (Whitty *et al.*, 1994a, b), the strong framing of scientific discourses prevented teachers and students from recognising health issues within subject lessons. Within the present political climate in the United Kingdom, sex is even less likely to be a topic that teachers will be willing to address. There is an urgent need to re-examine the role of education within society.

Acknowledgements

The author thanks Katie Featherstone and William Housley for comments on earlier versions of this paper.

Note

1. Examples are drawn from classroom observations undertaken as part of two funded research projects: 'Assessing Quality in Cross Curricular Contexts', ESRC Project Directors Prof. G.J. Whitty and Prof. P. Aggleton (1991–1993) (example from science lesson), and 'Investigating Teaching and Learning in Single Sex Classes', Open University Project Directors Patricia

Murphy and Gabrielle Ivinson (1998–2000) (examples from English, art, PE and PSHE lessons).

References

Bernstein, B. (1974) *Class, codes and control 1, theoretical studies towards a sociology of language* (2nd rev edn) (London, Routledge).

Bernstein, B. (1990) *The structuring of pedagogic discourse* (London & New York, Routledge).

Bernstein, B. (1996) *Pedagogy symbolic control and identity theory, research, critique* (London & Bristol, Taylor & Francis).

Bernstein, B. (1999) Vertical and horizontal discourse: an essay, *British Journal of Sociology of Education*, 20(2), 157–173.

Cleland, A. & McKay, L. (1992) *Studying the effectiveness of sexuality education programmes* Research report (University of Auckland, New Zealand).

Devereux, G. (1967) *From anxiety to method in the social sciences* (The Hague & Paris, Mouton & Co.).

Diorio, J. & Munro, J. (2000) Doing harm in the name of protection: menstruation as a topic for sex education, *Gender and Education*, 12(3), 347–365.

Dowling, P. (1998) *The sociology of mathematics education: mathematical myths, pedagogic texts* (London & Washington, DC, Falmer Press).

Duveen, G. (2001) Representations, identities, resistance, in: K. Deaux & G. Philgène (Eds) *Representations of the Social* (Oxford, Blackwell).

Elliott, K. J. (2003) The hostile vaginal: reading vaginal discourse in school health texts, *Sex Education*, 3(2), 133–144.

Epstein, D., O'Flynn, S. & Telford, D. (2003) *Silenced sexualities in schools and universities* (Stoke on Trent, Trentham).

Foucault, M. (1972) *The archaeology of knowledge* (A. M. Sheridan Smith, Trans.) (New York, Pantheon Books).

Gamble, J. (2002) Teaching without words: tacit knowledge in apprenticeship, paper presented at the *2nd International Bernstein Symposium*, Cape Town, July.

Gard, M. (2003) Moving and belonging: dance, sport and sexuality, *Sex Education*, 3(2), 105–118.

Heider, F. (1958) *The psychology of interpersonal relations* (New York, Wiley).

Ivinson, G. & Murphy, P. (2003) Boys don't write romance: the construction of knowledge and social gender identities in English classrooms, *Pedagogy, Culture and Society*, 11(1), 89–111.

Ivinson, G. & Murphy, P. (forthcoming) *Working with gender: sex groupings and subject teaching* (Buckingham, Open University Press).

Jodelet, D. (1991) *Madness and social representation* (London & New York, Wheatsheaf).

Kehily, J. M. (2002) *Sexuality, gender and schooling: shifting agendas in social learning* (London, Routledge Falmer).

Kirk, D. (1998) *Schooling bodies: school practice and public discourse 1880–1950* (London, Leicester University Press).

Kirk, D. (1999) Physical culture, physical education and relational analysis, *Sport, Education and Society*, 4(1), 63–73.

Latour, B. (1993) *We have never been modern* (Hemel Hempstead, Harvester Wheatsheaf).

Lave, J. (1988) *Cognition in practice* (Cambridge, Cambridge University Press).

Luke, A. (1995) Getting our hands dirty: provisional politics in postmodern conditions, in: C. Luke & J. Gore (Eds) *Feminisms and critical pedagogy* (London, Routledge).

Lévy-Bruhl, L. (1925/1926) *How natives think* (Lillian Clare, Trans.) (London, George Allen & Unwin).

Mauss, M. (1950) *Sociologie et anthropologie* (Paris, Presses Universitaires de France).

Macdonald, D. (1993) Knowledge, gender and power in physical education teacher education, *Australian Journal of Education*, 37(3), 259–278.

McKay, J., Gore, J. M. & Kirk, D. (1990) Beyond the limits of technocratic physical education, *Quest*, 42(1), 52–76.

Moscovici, S. (1961 [rev edn 1976]) *La Psychoanalyse, son image et son public* (Paris, Presses Universitaires de France).

Moscovici, S. (1981) On social representation, in: J. Forgas (Ed.) *Social cognition* (London, Academic Press).

Moscovici, S. (1984) The phenomena of social representations, in: R. M. Farr & S. Moscovici (Eds) *Social representations* (Cambridge, Cambridge University Press), 3–69.

Moscovici, S. (2001) *Social representations: exploration in social psychology* (G. Duveen, Ed.) (New York, New York University Press).

Peim, N. (2004) Bernstein and curriculum politics: rethinking theory, English and English teaching', paper presented at the *Third International Bernstein Symposium*, Cambridge, 15–17 July.

Pronger, B. (1995) Rendering the body: the implicit lessons of gross anatomy, *Quest*, 47(4), 427–446.

Renold, E. (2000) 'Coming out': gender, (hetro)sexuality and the primary school, *Gender and Education*, 12(3), 309–326.

Renold, E. (2001) Presumed innocence: sexualised bullying and harassment in primary school, paper presented at the *5th Conference of the European Sociological Association*, Helsinki, Finland, 28 August–1 September.

Singh, P. (2002) Pedagogising knowledge: Bernstein's theory of the pedagogic device, *British Journal of Sociology of Education*, 23(4), 571–582.

Sontag, S. (1978) *Illness as metaphor: and AIDS and its metaphors* (London, Penguin Modern Classics).

Warwick, I., Douglas, N., Aggleton, P. & Boyce, P. (2003) Young gay men and HIV/AIDS: towards a contextual understanding of sexual risk, *Sex Education*, 3(3), 215–229.

Whitty, G., Rowe, G. & Aggleton, P. (1994a) Discourse in cross-curricular contexts: Limits to empowerment, *International Studies in the Sociology of Education*, 4(1), 25–41.

Whitty, G., Rowe, G. & Aggleton, P. (1994b) Subjects and themes in secondary school curriculum, *Research Papers in Education*, 9(2), 159–181.

7 From psychic defences to social defences

Recontextualizing strategies and Klein's theory of ego development

Claudia Lapping

Introduction: psychical aspects of recontextualization

I am beginning with a deviation to reflect briefly on the relation between sociology and psychoanalysis, before moving on to outline the more central focus of this chapter. Pierre Bourdieu and Basil Bernstein were both major sociologists working from the 1960s to the beginning of the twenty first-century. Both were interested in the relation between class and knowledge and their work in this area was central to the development of the field that became known as the new sociology of knowledge (Young, 1971). In addition, the work of both men suggests that they were influenced by the psychoanalytic theories that dominated in their respective countries at the time they were writing: for Bourdieu, in France, Lacanian ideas; for Bernstein, in the UK, the ideas of Melanie Klein. And finally, neither appears to have fully acknowledged the relation to psychoanalysis within their work. The similarity in the use and suppression of psychoanalytic ideas in the work of these two sociological theorists provides a basis for speculation on the relation between the two fields, sociology and psychoanalysis. It raises the possibility that the field of sociology did not find it easy to accommodate the insights of psychoanalysis. This constitutes, I think, an important context for a consideration of moments in their individual writings where psychoanalytic sources are either rejected or ignored.

George Steinmetz (2006) has argued that Bourdieu's relation to psychoanalysis can be understood in terms of the Freudian concept of (de)negation, in which a repressed idea is admitted to consciousness, but is not fully recognized or accepted by the subject (p. 445). He explains:

> In some writings, especially the earlier ones, Bourdieu rejects psychoanalysis out-right. In *Outline of a Theory of Practice*, for example, psychoanalysis is reduced to a biological reductionism, completely ignoring Freud's shift from the theory of childhood abuse in the early *Studies in Hysteria* to the theory of sexual fantasy that he developed in the course of his self-analysis. But his treatment of Freudian psychoanalysis more often takes the form of admitting Freudian terminology

> and even some psychoanalytic arguments into his texts while surrounding these passages with rhetorical devices that seem to condemn psychoanalysis.
>
> (ibid., pp. 445–446)

While he says it is not his aim to psychoanalyse Bourdieu, Steinmetz speculates on possible reasons for this refusal to acknowledge the influence of psychoanalytic or, more specifically, Lacanian ideas on his work. He suggests, for example that 'Lacan's combination of "nobility," externality to the academic field, and his disregard for rational scientific discourse were obviously distasteful to Bourdieu' (p. 459). However, Steinmetz proposes that a 'deeper' reason can be found in Bourdieu's statements asserting a distinction between sociology and psychoanalysis: '*Sociology does not claim to substitute its mode of explanation for that of psychoanalysis*; it is concerned only to construct differently certain givens that psychoanalysis also takes as its object' (Bourdieu, cited in Steinmetz, pp. 446 and 459, Steinmetz's emphasis). Steinmetz argues that 'while expressing a desire for differentiation from psychoanalysis, [Bourdieu] does not actually explain what the difference would be' (p. 446):

> If Bourdieu had explored this relationship in more depth he might have seen that they were not alternatives, but that psychoanalysis filled some of the lacunae in his own theoretical approach. His sociology did not so much construct the same object in a different manner as to construct it inadequately.
>
> (p. 459)

There are two strands to Steinmetz's argument. Firstly there is an exploration of psychical relations within Bourdieu's articulation of his theory; and second there is an attempt to demonstrate how Lacanian psychoanalytic theory might enhance the central concepts of this theory. Steinmetz's paper goes on to offer an account of the relation between Bourdieu's conceptualization of 'symbolic capital' and 'habitus' and Lacan's symbolic and imaginary orders, suggesting that the Lacanian theoretical framework can solve some of the problems associated with Bourdieu's ideas.

This chapter is imitative of both aspects of Steinmetz's approach. I am exploring ways in which Basil Bernstein both uses and suppresses ideas associated with Melanie Klein's theorization of the psychic defences, and I am also attempting to reconstruct these aspects of Bernstein's work, elaborating his use of Kleinian terminology to show how a further engagement with psychoanalytic ideas might enhance his conceptualization of processes of recontextualization. It should be noted that the notion of recontextualization appears twice within my argument: I am looking at the way Bernstein recontextualizes psychoanalytic ideas in his conceptualization of processes of recontextualization. However, his is not the only example I am drawing on to explore the recontextualization of Kleinian ideas. The chapter also looks at two studies emerging from the Tavistock Institute of Human Relations, a therapeutically oriented consultancy that integrates psychoanalytic approaches into the social scientific study of organizations: Elliott Jaques' (1951) consultancy/research into industrial relations in a factory and Isabel Menzies Lyth's study of a nursing service in a large teaching hospital (1959). Where Bourdieu and Bernstein suppress the relation to psychoanalysis, the Tavistock studies explicitly advertise their psychoanalytic origins.

I am using my exploration of contrasting recontextualizations of Kleinian ideas to develop existing conceptual frameworks within the sociology of knowledge, and I will use the remainder of this introduction to briefly sketch out some of the antecedents of my analysis.

Paul Dowling's theory of constructive description, or 'social activity method' (Dowling, 2009) foregrounds the ongoing process of construction of any social formation. Dowling's approach conceptualizes any instantiation of knowledge as a part of an ongoing social engagement, an enactment that forms social alliances or oppositions. He defines these social engagements as strategies and his work has developed several analytic schemas for describing the strategies deployed in the recontextualization of disciplinary knowledge. One example is the 'domains of action schema' which distinguishes between articulation of content (signified) and expression (signifier) in the formulation of knowledge. In his analysis of the recontextualization of mathematics in school textbooks Dowling (1998) argued that both content and expression can be either highly specialized (strongly institutionalized) or less specialized (weakly institutionalized). The analysis thus developed an account of four possible recontextualizing strategies. The language of academic mathematics is usually articulated in a highly specialized mode of expression that signifies highly specialized meanings, or content. Dowling describes instances of such specialized content and expression as strategies within the esoteric domain. Mathematics textbooks, in contrast to academic mathematics, tend to recontextualize mathematical knowledge in two possible ways. The first of these maintains the specialized content, but expresses this content in a more accessible, less specialized language; Dowling calls this the expressive domain. The other strategy is to deploy the specialized language of academic mathematics, but to transform or simplify the content to which the language refers: the descriptive domain. The final possibility is to use neither the specialized content, nor the specialized vocabulary, to establish something that may be called mathematics within a school context but that appears to have no relation to what is called mathematics by mathematicians: this type of action constitutes what Dowling calls the public domain.

The question is: In what way are the terms of one discourse repeated and transformed in a new setting? This question is significant in relation to the further question: In what way does the repetition and transformation of the terms of a discourse constitute social alliances and oppositions? Dowling's analysis suggests ways in which the recontextualizing strategies articulated in school textbooks aimed at contrasting groups of students might contribute to the socially differentiated distribution of educational opportunities.

This approach to the analysis of social activity might be productive in exploring the relation between any two discourses. Steinmetz's analysis of Bourdieu's relation to psychoanalysis might be rearticulated in the terms of Dowling's language. According to Steinmetz, Bourdieu sometimes uses the specialized language of psychoanalysis, without taking on the full implications or meanings associated with these terms, while at other times his own language expresses, without acknowledgement, specialized meanings associated with Lacanian psychoanalysis. Steinmetz's account thus suggests that, in relation to psychoanalytic discourse, Bourdieu's work constitutes activity within Dowling's expressive and descriptive domains. However, in describing this activity in terms of (de)negation or disavowal, Steinmetz's analysis also suggests psychical aspects to Bourdieu's relation to psychoanalysis that are not accounted for within Dowling's schema.

In order to introduce an explicitly psychical relation into the analysis of recontextualizing strategies, we might think of texts as instances of either articulation or substitution of signifiers and signifieds. As discussed in Chapters 2 and 4, the concepts of articulation and substitution describe the relation between the symbolic order and discourse (Lacan, 1957; Laclau and Mouffe, 2001). The free floating signifiers of the symbolic order are ordered and articulated within discourse, but can also be excluded through psychical mechanisms of substitution, such as the disavowal that Steinmetz traces in Bourdieu's relation to Lacan. The articulation of a signifier within a specified discourse constitutes an identification (in Dowling's terms, perhaps, an alliance) between that discourse and other discourses in which the signifier is also situated. In contrast, when one signifier is substituted for another an oppositional relation is established with the discourse into which the expelled signifier is deposited. Steinmetz suggests that at times Bourdieu explicitly rejects psychoanalysis, accusing Freud of biological reductionism, thus constituting an opposition between sociology and the negative associations of biologism that are deposited onto the discourse of psychoanalysis. In addition, Steinmetz's analysis suggests that the articulation or substitution of signifiers of personal or disciplinary origins (mentioning or failing to mention Lacan, for example) may be of relevance to the analysis of recontextualizing strategies within disciplinary knowledge practices.

This understanding of processes of discursive articulation and substitution provides an initial frame for the exploration of contrasting uses of Melanie Klein's theoretical language presented in this chapter. The account developed in the chapter draws attention to the way contrasting pieces of research either articulate or substitute different aspects of Klein's theory of ego development, and also notes where the same pieces of work articulate or substitute a relation to 'Klein', the author, as a significant influence or origin. The analysis constructs a trajectory from Jacques' work, which repeats Klein's conceptual framework in more or less its original form, to Lyth's work, which extends and elaborates Klein's theory in recognition of the 'emotional world of the organisation' (Armstrong, 2005), and finally to an exploration of Bernstein's work, which deploys Kleinian vocabulary in a way that has the potential to radically subvert the association between notions of the psyche and notions of the individual.

Two aspects of Melanie Klein's theory: the development of the infant ego and the psychic defence mechanisms

In order to explore contrasting articulations of Klein's work it will be useful to distinguish two aspects of her theory: first, there is a speculative, inferential story about the development of the infant in the earliest stages of ego formation; and second there is a set of concepts that define possible relations between a subject and the objects that, in Kleinian terms, constitute the internal world of the subject. The speculative story narrates the infant's construction of an internal world of good and bad objects, and their development from a sense of being persecuted by dangerous part objects to a sense of whole objects that are ambivalent and vulnerable in nature. The different stages[1] in the story are characterized by different kinds of defences in the infant's construction of psychical objects: violent defences in the paranoid stage and more conciliatory defences as the infant perceives the wholeness of, and develops a more ambivalent relation towards, their objects. It is through their changing relation to these objects, mediated by the presence of the mother, that the infant begins to develop a more stable sense of their own identity. The second aspect of Klein's theory is her specification of different forms in which the psychic defences might appear. The concepts of splitting, projection and introjection are elaborated in Klein's articulation of principles that distinguish different possible instantiations of these relations between subject and object. I will explain both these aspects of Klein's theory in more detail in the following sections.

Within Klein's own work there is a relation between the interpretation of specified forms of defences within the behaviour of individual patients and her diagnosis of their current psychical position; and the generalized narrative of ego development is understood to be an inference based on the experience of these defences in clinical psychoanalytic work. This chapter explores the extent to which these kinds of inferences from the observation of specific psychical defences to psychologizing accounts of ego development are rearticulated or substituted in research carried out in non-clinical settings.

Klein's narrative of the development of the ego, the paranoid schizoid and the depressive positions

The first aspect of Klein's theory, then, is her narrative of the development of the ego. This narrative constructs an account of human infancy that prioritizes an intensely affective primary encounter with both internal drives and the external world. Klein's narration of this encounter suggests that experiences of the drives and the external world are internalized, gradually building up a parallel world of inner objects. However, this inner world is, in Klein's words, 'inaccessible to the child's accurate observation and judgment', and 'phantastic' – the product of unconscious fantasy – giving rise to an overwhelming sense of doubt and anxiety (1940, p. 149). This anxiety, for Klein, is related to the death drive, the infant's own destructive impulses, and also to the painful experience of bodily needs and functions, all of which are felt as persecuting and attributed to 'objects' over which the infant has no control:

> I hold that anxiety arises from the operation of the death instinct within the organism, is felt as fear of annihilation (death) and takes the form of fear of persecution. The fear of the destructive impulse seems to attach itself at once to an object – or rather it is experienced as the fear of an uncontrollable overpowering object. Other important sources of anxiety are the trauma of birth (separation anxiety) and frustration of bodily needs; and these experiences too are from the beginning felt as being caused by objects.
>
> (1946, p. 179)

This extract suggests the transformation of the direct experience of an internal drive, the 'destructive impulse', into an inner object that the infant experiences as 'uncontrollable and overpowering'. Similarly, the infant's experience of the external frustration of bodily needs is transformed into an inner object that is the cause of its distress. The conceptualization of 'inner objects' provides a powerful metaphor for the infant's initial, unstable relation to the sensations that arise in response to its experience of both inner drives and external world. In these early stages of development, external objects are only partially represented internally, as they are only experienced in so far as they relate to an immediate bodily need and are thus satisfying or frustrating, good or bad. The concepts of 'inner object', 'part object' and, later on, 'whole object' are integral to Klein's account of infant development.

According to Klein, then, at this early stage the infant does not have a sense of itself as differentiated from the external world. This inability to separate leads to a sense of overwhelming persecution, as the infant feels itself subject to attack from internal bodily sensations and from frustrating part objects that fail to gratify bodily needs. This sense of persecution gives rise to great anxiety and fear of annihilation. According to Klein, the infant defends against this anxiety by attempting to control the attacking objects, which s/he does by the interrelated processes of splitting, projection and introjection (1946, p. 182): in phantasy, the infant splits off the good and bad parts of the object, and is thus able to control them, through processes of denial, idealization, projection and introjection, thus gaining some relief from the persecutory anxiety. However, the relief is incomplete, as the defences in this stage are largely destructive. Klein summarizes: 'In paranoia the characteristic defences are chiefly aimed at annihilating the 'persecutors', while anxiety on the ego's account occupies a prominent place in the picture' (1935, p. 118).

Klein emphasizes the unconscious, phantasmatic nature of these processes, and also their psychical effects:

> It is in phantasy that the infant splits the object and the self, but the effect of this phantasy is a very real one, because it leads to feelings and relations (and later on, thought processes) being in fact cut off from one another.
>
> (1946, p. 181)

This is what Klein terms the paranoid schizoid position. According to Klein, this is the dominant position of the infant in the very early development of the ego: the unconscious defences bring relief from the overwhelming sensation of destruction, but they also weaken the ego and impede integration and stability.

In the normal development of the infant, according to Klein, the dominance of the paranoid schizoid position is followed by dominance of the depressive position, within which the infant begins to recognize whole objects that contain both good and bad aspects. At this stage the infant begins to learn to tolerate ambivalence, but this brings with it a new array of difficult feelings. Klein argues:

> in my view, already during the sucking period, when it comes to know its mother as a whole person and when it progresses from the introjection of part objects to the introjection of the whole object, the infant experiences some of the feelings of guilt and remorse, some of the pain which results from the conflict between love and uncontrollable hatred, some of the anxieties of the impending death of the loved internalized and external objects...
>
> (1935, p. 142)

Whereas in the paranoid schizoid position, the infant is only concerned with its own survival, in the depressive position it comes to recognize other objects as also vulnerable, and experiences guilt related to its own feelings of hatred and its destructive attacks on these objects, both internally and in the external world. While paranoid fears are reduced in the depressive position, feelings of guilt, remorse and responsibility for loved objects come to the fore. Klein clarifies:

> I am aware how difficult it is to draw a sharp line between the anxiety contents and feelings of the paranoiac and those of the depressive, since they are so closely linked up with each other. But they can be distinguished one from the other if, as a criterion of differentiation, one considers whether the persecution anxiety is mainly related to the preservation of the ego – in which case it is paranoiac – or to the preservation of the good internalized objects with whom the ego is identified as a whole. In the latter case – which is the case of the depressive – the anxiety and feelings of suffering are of a much more complex nature.
> (ibid., p. 124)

For Klein, these positions are first experienced in early infancy, but they are the basis for our engagement with the world in later life, when we continue to shift between the paranoid schizoid and the depressive positions. This story of the shifts between the persecutory anxieties of the paranoid schizoid position and the anxious guilt and remorse of the depressive position, through the development of an inner world of partial and whole objects, constitutes Melanie Klein's account of infant development and its continuing effects in adult mental life. I have suggested that this account of what constitutes normal infant development, the inner world of the infant and the implications this might have for adult mental life, is a speculative inference based on clinical observation. However, the conceptual structure that frames these clinical observations can be broken down into constitutive elements that are not dependent on, and that do not necessarily imply, the more individualized narrative aspect of Klein's theory.

The psychic defences: identification, introjection, projection and projective identification

Klein's account of the way introjective and projective processes construct an inner representational world, which replicates the infant's experience of both inner drives and external interactions, constitutes one aspect of the concept of psychic defences. However, the theorization of these psychical mechanisms also has a second aspect which supports empirical analysis. Processes of internalization or introjection are suggested where we get a sense of separate elements within the psyche, and where there is some reference to an external source for these elements. In contrast to introjection, processes of projection are suggested when we get a sense that the subject's own feelings or characteristics are being attributed to another object. So when a child talking about seeing their old primary school building being knocked down says, 'It makes me feel sad. It's not nice for the building for that to happen. I feel sorry for it', we might interpret this as a projection of the child's unwanted feelings of sadness onto the building.[2] Klein's theorization of an inner world made up of part and whole objects that represent our feelings and experiences provides a vivid metaphorical language for the development of these kinds of interpretations. However, it is not necessary to incorporate her narrative of infant development into the analysis of psychical defence mechanisms.

The psychoanalytic literature elaborates possible distinctions between the closely related processes of identification, internalization and introjection.[3] Sandler (1988) distinguishes different forms of internalization in Freud's writing: 'the internalization of external prohibitions and regulations' and the 'internalization of aggression, the turning of aggressive impulses inwards' (p. 7). In his discussion of melancholia Freud makes a distinction between the internalization of social sanctions or prohibitions and the internalization of the parents/lost object (1923). The use of either 'internalization' or 'introjection' to refer to these different psychic relations is inconsistent, blurring the definitions of the terms. Nevertheless, some theorists articulate productive distinctions, between, for example, identification, which involves an alteration in the subject's self-representation, and introjection, in which the internalized object is kept apart from the sense of self. Sandler suggests:

> From a representational point of view it is valuable to make a sharp distinction between identification as a modification of the self-representation on the one hand, and introjection as the setting up of unconscious, internal 'phantom' companions, felt to be part of one's inner world, yet external to one's self-representation, on the other.
>
> (1988, p. 11)

For example, when a child says that it is important for her to keep her room tidy to help mummy, we might interpret this as an internalization of adult praise or sanction. This internalized object might support the child in ordering and controlling her world. In such a case we might say that she has identified with the object, that a 'modification of the self-representation' has taken place. Alternatively, the injunction to keep her room tidy might act as a critical voice of sanction, pointing out when she fails to live up to the internalized regulation. Following Sandler, we might describe this as an instance of introjection without identification, where the introjected object constitutes an 'internal phantom companion', an inner voice that is not integrated into the child's self representation.

A similar range of theoretical distinctions is evident in debates over the meanings of projection and/or projective identification. In general, projection is understood as the attribution of one's own feelings or aspects of one's character to an external object. The term projective identification is sometimes used to suggest the way in which this process has effects that go beyond the subject's image of the object, into the object itself: i.e. the object of the projection will in some way either respond to, or take on the elements attributed to them. The nature of the process of projective identification is the subject of debate: is it an intense form of projection that nevertheless occurs only in the phantasy of the subject; is it a more concrete response by the object of the projection to communication of the projection by the subject; or is it a more mystical sounding movement of affect between two subjects (Sandler, 1988; Meissner, 1988, see p. 62; Jervis, 2009)?[4] Klein's own position is probably closer to the first of these. She describes the process as 'the phantasy of forcefully entering the object' (1946, p. 186), limiting its effects to the subject, and not the object, of the projection. Contemporary post-Kleinians, following the ideas of Wilfred Bion (1961), tend to adhere to the second interpretation, which suggests an interpersonal model of projective identification.

Joseph (1988) provides a useful summary of some forms of projective identification suggested in Klein's work:

> She discussed the manifold aims of different types of projective identification, for example, splitting off and getting rid of unwanted parts of the self that cause anxiety or pain; projecting the self or parts of the self into an object to dominate and control it and thus avoid any feelings of being separate; getting into an object to take over its capacities and make them its own; invading in order to damage or destroy the object. Thus the infant, or adult who goes on using such mechanisms powerfully, can avoid any awareness of separateness, dependence or admiration or of the concomitant sense of loss, anger, envy, etc. But it sets up persecutory anxieties, claustrophobia, panics and the like.
>
> (Joseph, 1988, pp. 65–66; see also Klein, 1946, p. 183)

This account suggests three different instantiations of projective identification. The first of these, 'splitting off and getting rid of unwanted parts of the self that cause anxiety or pain', is probably the meaning that is most assimilated into everyday language. If I am deeply competitive and yet ashamed of my competitive feelings, I may project this characteristic of mine onto those around me, so that, for example, I fear others' envy of my success. This is an unconscious identification in which I deny my own feelings and in phantasy project them onto the other.

Joseph describes two further instantiations of projective identification: 'projecting parts of the self into an object to dominate and control it and thus avoid any feelings of being separate'; and 'getting into an object to take over its capacities'. The first of these describes instances where the unconscious assumption of sameness can be a mechanism for control and exploitation. The second describes a different kind of merging, where the subject seeks to construct an identity from the characteristics of the other.

These processes can protect against painful feelings of separateness, but can evoke difficult feelings when the object in some way reasserts its separate identity. The documentary *Man on Wire* provides an instance where it is possible to see the interrelation between these two types of projective identification.

Man on Wire tells the story of the wire walker Philipe Petit, and his successful plot to walk on a high wire between the Twin Towers in New York. The story is narrated by Petit himself, and is told through a combination of dramatic reconstruction and interviews with the friends who helped him to carry out his plan. Petit comes across as a fascinating, seductive character, totally overwhelmed by his own desire to perform between the Towers that he feels were constructed almost for this purpose: to tantalize, seduce and finally to be conquered by his skills on the wire. However, in order to achieve this goal, he requires the support of a group of co-conspirators who will help him to enter the towers and set up his wire. The most committed of these is a childhood friend who has helped to set up his wires for previous dangerous and illegal walks. When Petit calls to ask for his help, his friend flies over from France to take his part in the performance. Petit also recruits an Australian and two New Yorkers, each of whom drops out before the wire is in place: they are scared by the mortal risk to Petit if the walk is unsuccessful. Clearly, for Petit, the necessity to walk obliterates the immensity of what he is asking of his friends. This is what enables him to persuade them to help him to put himself at risk. He projects his own commitment onto those around him, charismatically merging their desires with his own. In Petit's case, perhaps, this projection is not related to a fear of separateness, but to other aspects of his overwhelming commitment to his art. For his friend the inverse mode of projective identification seems to be taking place. He seems to find an identity of his own in Petit's desire. He becomes deeply engaged in refining the details of the plans and its final execution, and revels in his position as the member of the group who has the greatest understanding and experience of how Petit sets up his wires. We might describe his relation to Petit as a way of constructing an identity by 'getting into an object to take over its capacities'.

The walk is successful, and Petit is lauded by the New York public, who are overwhelmed and grateful for the feat he has performed for them. Petit succumbs to his celebrity, apparently oblivious to his friend's contribution, and it seems that the friendship between the two men is broken. At the end of the documentary, which is enthusiastically narrated by Petit, his friend weeps, and cannot finish telling his part in the story. This example, I think, implicitly suggests how projective identification might be understood as an interpersonal experience in which the projections of each party influence or intensify the responses of the other, rather than as a purely individual phenomenon.[5]

Within Kleinian and post-Kleinian psychoanalysis these conceptualizations of projection and introjection are used to describe individual and interpersonal relations. However these different forms of psychic defences have also been used to explore the construction of social and institutional identities. Examples from organization studies and sociology can illustrate the productivity of this usage. As I have suggested, though, it is possible to mark out a distinction within this work between studies that articulate conceptualizations of both the psychical defence mechanisms and the narrative of the internal world, and studies that substitute or supplement the narrative of ego development with a conceptualization of social structures and institutions. The conceptual tussle taking place is over the centrality, or not, of the individual as the site of psychical identity.

From psychic defence to social defence: the recontextualization of Kleinian ideas into organizational analysis

Within psychoanalytically informed organization studies, it is possible to mark out a distinction between work that continues to conceptualize anxiety in the context of individual development and work that reconceptualizes anxiety in the context of the organization. Writing some time after the first studies published by the Tavistock group, David Armstrong suggests this distinction in his analysis of the field of psychoanalytically oriented organizational research and consultancy. He points out that work within this field can focus too much on individual or group relations, missing out what he describes as 'the organization as an independent variable':

> I am thinking, for example of the work done on narcissistic leadership, or the role of oedipal configurations, or some of the work on group and team dynamics or on inter- and intra group relations. Within this body of work, the organization as an independent variable, with its own internal logic – political, socio-technical, but also psychic – can easily get lost. Or, to put this the other way round, the emotional world of the organization can appear simply as a function, a kind of artifact, of human relations within it.
>
> (Armstrong, 2005, p. 93)

Armstrong suggests that there is a psychic logic that is specific to organizations that should not be subordinated to theories of individual or group development. In doing this he suggests the possibility of substituting or supplementing the conceptualization of the individual within Kleinian discourse with a conceptualization of the institution.

It is worth noting Armstrong's use of the term 'independent variable' to describe the logics of the organization. This maintains a sense of organization and individual as separate entities that prefigure the analysis; so he is not rejecting a notion of individual psychic development, but simply introducing the organization as a psychical entity, an 'emotional world' in its own right. It would be possible to go further than this; to begin to trouble the distinction between 'individual development' and 'organization' in the constitution of subjectivity. It is perhaps an artefact of the position of the field of psychoanalytically informed organization studies as a direct offshoot of traditional schools of psychoanalytic training, and specifically the Kleinian oriented Tavistock Clinic, that it articulates such clear continuities with traditional, individualizing psychoanalytic notions of development.

The rest of this section maps out the trajectory Armstrong constructs, from the prioritization of individualized conceptions of defences against anxiety, to a fuller recognition of anxiety as a part of the 'emotional world of the organization'. My account constructs Elliott Jaques' work as an instance of the former, and the work of Isabel Menzies Lyth as an instance of the latter. Jaques' exploration of relations between workers, workers representatives and management representatives in a wage negotiation uses Kleinian concepts to explore group processes as social, rather than purely psychical, instantiations of the defences of projection and introjection. However he does not extend his analysis to include structures or practices inherent to the institution. Lyth's study of a hospital nursing service, in contrast, focuses on ways specific practices within the service can be understood as institutionalized social defences against anxieties that inhere within the work of the hospital. She thus shifts the focus away from the individual as the source of anxiety, and away from interpersonal relations as the site of defences. The shift away from an understanding of anxiety as originating in internal drives to an understanding of anxiety as embedded within social organizations represents a move away from Klein's narrative of infant development, while still making use of her theorization of the psychic defences. Jaques' and Lyth's contrasting approaches can be understood as distinct recontextualizing strategies in relation to a Kleinian psychoanalytic discourse.

Elliott Jaques: group processes, 'social defences' and a Kleinian language of individual ego development

There are three aspects of Jaques' work that are of analytical interest in relation to the recontextualization of the concept of 'psychic defences' in organizational research and consultancy. First, his development of an understanding of 'social defences', as mechanisms that are similar to 'psychic defences', but that are common to groups of individuals, socially sanctioned in a way that is not the case with the original Kleinian concept. Second, his reiteration of both Klein's theory of ego development and her conceptual language of 'projection', 'introjection' and 'splitting'. And finally, his conceptualization of the therapeutic effects of his own analysis and interpretations.

Between 1948 and 1951, Jaques carried out an exploration of processes of cultural change and industrial conflict in the Glacier Metal Company (Jaques, 1951). He presents this exploration as somewhere between a consultancy project, a therapeutic intervention, and a piece of research. In reporting the project Jaques sometimes refers to 'the research team' or 'the researchers' and sometimes to 'the consultant', and it is clear that 'the consultant' offered interpretations during meetings that were designed to draw participants' attention to the psychical construction of their interactions. For example, when workers' representatives in a meeting to negotiate a new payment system expressed the view that 'all supervisors were on management's side', Jaques notes that this comment appeared to reiterate earlier suspicions expressed about the role of the research team. He reports: 'The consultant therefore interpreted this to them as a displacement on to supervision of suspicion towards himself and the research team, representing once again their own suspicion of each other at the moment' (1951, p. 383). The consultant suggests that the general suspicions the participants have of each other are being 'displaced' from one group to another. This kind of interpretation is understood to have a direct influence on the progress of the negotiations. Jaques' comments that the interpretation was 'vigorously denied'; but he also notes that after the denial the participants noticed that supervisors were not represented at the meeting, and they agreed to make sure they were present in future meetings (ibid., p. 383). There is an implication that the consultant's intervention might have contributed to the realization that supervisors should be invited to join the negotiations, and this constitutes a therapeutic aspect to Jaques' intervention in the Glacier Metal Company.

The consultant's intervention in the pay negotiations uses a psychoanalytic language to rearticulate what is going on in the meeting. The interpretation, noting the way feelings of mistrust or suspicion are moved from one object to another, suggests the comment that 'all supervisors were on managements' side' can be understood as an instance of projection, whereby bad or unwanted aspects of the self are 'displaced' onto the other. Within a Kleinian framework, it is possible to suggest that the workers' representatives' doubts and uncertainties in relation both to the potential change in the payment system and to their own role in the negotiations are displaced, in turn, onto the researchers, the supervisors and the managers, in order to defend against persecutory anxieties. What is of note here, for Jaques, is the social aspect of the projective process: the workers' representatives find a shared object through which to defend against their anxieties. Because the workers' representatives constitute their supervisors as a shared object of projection, Jaques suggests that the process should be understood as a social, rather than a psychical defence mechanism. In such instances, he suggests, the aggression directed at the object by the ego is sanctioned within the shared practice: 'Social sanction means that denial of unconscious hatred and destructive impulses against internal objects can be reinforced by turning these impulses against a publicly hated real external enemy' (1951, p. 427). He goes on to elaborate the psychical function of social legitimation. He suggests that the social sanction of destructive impulses is introjected, and supports the ego in its denial of aggression and avoidance of the associated anxiety and guilt (p. 427). For Jaques the social here refers merely to a similar psychical process experienced by a group of individuals. He does not elaborate more specific features of the social context, such as the differential roles of the various participants in the negotiations, which might constitute a significant aspect of these projective processes.

In addition to this reiteration of the association between the psychic defences and the individual, Jaques' account also invokes elements of Klein's developmental narrative, explicitly referring back to the paranoid schizoid and depressive positions that she theorizes as constitutive of the early stages of development of the ego. He suggests: 'institutions are used by their individual members to reinforce mechanisms of defence against anxiety, and in particular against recurrence of the early paranoid and depressive anxieties first described by Melanie Klein' (p. 420). This kind of assertion reconstructs Klein's inference from interpretations of mechanisms such as projection and displacement to, in Jaques' words, 'processes of working through the unresolved conflicts of the infantile depressive position' (p. 429). Jaques thus detaches the interpretation from the context of the institution and reinserts it into the story of the development and integration of the ego. This constitutes the role of social defences such as shared processes of displacement and projection as one of helping individuals to 'find relief from their own internal persecution' (p. 426). The repeated inference from psychical defence mechanisms back to individualized anxieties obscures the specific tensions and anxieties of the factory within Jaques' analysis.

Similar moves, identifying interactions as instances of developmental positions, can be seen in other examples in Jaques' analysis of the pay negotiations at the Glacier Metal Company. He suggests that when the workers expressed suspicion of their elected representatives, their own 'bad' impulses are first projected (onto their representatives) and then re-introjected in such a way that they can be 'maintained as a segregated part of the ego' (p. 433). This process is, again, supported through social sanction:

> In addition to defence against internal persecution, the introjection of the other workers provided social sanction for considering the internalized representatives as bad, offsetting the harshness of super-ego recriminations for attacking objects which contained good as well as a persecuting component.
>
> (p. 433)

The reference to 'super-ego recriminations for attacking objects which contained good as well as a persecuting components' invokes Klein's depressive position, and the guilt introduced with the recognition of ambivalence.

Both the managers and the elected representatives are similarly inscribed within the terms of infant development towards an integrated ego. The managers' expressions of trust in the workers are described as an 'idealization' that is interpreted as a way of avoiding the implications of the exercise of managerial authority:

> The idealization can be understood as an unconscious mechanism for diminishing guilt which was stimulated by fears of injuring or destroying workers in the day to day situation through the exercise of managerial authority – an authority which, there is good reason to believe is, at least to some extent, unconsciously felt to be uncontrolled and omnipotent.
>
> (p. 433)

This interpretation constructs the managers as overwhelmed by a sense of their own authority, and of the damage this might inflict on their subordinates. It mirrors Melanie Klein's account of the infant's sense of its destructive impulses as dangerously omnipotent, and able to bring about the death of good objects. However, there are other possible interpretations of the managers' expressions of trust in the workers; and the inference from an interpretation of mechanisms of idealization back to positions associated with early development pathologizes and infantalizes the managers' approach.

In a similar way, the 'suspicion and hostility' expressed by the workers' representatives during meetings with managers are interpreted in terms of their 'anxiety and guilt about damaging the good managers': a further iteration of the depressive position. Jaques suggests:

> The primary defence mechanism against the onset of depressive anxiety was that of retreat to the paranoid schizoid position. This came out as a rigid clinging to attitudes of suspicion and hostility even in situations where there was a conscious feeling that some of this suspicion was not justified by the situation actually being experienced by the representatives.
>
> (p. 433)

The description of 'retreat to the paranoid schizoid position' re-inscribes the participants within a Kleinian trajectory of infant ego development. In its rigid reiteration of this narrative, Jaques' analysis might be said to displace alternative interpretations that might situate the suspicion and hostility observed within the hierarchically differentiated structures of the setting.

Finally, it is worth briefly noting Jaques' claims regarding the therapeutic effects of his interpretations within the process of negotiation. He suggests that the conflict between the parties in the negotiations was 'partly resolved' by the 'open interpretation' of the suspicions and idealizations articulated by participants (p. 436). However, he also acknowledges an important social mechanism that supported the resolution. This was the setting up of a Council of workers and management with an ongoing role in determining policy within the department. Jaques describes the Council as 'an explicit social institution ... which allowed for the establishment of unconscious mechanisms at the phantasy level for dealing with paranoid and depressive anxieties'. He suggests that both the consultant's interpretations and the mechanism of the Council 'helped individuals to deal with anxiety' (p. 436). He thus conceptualizes therapeutic support as something directed at individual anxieties, rather than at the emotional configuration of the institution as a whole.

As David Armstrong has suggested, Jaques' focus on individual anxiety does not only fail to recognize the significance of the emotional life of organizations, it also pushes the therapeutic resources of the consultant in the wrong direction, and misdiagnoses the object of treatment as the emotional well being of individuals. For Armstrong, emotions interpreted in the analysis are not the object of treatment, but rather a clue in coming to understand the life of the organization: 'No emotional experience in organizational life is a suitable case for treatment. Rather, a resource for thinking, for releasing intelligence' (2005, p. 109). Emotional experience may be articulated by individuals, but the intelligence it offers relates to the structuring of the organization.

Isabel Menzies Lyth: the location of anxiety within the social system

The organizational analysis developed by Isabel Menzies Lyth (1959) references Jaques' work and at several points it echoes his recourse to the language of individual psychical development. However, Lyth's analysis also constitutes a precise articulation of the social aspects of anxiety: the production of anxiety within social systems and organizations. As we have seen, Jaques analyses the projections of parties in the pay negotiations, but he does not situate these projections in an analysis of organizational structures or of the substantive content of organizational activities. Lyth's study of the nursing service in a teaching hospital contextualizes the social defences against anxiety in a way that shifts the analysis from individuals or groups of individuals to the broader structures and purposes of the organization. The empirical basis of the study comprised observations, interviews and group discussions, which fed into more 'therapeutic' activities with five senior nurses.[6] Lyth's publications on the study focus largely on the initial analysis, rather than on the more therapeutic work. There are two stages to this analysis.

The first stage contextualizes the production of anxiety within the nursing service in relation to the objectives, or 'primary task', of the hospital. Lyth suggests that the emotions related to the 'objective situation' of the hospital 'stimulate afresh' the 'primitive levels of the mind' associated with 'early situations' (1959, pp. 46–47). The detail of her analysis foregrounds features of the 'objective situation': the nurses' relations to illness and to patients and relatives within the hospital:

> The direct impact on the nurse of physical illness is intensified by her task of meeting and dealing with psychological stress in other people, including her own colleagues. It is by no means easy to tolerate such stress even if one is not under similar stress oneself. Quite short conversations with patients or relatives showed that their conscious concept of illness and treatment is a rich intermixture of objective knowledge, logical deduction and fantasy. The degree of stress is heavily conditioned by the fantasy, which is in turn conditioned, as in nurses, by the early phantasy situations. Unconsciously, the nurse associates the patients' and relatives' distress with that experienced by the people in her phantasy world, which increases her own anxiety and difficulty in handling it.
>
> (p. 48)

This analysis gives equal weight to the 'objective' features of the hospital and to the internal objects of the nurses' inner representational world. The objective features include the 'direct impact on the nurse of physical illness' and the mixture of knowledge and fantasy in patients' and relatives' 'concept of illness and treatment', all of which constitute a part of the everyday working context of nurses in the department. The emotions associated with a nurse's inner representational world are evoked where s/he is not able to maintain a distinction between 'objective reality' and the 'phantasy situations' of her inner world. Lyth suggests that this distinction is achieved through symbolization: 'To be effective, such symbolization requires that the symbol *represents* the phantasy object, but *is not equated* with it'. She continues: 'If, for any reason, the symbol and the phantasy object become almost or completely equated, the anxieties aroused by the phantasy object are aroused in full intensity by the symbolic object' (p. 49). Lyth describes an instance when the distinction between symbol and phantasy object was not sustained: 'a nurse whose mother had had several gynaecological operations broke down and had to give up nursing shortly after beginning her tour of duty on the gynaecological ward' (p. 50).

Through this analysis of 'objective features' of the setting and their relation to the 'phantasy world' of the nurses, Lyth constitutes a link between the two as inherent to her analysis of the nursing service: the anxieties experienced by the nurses cannot be separated from the organizational context of the hospital. A similar analysis in Jaques study of the Glacier

Metal Company might have foregrounded the contrasting objectives of workers and managers within the organization, and the ways in which the fantasies they constructed might be accounted for in relation to specific features of their differential positioning.

In concluding this first stage of her analysis Lyth argues that nurses' relations to illness, patients and relatives are not sufficient to account for the high levels of anxiety observed during the study. The second stage of her analysis explores the social defences established within the nursing service: the institutionalized practices constructed to alleviate anxiety. Lyth argues that institutional practices that might appear to protect against anxieties related to the primary task of hospital care can fail in this function, or can themselves become the source of secondary anxieties within the nursing service.

Lyth suggests that the members of an organization, in this case the nursing service, 'use' the organization to avoid anxiety: to do this they develop 'socially structured defence mechanisms which appear as elements in the organization's structure, culture and mode of functioning' (p. 50). For example, in order to avoid the intense anxieties likely to be provoked in personal relations with severely ill patients, the service is organized to limit the development of such relations, by dividing the care of individual patients into 'tasks' allocated to several nurses:

> The nursing service attempts to protect her from the anxiety by splitting up her contact with patients. It is hardly too much to say that the nurse does not nurse patients. The total workload of a ward or department is broken down into lists of tasks, each of which is allocated to a particular nurse. She performs her patient centred tasks for a large number of patients – perhaps as many as all the patients in the ward, often thirty or more. As a corollary, she performs only a few tasks for, and has restricted contact with, any one patient. This prevents her from coming effectively into contact with the totality of any one patient and his illness and offers protection from the anxiety this arouses.
>
> (p. 51)

Lyth's interpretation of the 'task list' as a mechanism for organizing nurses' practice suggests that it aids 'depersonalization' and the 'elimination of individual distinctiveness in both nurse and patient' (p. 52). This contributes to 'an almost explicit 'ethic' that any patient must be the same as any other patient' (p. 52), so that nurses avoid or suppress preferences for or relationships with individual patients. This ethic is also instantiated in a general denial of the disturbing feelings and emotional strain that arise in response to distressing situations nurses face within their work. Lyth reports, for example, that when a student nurse makes a mistake, 'she is usually reprimanded rather than helped' (p. 54). Thus, while the division of labour instantiated in the task list might reduce the likelihood of nurses developing relations with patients that might cause them anxiety, it also contributes to an ethos that denies support and recognition of necessarily distressing situations.

Lyth also notes an underlying fear within the service that practitioners will behave irresponsibly. This fear is instantiated in the regulation of practice by means of the task list, but also in the ways that nurses talked about each other. Lyth reports:

> Nurses habitually complain that other nurses are irresponsible, behave carelessly and impulsively, and in consequence must be ceaselessly supervised and disciplined. The complaints commonly refer not to individuals or to specific incidents but to whole categories of nurses, usually a category junior to the speaker.
>
> (p. 57)

Lyth argues that these complaints, usually targeted at a group rather than an individual, 'stem from a collusive system of denial, splitting and projection'. She suggests that all nurses have greater or lesser tendencies towards irresponsibility, and that in order to deal with these frightening tendencies they split them off, and project them onto their colleagues, so that: 'Her irresponsible impulses, which she fears she cannot control, are attributed to her juniors' (p. 57). The shared objectification of junior nurses as irresponsible can thus be understood as a social defence against anxieties more senior nurses have about their own irresponsibility. In addition, these processes of projection support a strict disciplinary regime, within which mistakes are treated as irresponsibility and suitably reprimanded. As with the task list, the effect is to suppress the justified anxiety related to the primary task of nursing, and to construct ways in which the practice of the department was likely to evoke secondary anxieties, not directly related to the primary task, but related instead to the strict hierarchical regime within the service.

Lyth concludes that the system of social defences within the nursing service 'itself arouses a good deal of secondary anxiety as well as failing to alleviate primary anxiety' (p. 65). She argues, further, that the effect of the defences is to prevent individuals from experiencing or confronting their anxieties:

> Thus the individual cannot bring the content of the phantasy anxiety situations into effective contact with reality. Unrealistic or pathological anxiety cannot be differentiated from realistic anxiety arising from real dangers ... The forced introjection of the hospital defence system, therefore, perpetuates in the individual a considerable degree of pathological anxiety.
>
> (pp. 74–75)

The suggestion is that the social defences are internalized by those working within the system and that the internalized social defences cover over unbearable feelings of anxiety, rather than addressing or coming to a more considered understanding of their source. For Lyth, as we have seen, the source of the nurses' anxieties must be contextualized within the primary task of the hospital: relations to illness, patients and relatives. Her articulation of a conception of institutionally structured defence mechanisms supplements Klein's psychic defences and at points substitutes the institution for the individual as the site of anxiety. This disrupts the individualized narrative of ego development as a progression from the paranoid schizoid to the depressive position, and places the emotional life of the organization at the centre of the analysis.

Modes of recontextualization of Kleinian discourse

As I have suggested, it is possible to interpret Jaques' work and Lyth's study as instantiations of contrasting strategies for the recontextualization of Kleinian discourse. Jaques' work articulates identifications with both aspects of Klein's theory and substitutes her conceptualization of the paranoid schizoid and depressive positions for an account of the social structure of the factory. In so far as he reiterates her prioritization of the individual over a notion of social structure, Jaques' account also constitutes an identification with the management of the factory that already functions to individualize roles and responsibilities within the workplace. We might perhaps interpret this as a form of disavowal in which he sees but does not acknowledge the differential status of managers and workers. The factory is right in front of him, but all that Jaques sees is the infantile defences of the paranoid schizoid and depressive position. In contrast, Lyth's analysis both rearticulates Kleinian concepts and at the same time introduces supplementary terms into the discourse. These contrasting strategies might be understood in terms of Laclau and Mouffe's conceptualization of the logics of equivalence and difference (2001).[7] A logic of equivalence involves the metaphorical substitution of one term for another, while a logic of difference supports multiple meanings within the signifying system. Either strategy might act either to maintain or to subvert hegemonic social formations (see Howarth, 2000b, Marchart, 2004; Lapping, 2008). In this instance, Jaques' interpretive activity constitutes a logic that equates the factory with psychodynamics and obliterates the differences between social structure and individual. This equivalence extends the authority of the individualizing discourse of Kleinian psychoanalysis from the clinic to the factory. Lyth's strategy, in contrast, introduces a differential element which might act to limit or subvert psychoanalytic authority. However, while her conceptualization of the social defences shifts the focus from individual to social organization, she does not develop this as an explicit critique of psychoanalytic orthodoxy.

It is worth noting the dangers that might be associated with an explicit subversion of this kind of a hegemonic formation. In an interview with Ann Scott and Robert M. Young, while Lyth noted that she felt it was important for people involved in work with organizations to have a background in social science as well as a psychoanalytic training (Lyth, 1988, p. 8), she also talked about pressure she came under from the psychoanalytic community in relation to her work:

> when I continued my [organizational] work at the Tavi after I had qualified in psychoanalysis, I did come under a lot of pressure from senior Kleinian analysts who felt I was wasting my time and my gifts staying there when I could have been working full-time in psychoanalysis. That subsided a bit when my papers began to appear, which showed how I was using psychoanalysis, and also when I made fairly rapid progress in psychoanalysis, becoming a full member of the Society and a training analyst pretty quickly.
>
> (ibid., p. 33)

Insofar as it is possible to interpret Lyth's lack of acknowledgment of the disjunctures between her work and Klein's ideas – and her uncritical referencing of work by other researchers at the Tavistock – as a disavowal of the distinctiveness of her own work, this disavowal should be understood in relation to the pressure to conform to the powerful regulative authority of senior members of the psychoanalytic community. Just as Paul Dowling's (1998) work on school mathematics suggests the way different modes of recontextualization both construct and limit educational opportunities, so the mode of recontextualization of psychoanalytic ideas constructs and limits professional trajectories.

The articulation of 'psychic defences' within Basil Bernstein's theory of recontextualization

Where Jaques and Lyth were both professionally located within the Tavistock Institute of Human Relations, Bernstein, like Bourdieu, held a university post as a sociologist, and therefore did not require legitimization from psychoanalytic authorities. Nevertheless, the lack of reference to psychoanalytic theorists as sources for some of his ideas is noteworthy, since in other instances he does not conserve energy in trying to establish correct interpretations of his relations to other authors and fields. He devotes a paper to an account of his relation to the field of sociolinguistics, acknowledging his intellectual debt to Hallidayan linguistics and tracing his relation to other researchers within the field (Bernstein, 2000, pp. 145–153). Bernstein also spends considerable time distinguishing his theory from that of Bourdieu, providing evidence that Bourdieu's critique of his work is based on a misreading, and rejecting the suggestion that his own work might be seen as a development of Bourdieu's ideas (ibid., pp. 175–189):

> Harker and May state that my analysis of pedagogic discourse 'starts where Bourdieu and Passeron ... left off'. This is nonsense. The basic recontextualizing model is set out in the Introduction to *Class, Codes and Control*, Vol. III, 1975, p. 31, developed in Bernstein, 1981, whilst the concepts of instructional and regulative discourse go back much earlier (Bernstein, 1965) ... I have clearly gained much from reading Bourdieu; in particular, the concept of field. But there is a considerable difference which emerges out of my development of the importance of exploring within/between relationships ... *Homo academicus* is not about the constitution of academic discourses, their systems of transmission, their formations of specialized consciousness, it is about power games and their strategies.
>
> (pp. 188–189)

It would be possible to argue that Bernstein's refutation of the overlap between his work and that of Bourdieu has the structure of disavowal. Somewhat ironically, in refuting Bourdieu's interpretation of his work, Bernstein accuses him of 'reading omnipotence', which he defines as 'a clinical condition which renders texts which disturb one's own interpretation unread, even when they are' (p. 177). This would seem to be a version of Freudian disavowal, but Freud is not referenced. Indeed, in the collection of essays in which the comment appears, Freud's name appears once, in a long list of other major sociological and psychological theorists, and Melanie Klein is not referenced at all, despite Bernstein's use of the vocabulary of Kleinian psychic defences in his account of key concepts throughout the collection. Where psychotherapy is mentioned it is as a potential object of analysis, not as a source for his ideas (p. 212).

It is worth noting Bernstein's complicated strategies in relation to the acknowledgement of individual and disciplinary origins, but I don't want to speculate further about the possible meaning of these strategies.[8] Or at least, I simply want to note the productivity of reading Bernstein's suppression of a relation to psychoanalysis alongside Steinmetz's (2006) account of similar moves in Bourdieu's writing, which might mitigate any tendency to interpret either in terms of individual pathology. Instead we might speculate on the apparently allergic relation between the disciplinary field of sociology and the acknowledgement of key authors and theories from psychoanalysis. In the remainder of this chapter, however, I want to explore the potential productivity of Bernstein's unelaborated inclusion of Kleinian terms, to see what these psychoanalytic ideas might contribute to his theorization of processes of recontextualization.

Bernstein's work within the sociology of knowledge develops conceptual models that suggest how forms of knowledge are constituted in relation to the social contexts in which they are articulated. For example, he describes how the strength of boundaries between fields of disciplinary knowledge relates to organizational structures, and how this relationship will tend to serve the interests of one social group over another. For Bernstein, the strength of the boundaries between fields of knowledge constitutes a key feature in processes of recontextualization. He refers to this feature, the strength of the boundary insulating fields from each other, as 'classification'.

Bernstein invokes the notion of 'psychic defences' in relation to the principle of classification, that which constitutes distinctions between fields of knowledge, or discourses. He suggests that the principle of classification, the basis of differentiation, is always related to power and acts to naturalize what are in fact arbitrary power relations: 'the arbitrary nature of these power relations is disguised, hidden by the principle of classification' (2000, p. 7). In its function of disguise, Bernstein suggests, the principle of classification relates not only to external social relations, but also to 'relations within individuals'. It is this internal function of the principle of classification that Bernstein describes as 'a system of psychic defences':

> externally, the classificatory principle creates order, and the contradictions, cleavages and dilemmas which necessarily inhere in the principle of a classification are suppressed by the insulation. Within the individual, the insulation becomes a system of psychic defences against the possibility of the weakening of the insulation, which would then reveal the suppressed contradictions, cleavages and dilemmas. So the internal reality of insulation is a system of psychic defences to maintain the integrity of a category.
>
> (ibid., p. 7)

What Bernstein articulates here is the psychic structuring of fields of knowledge. The order or coherence that appears to underlie the construction of disciplinary fields or systems of knowledge is achieved through 'a system of psychic defences'. The broader point is that any form of knowledge will serve the interests of a specific social group, and it is this aspect of knowledge that is repressed, both in organizational discourses of legitimate knowledge and in the individual construction of psychical objects. Thus, 'the principle of classification comes to have the force of the natural order' (p. 7).

In two of his later papers, 'Pedagogising Knowledge: Studies in Recontextualising' and 'Official Knowledge and Pedagogic Identities: The Politics of Recontextualisation' (in Bernstein, 2000), Bernstein uses the vocabulary of the defences in his account of contemporary forms of disciplinary knowledge within educational institutions. In particular, he describes disciplinary and institutional identities as constructed through processes of projection and introjection. Thus, although in the extract quoted above, he appears to associate the defences with the construction of individual rather than collective identities, in his discussion of particular modes of knowledge and institution this distinction seems to get lost, and psychical processes appear to be attributed to collective identities. However, Bernstein never explains or elaborates the meaning of these psychical processes within his theory.

In the following sections I have taken extracts where Bernstein uses the vocabulary of psychical defence mechanisms and I have attempted to elaborate possible interpretations or meanings evoked by his use of these terms. I look at his conceptualization of three modes of knowledge that he suggests are to be found within formal educational settings. These are: *singulars*, rarified forms of knowledge that are considered discrete, strongly classified and autonomous or self-legitimating; *regions*, forms of knowledge that combine knowledge from singular disciplines and apply this knowledge in fields beyond the school or university; and *generic modes*, forms of knowledge that originate outside educational institutions and are imported into educational settings, typically in the construction of vocational qualifications. For Bernstein, each of these modes of knowledge serves an economic goal and can be considered as 'instrumental' (p. 54). However, the explicitness with which the instrumental goal of knowledge constitutes a part of the identity of the field varies according to mode. Similarly, in Bernstein's account, the psychic defences associated with fields of knowledge vary from mode to mode.

Singulars

Bernstein suggests that traditional disciplines such as classics, English and history, physics and chemistry, economics and the social sciences are all examples of singulars. He associates these knowledge structures with historical developments of the nineteenth century: nationalism, the development of the empire, new material technologies, and the development of the market and its associated 'management of subjectivities' (p. 54). He suggests:

> Classics provided privileged access to the administrative levels of the Civil Service. The specialized sciences provided the basis for material technologies. However, despite these external linkages singulars are like a coin with two faces, so that only one face can be seen at any one time. The sacred face sets them apart, legitimizes their otherness and creates dedicated identities with no reference other than to their calling. The profane face indicates their external linkage and internal power struggles. Organizationally and politically singulars construct strong boundary maintenance. From this point of view singulars develop strong autonomous self-sealing and narcissistic identities. These identities are constructed by procedures of *introjection*.
>
> (emphasis in original, pp. 54–55)

Thus the 'sacred face' of singular modes reveals aspects of knowledge that appear as pure intellectual activity, while the 'profane face' represents 'external linkages', instrumental aspects of knowledge that appear unrelated to the legitimized, intellectual activity. In defining these knowledge structures as 'narcissistic', Bernstein seems to suggest the direction of libido towards specialized disciplinary characteristics, the 'sacred elements', and the repression or denial of characteristics associated with external linkages. This might be consistent with the projection of the profane 'external linkages' onto other objects/disciplines/contexts. Yet Bernstein describes these identities as 'constructed by procedures of *introjection*'. This is consistent with a Kleinian account of narcissism as 'love for and relation with the internalized good object' (Kleing, 1946, p. 204), and this formulation reminds us of the idealized and phantasmatic nature of the characteristic that is here the object of narcissistic love: idealized because intellectual values can never be abstracted from their interdependency with social contexts; phantasmatic because the splitting off of the idealized object is a product of unconscious phantasy. However, it is not clear why Bernstein wants to claim that introjection is more significant than processes of projection in the establishment of 'singular' identities. This may be related to his tendency to produce slightly homogenizing, static models. The terms 'projection' and 'introjection' are partly deployed to construct a distinction between 'singulars' and more externally oriented knowledge structures (regional and generic modes). He claims: 'If the procedures of introjection construct the identities produced by singulars then the procedures of projection construct the identities produces by the new regionalization of knowledge' (Bernstein, 2000, p. 55). But he revises this homogenizing claim a few paragraphs later, when he acknowledges both processes within the singular mode:

> The 'autonomous' [singular] mode is ambiguous as the context acts selectively upon whether autonomy is emphasized and dependency masked or dependency is pragmatically embraced. Thus the identity here is split but manageable when introjected elements and projected elements can be actualized in discrete contexts.
>
> (p. 55)

Both the tendency to construct static, homogenizing models and the inconsistency illustrated here are characteristic of Bernstein's theorizing.

It is also worth speculating a little more on Bernstein's claim that the identity of singular modes 'is split but manageable'. Splitting arises here because of the need to defend against profane elements by separating (bad) dependency from (good) autonomy. Bernstein suggests that this split is manageable as long as the institution instantiates separate sites for the articulation of these contrasting elements of the identity, e.g. teaching and research versus committees and administration. It seems plausible that the provision of 'discrete contexts' allows the de-toxification of the dependency that is otherwise likely to remain as a persecuting 'bad object'. However, some settings might support a more integrated and ambivalent understanding of these disciplinary identities. In these instances, there would be no need for the splitting that Bernstein suggests, so that a singular mode might be instantiated within a 'depressive' rather than a 'paranoid schizoid' position.

It is worth noting here that Lyth's account of the nursing service would suggest that the instantiation of the 'depressive' or 'paranoid schizoid' position might be dependent not just on institutional context, but also on individual disciplinary subjects: the combination of dependency and autonomy might be felt as an unbearable attack by some but as a bearable ambivalence by others. There is a clear distinction between the perspectives of the two authors. Lyth's account of the hospital foregrounds instances where individual psychical histories come into contact with the psychical logic of the organization. Bernstein's models, in contrast, conceptualize knowledge modes as social identities, and the individual emerges only as a type within the social, not as a subject with its own psychical identity.

Regions

Bernstein defines regional modes as fields of knowledge that relate both to the specialized intellectual field of singular academic disciplines and to external fields of practices. Examples include medicine, engineering and architecture each of which incorporates ideas from several singular disciplines for application in settings beyond the university. Bernstein suggests that one feature of regional modes is their construction through processes of projection:

> Regions are recontextualiasations of singulars and face inwards towards singulars and outwards towards external fields of practice [...] Identities produced by the *new* regions are more likely to face outwards to fields of practice and thus their contents are likely to be dependent on the requirements of these fields. Identities here are what they are, and what they will become, as a consequence of the *projection* of that knowledge as a practice in some context.
>
> (emphasis in original, p. 55)

The suggestion that regions are constructed through projection requires some elaboration. The distinction between 'projection' and 'projective identification' might help to clarify this process. One interpretation of projective identification suggests a process whereby the ego does not merely split off a part of itself and project it into an object, but, in addition, the ego then identifies with the object of the projection (Mitchell, 1991, p. 20). Another variation suggests that the object of projection takes on the identity projected onto it by the ego. If we consider the identity of regional knowledge modes, analogous processes might be inferred. Regional knowledge structures – disciplinary fields situated within higher education – might first project meanings or concepts onto external practices, and then, following the projection, they will identify with the external practice. So, for example, medical researchers might identify with doctors, or educational researchers with teachers. Or, alternatively, it might be the case that ideas and concepts from the regional mode will not just be projected onto the contextualized practice of engineering, medicine or education, but will be taken in as a part of the identity of this external object. Where professional bodies and individual professionals construct their identities by reference to knowledge developed within an academic context, when professional practice comes to be evaluated in the terms of a recontextualized academic language, we might describe this as a process of projective identification. However, there is also likely to be some movement the other way, i.e. 'regional' knowledge structures taking in (introjecting) idealized aspects of the contextualized external practice. There remains a question, though, as to the extent to which this might be understood as an individual or a collective process, and also as to the conceptualization of the unconscious within these processes.

In more Lacanian terms, we could describe both of these processes – the introjection of knowledge from external practice into the academy and also the projection of knowledge from the academy into external practice – in terms of the master discourse (Lacan, 2007). The process of recontextualisation transforms knowledge from S2, the chain of signifiers, into S1, the master signifier. Lacan describes these as 'the two aspects of knowledge', embedded knowledge or 'know how', represented by S2, and 'articulated knowledge', S1 (ibid., p. 22). The point of articulation, S1, abstracts knowledge from its context to assert it as a regulatory reference point, initiating new chains of signification.[9] This occurs when a particular aspect of professional practice is taken up to be researched within the university, but also when knowledge produced within the university is inserted into the regulatory systems of professional practice. Both processes involve the extraction of knowledge for the purposes of the master, or, Lacan says 'betrayal, of the slave's knowledge, in order to obtain its transmutation into the master's knowledge' (p. 22).

Generic modes

A third mode of educational knowledge that Bernstein distinguishes within the contemporary context is what he calls 'generic'. As this term (perhaps) suggests, this mode incorporates a wide range of practices within the category of 'knowledge'. It includes practices and experiences that do not originate within the traditional disciplinary regimes of higher education.[10] The value of these modes originates outside formal educational settings, as they are 'essentially directed to extra school experiences: work and 'life'' (2000, p. 53). He suggests that they are produced through 'a functional analysis' (p. 53) of 'a set of general skills underlying a range of specific performances' (p. 55). However, he also says:

> generic modes and the performances to which they give rise are directly linked to instrumentalities of the market, to the construction of what are considered to be flexible performances. From this point of view their identity is constructed by procedures of projection.
>
> (p. 55)

Joseph's account of Kleinian forms of projective identification can help us to make sense of Bernstein's use of 'projection' here. She suggested that one form of projective identification consisted in 'getting into an object to take over its capacities and make them its own' (1988, p. 65). If we recontextualize this idea, we can think of pedagogic identities as forced to project themselves into the values of the market. If all worth appears to be attributed to something other than pedagogic values, pedagogic identities, full of worthlessness, will, in phantasy at least, take over the capacities of the market and make them their own. This is, of course, only a phantasy, and the production of pedagogic identity through this violently defensive mechanism is likely to produce something approximating the paranoid schizoid, or, in Bernstein's reformulation, the 'pedagogic schizoid' (2000, p. 71) position.

A similarly violent psychical process is suggested in Bernstein's account of the psychical construction of the identity of higher education institutions in an era where funding is tied to performance indicators such as research output in 'prestigious' journals. He describes the way the identity of elite universities is bound up in their ability to attract appropriately productive members of the academic staff:

> Elite universities can maintain their position by buying in research leaders, and as a consequence will have *less* need to change their discourse or its organization to maintain their power and position ... [T] he identities formed in elite institutions are likely to be formed by introjection of knowledge. That is the identity finds its core in its place in an organization of knowledge and practice.
>
> (p. 70)

The suggestion is that elite universities introject aspects of knowledge found in other objects (research leaders) and incorporate these into their identities. Reading this example alongside Julia Segal's account of introjection can help us to develop a more elaborated picture of the psychical relations that may constitute the institutional identities that Bernstein is describing. She suggests:

> Phantasies in which parts of others are taken into the self (introjection) are also extremely important. Where this takes place under the influence of the paranoid schizoid position the parts taken in will be split and idealized: larger than life and wonderful or excessively persecuting and dangerous. The boundary between self and other is in some way denied, and the self may be felt to be attached to or identical with a very powerful idealized other who can do no wrong. This idealization covers a conviction that this other is really frightening and aggressive, diminishing the self, humiliating and destructive....
>
> (Segal, 1992, p. 35)

Both aspects of this account, the idealization of the object and the denial of the boundary between self and other, might be applicable to the relation between academic institutions and certain celebrated members of academic staff. The further suggestion that this relation 'covers a conviction that this other is really frightening and aggressive', and that the idealized other in some way diminishes the self is also insightful as an account of the institutional insecurities that exist within higher education.

The productivity of Bernstein's use of Kleinian vocabularies

Bernstein does not elaborate the conceptual implications of his introduction of the language of psychic defences into his account of educational practices. Apart from a joking reference to 'a new pathological position at work in education' which he terms 'the pedagogic schizoid position', there are no traces of Klein's individualized, developmental narrative in his models of contemporary forms of knowledge. The productivity of his use of Klein's terms seems to lie in the meanings associated with the signifiers 'projection' and 'introjection', and in the potential these have to articulate relations between educational identities and the 'internal' and 'external' objects in relation to which these identities are constructed. They offer a language through which we might begin to conceptualize psychical aspects to processes of recontextualization.

Bernstein's introduction of unelaborated, and unacknowledged, instances of Kleinian psychoanalytic vocabulary – signifiers without signifieds – into his conceptual apparatus also invites us to play, and to move beyond the models that he has constructed. I have argued elsewhere that there are congruencies between Bernstein and Lacan, especially in their shared interest in the production of codified meanings and their conceptualization of the gap that is that site of unthinkable, that which is excluded from codified knowledge (Lapping, 2004; see also Davis, 2004). So, I would argue, there is some basis for drawing on a Lacanian framework to explore possible connotations of the psychoanalytic references in Bernstein's work. A more Lacanian approach, I have suggested, might help to articulate discursive aspects of knowledge practices, emphasizing the instantiation of knowledge and subjectivity within symbolic systems of power that are not so clearly captured in the Kleinian language with its psychologizing metaphors of internal world and individual ego (see also Kracke and Villela, 2004, pp. 181–182). By tracing the articulation, extraction and substitution of signifiers across different contexts, in a re-articulation of Bernstein's models, we might begin to map shifts in the political and symbolic regulation of academic and professional contexts and the interdependencies of these contexts in the production of regulatory codes.

Bernstein's detachment of the psychic defences from Klein's developmental conceptualization of the ego and from notions of an integrated and individualized subject creates possibilities for analysing the defences as constitutive of institutional identities or discursive fields. This move expands the potential productivity of the concept for social scientific analysis. It might also be understood to take us closer to a Lacanian conception of the defences, which suggests that what is defended against is not the disintegration of the ego, but the power of unconscious meanings. Ragland-Sullivan explains: 'Because Lacan delimits consciousness and makes consciousness and language themselves defences against unconscious meaning, he is not generally understood by ego psychologists who place defences in the ego itself' (1986, p. 120).

This radically extends the notion of the defences. Rather than conceptualizing defensive mechanisms such as splitting and projection as distorted linguistic representations of real relations, language itself is understood as a distorting, defensive mechanism. Consciousness does not represent a normalized, rational relation to reality, but a necessary defence against the unconscious. From this perspective, unconscious meanings pose a threat to individualized human identities, but no more so than they pose a threat to institutional or social identities. The strong association between Kleinian theory and invocations of the psychical defences seems to set an unnecessary limit on the use of this conceptual tool in the analysis of social relations.

Conclusion: contrasting recontextualizations and the unconscious of power

It seems relatively mundane to suggest that the contrasting positioning of Jaques and Lyth, within the psychoanalytically regulated Tavistock Institute of Human Relations, in comparison with Bernstein and Bourdieu, as academic sociologists, can explain their differential articulations of psychoanalytic ideas. The sociology of knowledge provides a more precise analytical framework for exploring these recontextualizations, one that constructs disciplinary fields and concepts as social objects that are neither unified nor separate from the contexts in relation to which they are articulated. Dowling's 'domains of action' schema foregrounds the constitution of disciplinary languages in signifiers and signifieds that articulate relations to a variety of differential discourses and social positions. Bernstein's conceptualization of 'singulars', 'regions' and 'generic modes' foregrounds the economic relation of disciplinary fields of knowledge. These analytical languages help us to construct a more precise account of contrasting articulations of knowledge and of the discursive/social alliances and oppositions that they enact. The chapter has also attempted to articulate the psychical aspect of these recontextualizing strategies, suggesting that the articulation or substitution of signifiers and their relation to different signifieds can be understood as constitutive of psychical relations within discourse. Thus strategies of acknowledgement or suppression of psychoanalytic antecedents in the work of Jaques and Lyth, and of Bernstein and Bourdieu, might be understood as unconscious articulations of the complex alliances and oppositions necessary to the production of their particular professional and intellectual identities.

I want to finish this chapter with two thoughts. The first relates to the contrast between the empirically or ontically oriented conceptual frameworks within the sociology of knowledge and more abstracted, theoretically or ontologically oriented conceptual frameworks. The second relates to the notion of the unconscious.

At various points throughout the book I have set up an opposition between the empirical and the speculative, the particular and the universal; and a question remains about the relation between these two modes of investigation. This has been described by Laclau as the 'complex dialectic between particularity and universality, between ontic content and ontological dimension' (cited in Marchart, 2004, p. 57) and he refers to the impossibility of achieving either pure universality or pure particularity (Laclau, 2004, p. 310). We might consider the move between the more abstracted terms of the ontological dimension and the more particularized concepts of ontic analysis as the space within which psychoanalytic terms are recontextualized in the analysis of both clinical and non clinical material. The distinction between Laclau and Mouffe's more abstracted conceptualization of the logics of equivalence and difference and the specificity of models developed within the sociology of knowledge is an example of this kind of shift in levels of analysis. The introduction of the unconscious at the ontological level will carry through into the ontic account of the particularity of the setting, but the ontic always contains an excess that, in Zizek's words, 'eludes …the ontological clearance within which entities appear' (1994, p. 181; see also Laclau, 2004., p. 305).

Finally, I want to reflect briefly on the shifts in the meaning of the unconscious that are necessitated when we begin to conceptualize the defences as constituted within organizational and social structures. Where for Klein the unconscious is a force that acts in relation to an individual ego, it is not clear what constitutes the unconscious in Bernstein's models of different modes of knowledge. It is certainly not an individualized unconscious. Indeed, it seems far more like the Lacanian appearance of the unconscious in the symbolic punctuations in the signifying chain. Or perhaps we might understand the very conceptualization of the force that constitutes legitimized fields of knowledge in relation to economic and social hierarchies in terms of something more like Butler's unconscious of power. If, as Butler suggests, the unconscious is 'whatever resists the normative demands by which subjects are instituted' (1997, p. 86), then the relation between fields of disciplinary knowledge and the economic field that is foregrounded in Bernstein's models can be understood as an element positioned within the unconscious. It is precisely this *relation* that resists the normative demands of objective, scientific knowledge. When this relation, then, is foregrounded within the terms of knowledge itself, within the conceptual frameworks of the sociology of knowledge, this may become something like the mobilization of subjection against subjection that Butler defines as the unconscious of power (ibid., p. 104). Where the unconscious is that which resists articulation, the unconscious of power is the mobilization of articulated terms against the normative conditions of articulation.

Index

Note: Figures are indicated by *italic* text, tables by **bold** text, and endnotes by "n" and the number of the endnote after the page number.